W9-APQ-717

NOV 2 8 2008
DEC 1 3 2008

JAN 0 3 2009

MAR 1 6 2009

APR 2 5 2009

Withdrawn

Northville District Library
212 W. Cady Street
Northville, MI 48167-1580

More Advance Praise for *Scheisshaus Luck*

"Pierre Berg deserves praise for his absorbing account. He has achieved a rare balance of accuracy and dispassion, allowing readers to enter his memories without need of extraneous literary embellishment. An important contribution to the growing library of Holocaust testimony."

—Joshua M. Greene, Hofstra University; author of *Justice at Dachau: The Trials of an American Prosecutor*

"Mesmerizing, devastating, haunting, *Scheisshaus Luck* is as gripping as *Schindler's List*. Berg's story is a monument to the human spirit that prevails beyond every jackbooted attempt to stamp it out. That Berg survived to tell the tale is as astonishing and miraculous as the book itself. This is riveting reading, a page-turner, an unforgettable experience. It should be required reading in every 20th century history class that dares to deal with the Holocaust."

—Duff Brenna, author of *The Book of Mamie*

"The cinematic quality of his [Berg's] narrative takes you over an abyss into the Auschwitz that really was. Would you have made it through? Berg's talents served him well, but there were many close calls. There is suspense here—a lot of it—along with irony, cynicism, loyalty, and love. Vetted against Nazi archival sources, this is the real thing with no detail spared for delicacy's sake."

—Steven Sage, author of *Ibsen and Hitler: The Playwright, the Plagiarist, and the Plot for the Third Reich*

"A staggering voyage through the hell of Nazi death camps with a sensitive young Frenchman determined to emerge alive. . . . Pierre Berg's day-to-day details of his slavery and survival are searing."

—Richard Z. Chesnoff, columnist, the *New York Daily News;* and author of *Pack of Thieves: How Hitler & Europe Plundered the Jews*

"Through the fog of memory comes a powerful new read about survival in the Auschwitz abyss. This is the warts-and-all story of an 18-year old political prisoner's incarceration as a slave laborer in the Monowitz labor camp, part of the Auschwitz complex, and in Dora, which provided labor for the Nazi's V-2 rocket program. Pierre Berg, a non-Jew from Nice in France, tells his story with utter frankness, and hides nothing of man's bestiality to man, and what people will do to survive. My book of the year."

—William Bemister, Emmy-winning Producer-Correspondent of *The Hunter and the Hunted* and *The Search for Mengele*

"Pierre Berg's touching memoir considerably deepens our knowledge not only of the horror faced by Jewish victims during the Holocaust, but also underscores their bravery and humanity. It is essential reading for those interested in a deeper understanding of the Holocaust."

—David M. Crowe, Elon University; author of *The Holocaust: Roots, History, and Aftermath* and *Oskar Schindler: The Untold Account of His Life, Wartime Activities, and the True Story Behind "The List"*

"*Scheisshaus Luck* is an important contribution to Holocaust literature in general, but in particular to that written by non-Jewish survivors. While there was little difference in the daily hellishness that both groups endured—starvation, disease, the numbing torture of mindless hard labor—many Jews considered their faith essential to their survival. After all, they were targeted for extermination not for anything they did or might have done, but simply for who they were: Jews. Even the most secular couldn't escape the Nazis' cynical ethnic calculation. Thus, Jewish identity inevitably anchors many survivor accounts, religious and secular. Pierre Berg didn't have the arguable luxury of faith to buffer his suffering, and so the retelling of it—in astonishing detail worthy of thriller fiction—is raw, jarring, and as agonizing as the slash of a bullwhip. Berg's exhausting daily struggle to survive the next beating, the next freezing roll call, the next gun-wielding Nazi sadist, is as real as it gets. He doesn't aim for uplift or for answers to the great philosophical questions, but offers the hard currency of an ordinary person's experience recorded while still crisply recalled. I found Berg's honesty about how he coped with physical and emotional need under unimaginable pressure—how he processed loss, pain, and the Nazis' twisted reality—reassuring."

—Ellie Brecher, author of *Schindler's Legacy: True Stories of the List Survivors*; and General Assignment Reporter for *The Miami Herald*

"Pierre Berg's extraordinary survivor memoir *Scheisshaus Luck* is an invaluable contribution to a history we must never forget, further distinguished by the verve, vitality, and wry wit with which Berg tells his story. Paced like an adventure tale, laced with moving philosophical commentary, *Scheisshaus Luck* is a riveting, unforgettable read."

—Jenna Blum, author of *Those Who Save Us*

SCHEISSHAUS LUCK

Surviving the Unspeakable in Auschwitz and Dora

Pierre Berg

with Brian Brock

⊹AMACOM

AMERICAN MANAGEMENT ASSOCIATION

New York • Atlanta • Brussels • Chicago • Mexico City • San Francisco
Shanghai • Tokyo • Toronto • Washington, D.C.

Special discounts on bulk quantities of AMACOM books are
available to corporations, professional associations, and other
organizations. For details, contact Special Sales Department,
AMACOM, a division of American Management Association,
1601 Broadway, New York, NY 10019.
Tel.: 212–903–8316. Fax: 212–903–8083.
Web site: www.amacombooks.org

This publication is designed to provide accurate and authoritative
information in regard to the subject matter covered. It is sold with the
understanding that the publisher is not engaged in rendering legal,
accounting, or other professional service. If legal advice or other expert
assistance is required, the services of a competent professional person
should be sought.

Library of Congress Cataloging-in-Publication Data

Berg, Pierre.
  Scheisshaus luck : surviving the unspeakable in Auschwitz and Dora / Pierre Berg with
Brian Brock.—1st ed.
      p.   cm.
  Includes bibliographical references.
  ISBN 978-0-8144-1299-2
  1. Berg, Pierre.   2. Auschwitz (Concentration camp)   3. Political
prisoners—France—Biography.   4. World War, 1939–1945—Personal narratives,
French.   I. Brock, Brian.   II. Title.

  D805.5.A96B465   2008
  940.53'18092—dc22
  [B]

                                                                    2008003779

© 2008 Pierre Berg and Brian Brock.
All rights reserved.
Printed in the United States of America.

This publication may not be reproduced,
stored in a retrieval system,
or transmitted in whole or in part,
in any form or by any means, electronic,
mechanical, photocopying, recording, or otherwise,
without the prior written permission of AMACOM,
a division of American Management Association,
1601 Broadway, New York, NY 10019.

Printing Number

10   9   8   7   6   5   4   3   2   1

Northville District Library
212 W. Cady Street
Northville, MI 48167-1560

OCT 3 0 2008

3 9082 05753608 1

To all my comrades who didn't make it

CONTENTS

FOREWORD

In 1947, two years after Pierre Berg escaped from a Nazi concentration camp, he began writing down his experiences. His goal was to record his observations of those terrible eighteen months before he forgot them. He had no intention of ever publishing them. Nonetheless, he gave these recollections a title, *Odyssey of a Pajama*.

Pierre wrote his memoir in French, but since he was now living in America, he had it translated by a UCLA grad student. He then allowed a couple of people to read his odyssey, and they convinced him that a magazine or book publisher might be interested in his story. In 1954, after two rejection letters, one from the *Saturday Evening Post* and the other from *Harper's*, Pierre put his concentration camp memoir aside and got on with his new life in Los Angeles.

More than fifty years later, I was supplementing my income as a struggling writer by working the concession stand at a playhouse in Beverly Hills. Pierre, now retired, was working as an usher. During a Sunday matinee performance, Pierre and I struck up a conversation on the writer's life. He informed me that he had written something about his time in the camps. A few days later he handed me a 145-page manuscript. As I read *Odyssey of a Pajama* for the first time, it was obvious that Pierre's experiences in the camps were unique and compelling. His voice was frank and was tinged with irony, irreverence, and gallows humor. The situations he found himself in were horrifying, heartbreaking, perverse, and oddly enough, sometimes funny. I was fascinated by his tale and by the young man in it. I believed that Pierre's story would be a major addition to the Holocaust literature.

We decided to work together to amplify the original manuscript, which we did through both oral and written interviews. One of the problems I found was that many of the events that the young Pierre had written about lacked crucial details that would immerse the reader in that world and in what he had suffered. After my initial interviews, it also became evident that some of the incidents the teenager had endured or witnessed did not appear in the manuscript. It was no surprise to me that the original manuscript was incomplete: It was written as a private journal by a very young man who, in 1947, had no way to judge the significance of what he had just experienced. Also, because his mother was typing the manuscript for him, Pierre had left things out in order to spare her the details of some horrific events he had been involved in.

As Pierre's collaborator I felt that I had two major responsibilities. First, I needed to ensure that his personality came across on the page. Second, I wanted to be sure that we expressed as vividly as possible the emotional impact of the daily life-and-death struggle in Auschwitz. This latter goal proved to be the more difficult.

It is well known that those who have been brutalized and violated block those memories as a survival mechanism. Pierre was no different. He was resistant to talking about the emotions that gripped him during those eighteen months, saying many times that he didn't feel anything. But the details he related to me, and his gestures and expressions in regard to those events, said otherwise. When he was unwilling to delve into the emotions of a specific incident, I would present him with differing emotional points of view, and this would often ignite a dialogue that enabled us to capture his emotional state at that time.

We had many arguments, especially when I aggressively tried

to elicit Pierre's reactions and emotions. I pushed him relentlessly because I thought it was important that his story be told fully. It is a credit to Pierre's strength of character that he never wavered in his resolve that this story be told completely—and that he never took a swing at me.

Concentration camp inmates all wore triangles of varying colors to distinguish the different classes of prisoners. Pierre's was a red triangle (political prisoner). His story is vital because it is a reminder that it wasn't just yellow triangles (Jews) who were rounded up and killed by the Nazis. The Jewish people suffered the most, but Gypsies, Communists, Jehovah's Witnesses, homosexuals, and other men, women, and children from every country in Europe were imprisoned and perished alongside them. *Scheisshaus Luck* will remind everyone that none of us—no matter what race, religion, nationality, or political conviction—are immune from becoming a victim of genocide.

◆ ◆ ◆

To be faithful to the spirit of Pierre's original manuscript, we have purposely steered away from putting the events in a historical context or of adding the elderly Pierre's thoughts on what he had endured sixty-two years earlier.

This, then, is the autobiographical account of an eighteen-year-old *Häftling* (inmate).

Brian Brock

PREFACE

"Our lives begin to end the day we become silent about things that matter."
—MARTIN LUTHER KING, JR.

If you're seeking a Holocaust survivor's memoir with a profound philosophical or poetic statement on the reasons six million Jews and many millions of other unlucky souls were slaughtered, and why a person like myself survived the Nazi camps, you've opened the wrong book. I'd be lying if I said I knew the reason, or if I even believed there is a reason, I'm still alive. As far as I'm concerned it was all shithouse luck, which is to say—inelegantly—that I kept landing on the right side of the randomness of life.

I can rattle off the reasons for the Holocaust that I've read in books and magazines, and they definitely contain some truth, but for me they fall short of fully explaining how a place as inhumane as Auschwitz could exist. There's nothing I've perused or heard spoken by Holocaust experts that explains the sadistic cancer that sprang from the Nazi masterminds, spread so easily through their SS henchmen, poisoned the *Kapos* (supervisors) and underlings, then killed and maimed untold millions. When you lived with that cancer day in and day out for eighteen months, no words, no jargon, no hypothesis, no historical context or philosophical noodling or religious rhetoric can adequately explain the glee or stone-cold soullessness in those murderers' eyes. No philosophical discourse will make sense of the memories of the innocent men I saw hung, beaten to death, shot in the head, or trucked off to Birkenau. Or why the stench of death had to greet us every morning when we woke, befriend us while we slaved for our Nazi masters, then follow us back to camp every night.

All I can give you, I hope, dear reader, is an understanding of what it was like to be an able-bodied teenager torn from family, friends, and home, tossed into a Nazi death camp, and nearly reduced to what the Nazis considered all of us who were tattooed, *Untermensch* (subhuman).

Pierre Berg

ACKNOWLEDGMENTS

It has been a long odyssey. There were times I wondered if I would live to see my memoir in print. Thankfully, that's not a worry anymore. Brian and I couldn't have done it without the guidance and support of countless friends, and our agent, Regina Ryan.

We'd especially like to thank:
Joseph Robert White
Michelle Upchurch
Ed Sweeney
Siegfried Halbreich
Sean Mozal
Marlon West
Barry Dennen
Mark Protosevich
Irene Baran
Brad Brock
Joe Kusek
Sarah Aspen
And our wonderful editors at AMACOM Books: Bob Nirkind and Mike Sivilli.

PART I
DRANCY

CHAPTER 1

Drancy, January 1944: A door slammed. I turned and found that Stella and I were now all alone. A searchlight's beam passed by the rain-drenched windows. Stella's damp, red hair was matted against her forehead and hung in rattails down her neck. Tears had dulled her blue eyes.

The guards' shrill whistles and the murmur of fellow prisoners shuffling into formation outside bounced off the whitewashed walls. Stella buried her face against my shoulder. Her body shook. I held her closer so she wouldn't notice my own tremors. I pressed my mouth to her neck and found her racing pulse beating under my lips.

It was time to go. No sense getting dragged and kicked down two flights of stairs. I gently pried Stella's arms from around my neck and picked up my blanket roll and burlap bag of clothes. Strewn about the floor were vermin-infested mattresses, one of which had been my bed.

Neither of us spoke as we moved down the empty corridor. One wall was covered with old and newly scrawled farewell messages to loved ones not yet rounded up. I counted my footsteps in a vain attempt not to think about what was coming.

Going down the stairs, I wanted to comfort Stella, give her hope, but I kept silent. There wasn't a reassuring word I could squeak out with any conviction.

We walked out into the rain. Stella squeezed my hand at her waist. Standing before us in the cinder-lined courtyard were our traveling companions, twelve hundred prisoners of the Third Reich.

Stella's parents eagerly waved to her from the edge of the throng. Without a word, she released my hand and ran to them. I watched her hug her mother and father and wished I had kissed her. The tears I had held back in her presence now mixed with the cold rain.

"Hey, Pierre, are you coming or not?"

"What are you waiting for?"

My friends were calling. There had been fifty of us, single men and a handful of teenagers like myself, living in that barren second-floor room, and now we would travel together on the train. We had been snatched up from all corners of France. Some of us were members of the Maquis (French Resistance). Others had been shipped in from other camps or prisons. Many had been awakened in the middle of the night, swept away as they were, and then were stunned to find themselves staring at freedom from behind barbed wire in the Paris district of Drancy. The Germans had transformed a half-finished apartment complex into a transit internment camp from where all "undesirables," mainly Jews, were deported to various Nazi concentration camps east of the Rhine.

As I trotted over to my pals, the wind carried snatches of voices singing songs of the *maquisards* (Resistance fighters). Many more voices joined in the singing of the *"Marche de Lorraine,"* a hymn of the "Free French," and *"La Marseillaise,"* the French national anthem. I stared contemptuously at the SS in their field gray uniforms as they let loose random volleys of submachine gunfire in attempts to intimidate us. The *gendarmes* (French military police) and *gardes-mobiles* (French federal police) stood motionless in their warm coats.

I joined in the singing of our version of *"Le Chant des Marais."*

"*Le printemps refleurira, Liberté, Liberté chérie Je dirai: Tu es à moi.*"
(*But one day in our lives, spring flower, freedom, cherished freedom, I will
say: You are mine.*)

Others took up the chorus. "*Piocher, piocher.*" (Swing a pick axe,
swing a pick axe.)

The roar of diesel engines drowned out our voices. Pulling into
the courtyard with their headlights barely piercing the morning fog,
the Paris buses looked like milky-eyed monsters hungry for new
bones to mash. This is finally it, I said to myself.

Drancy had been the scene of much misery, but it was where I
nevertheless had spent some of the happiest moments of my eighteen years. I craned my neck for a glimpse of Stella, but had no luck.
I looked over at the camp's shithouse, Le Château, and wondered if
a new arrival would find a sliver of good fortune when inheriting
my duties as the lord of that rank domain. Behind Le Château was
the building where we had been searched the evening of our arrival.
Stella had a small gold coin, her good luck charm, that she didn't
want to lose, so while we waited our turn to be frisked I hid it in a
piece of bread I had saved. She squeezed my hand when I returned
the keepsake the next day.

Across from that building were the rooms where they housed
the new arrivals. No light shone in the windows, but I was sure that
shadowy figures were pressing their faces to the grimy panes of
glass, wondering when their time would come. That had been my
thought as I watched a group being herded out my first night. I had
hoped with all my heart that I wouldn't be forced onto one of those
buses, but I quickly learned that, from behind barbed wire, hope
hardly ever brought more than heartache.

A loaded bus drove by. Someone wiped their fogged-up window
and waved to me.

"Stella, Stella!" I cried.

Instinctively I started after her, but a strong hand fell on my
shoulder.

"Don't, kid. You'll see your Stella again," Jonny murmured.

"You think so?"

"I'm sure."

I turned to see the blue exhaust of Stella's bus swirling at the gate.

My group began to board one of the buses. A Paris *flic* (French slang for a policeman) was seated beside the driver. Two *gendarmes*, shouldering rifles with fixed bayonets, guarded the rear platform. I sat down next to Jonny, who mopped his bald head with a red bandana. He was a former circus strongman, a Parisian Jew whose imposing build and calm manner had made him a natural leader in Drancy. It was rumored that he was the illegitimate son of a "doughboy" (WW I American soldier).

Jonny always had a good word to say to me when we passed each other in the courtyard and a joke to tell us all as we settled in for the night. He put his thick arm around my shoulder as I stared out the window.

"Let's go!" shouted one of the *gendarmes*.

After making a sharp turn, our bus rumbled toward the exit. Those still standing in the rain continued to sing.

"*Ô terre, enfin libre, Où nous pourrons revivre, Aimer! Aimer!*" (Oh earth, finally free, where we can again live and love! Love!)

The gate swung open. A curly-haired boy furiously pedaling his bike shot by as our bus pulled onto the street. I had been riding my bike the day I got myself into this predicament.

CHAPTER 2

Nice, November 1943: One morning my friend Claude arrived at my house dirty, bloody, and out of breath. For several years he and I sat next to each other in school. I lost count of how many times we had been reprimanded for playing tic-tac-toe during lectures. Now that we were in the second stage of *lycee* (high school) we didn't see each other as often, since I had opted for philosophy as my major and Claude had chosen mathematics.

"Can you hide me?" he asked.

"Sure. Why?" I asked, disconcerted by his appearance.

"Two Vichy goons came to our house to arrest me."

Two months earlier, September 8, 1943, to be exact, the Nazis occupied southern France after the Italians had pulled out of the war. Emboldened by the influx of SS and Gestapo, the Fascist *milice* (militia) in our hometown of Nice became more active.

"Why did they want to arrest you?"

"They're rounding up more bodies to finish the *boches'* [derogatory slang for Germans] Atlantic wall. Hell, no. I jumped through my rear window right into a bush."

I had heard that the traitors were snatching people at random. Claude smiled when I glanced down our driveway.

"Don't worry. I lost them for good."

"Get washed and I'll patch you up."

Claude wasn't sure why they had chosen him. It could have been because his parents were Italian, or because he was born in the French colony of Indochina. It could be they figured he had a strong back. Claude was a head taller than I was, and very athletic.

It was no problem letting him hide in our house. My parents were gone and wouldn't be back for a month or more. Since I was ten, my parents had been in the habit of leaving me alone when my mother accompanied my father on his business trips to Paris, Geneva, or Berlin. There was always a maid, but since their concern was keeping the house tidy, and not my comings and goings, I was more or less left to my own devices.

Even though my parents were in the mountains above Monte Carlo, they weren't on vacation this time. My father had leukemia, a cancer he had been battling for two years with radiation and arsenic treatments. He had been in remission for months, but it was back and my mother had escorted him to a clinic.

After Claude's brothers and his girlfriend came to visit a few times, I began to worry that the foot traffic would attract the attention of my neighbors. You couldn't trust anybody, with the Germans posting rewards for reporting anything suspicious or out of the ordinary. I took Claude into our backyard and pointed to the toilet under the steps leading to a room over the garage.

"Claude, if those bastards ever show up, this should be the best place to hide."

It was a Thursday afternoon. In France there was no school on Thursdays. Claude was upstairs in my room checking my homework. The only reason I was still in school was to please my father. He wanted me to become a jeweler and watchmaker, to have a business of my own. I suppose if he hadn't sold off his leather wholesale business, which included a shoe factory in Berlin and a factory in the French Alps that manufactured gloves, after being diagnosed, he would have wanted me to join him. The only business I was interested in owning was a beauty shop, but my father wasn't about to entertain that idea. Maybe he saw through it, since being a beautician had more to do with my aspirations as a gigolo than as an entrepreneur.

I was in the kitchen putting the leftovers from lunch into the icebox. And as she did every Thursday, our maid, Madame Biondi, was washing the laundry in the concrete double basin in the backyard. Fists pounding against the front door suddenly broke the wonderful monotony of the last two weeks.

"*Aufmachen!*" (Open up!), a guttural voice barked.

I raced upstairs and peeked through the slats of the closed wooden shutters of my parents' bedroom. Two plainclothes Gestapo officers and two soldiers with guns drawn were banging at the door and ringing the bell. I ducked into my room.

"Let's go!"

Claude and I tumbled down the steps and out the back door. Madame Biondi wasn't at the washbasin and the toilet door was locked.

"Fire!" I hissed, knocking at the door. "Get out!"

Madame Biondi rushed out with her panties around her ankles. I told Claude to stand on the toilet seat because of the gap at the bottom of the door.

"Madame, look busy and pull up the panties."

"*Mais, monsieur.*" (But, sir.)

"The Germans are here."

"Yes, yes, I understand," she said, and went back to the basin.

I grabbed a rake and started playing gardener. Just in time. The Germans came trotting around the corner. They didn't say a word to either of us. The younger officer, who had dark hair and penetrating eyes, and was wearing a black leather coat and black hat, ordered one soldier to stay with us as the rest of them rushed through the rear door. On shaky legs I kept up my act as the gardener gathering leaves. I hoped they wouldn't notice me in the photographs on the walls or search the house too thoroughly. I had a document stashed in my father's study that could get me shot.

Ten minutes later the *boches* came back out. The other officer, a bald-headed fatso wearing a tweed suit with brown leather buttons, had my father's attaché case in his pudgy hand. The sides of the case were bulging and I wondered what they had swiped. The younger officer came up to me. He was definitely the man in charge.

"Who are you?" he asked in broken French.

I could tell from his accent that he was Austrian.

"I'm the gardener."

"Papers," he ordered, waving his Luger at the two of us.

Madame Biondi pulled her I.D. from the pocket of her apron.

"Ah, Italian," the Austrian said in German.

"Mama, I don't have my I.D. with me," I whimpered.

"*Mi figlio*" (My son), she pointed at me.

Fatso asked in French where the owners were.

"They're sick old people, both in the hospital." For once I almost volunteered the truth.

"There are dishes on the table," he said, pointing toward the kitchen.

"We had lunch."

"*Die Frau am Telephon hat gemeldet dass hier viele Leute sind*" (The woman on the phone mentioned a lot of people), the Austrian said to Fatso, who shrugged his shoulders.

"*Sind wir im falschen Haus?*" (Are we at the wrong house?)

"*Vielleicht*" (Maybe), said the Austrian.

They weren't hunting for Claude. They were hunting for Jews. The main reason for the flood of Gestapo and SS in Nice was that the Riviera had become a Jewish "Promised Land." Under the Italians, fleeing Jews were given legal residence and protection under the law, and the Italian police did everything they could to protect them. The goons were here to correct that.

The Austrian looked around.

"*Irgend etwas stimmt nicht. Wir werden die noch mal in der Nacht überraschen.*" (Something is fishy. We're going to surprise them again at night.)

Idiots. They didn't think that a gardener could understand

German and three other languages. All French students were required to learn two languages. I chose German and English. Italian was more or less a second language in southern France since it had been a part of Italy until Napoleon III took it. Our Italian maids had been good teachers. Spanish I picked up when the family of a Spanish general became our neighbors after the civil war. I taught their two sons French, and as a result I learned Spanish. They had wisely fled to Mexico not long after the German invasion.

"What's behind this green door?" the Austrian asked in German.

I struggled to stay calm. Fatso translated.

"A toilet," I said quickly. "The door has been jammed for a long time."

Fatso translated my response into German and the Austrian nodded. "Well, we will see."

He tried to pry it open, but it wouldn't budge. He grabbed one of the soldier's submachine guns and fired a volley at the bottom of the door. My heart stood still. Porcelain splinters came flying out the gap, followed by stinking brown ooze. Thankfully I saw no blood. The Austrian couldn't stomach the stench and called off the search.

After I made sure that they had left, I knocked at the toilet door. "Claude, open up."

He tumbled out, gasping as if he had been under water.

"Boy, you got splashed. You stink," I told him.

"When the bowl collapsed I added to the mess," he replied. "I shit in my pants."

Madame Biondi was sitting on the back steps, shaking and sobbing.

"I'm glad that I didn't flush," she squeaked.

Before curfew that night, Claude collected his things and went to stay with one of his brothers on the outskirts of town. For both our sakes I wasn't about to contact my friend until the Nazis were defeated.

A week later I rode my bike down Boulevard de Cimiez to visit my friend Bernard, a skinny seventeen-year-old whose thick glasses had made him the brunt of many of our classmates' jokes. I had known Bernard since elementary school. In high school we wrote and performed goofy skits on his shortwave transmitter. We loved to imitate Laurel and Hardy. In France, their movies had become extremely popular when the comedic duo chose to speak their lines in French instead of using subtitles. Hearing French spoken with a pronounced British accent was more hilarious than their slapstick, and Bernard and I lampooned their voices in our skits. The shortwave signal was weak, but our friends received our transmissions, and we would be the talk of the school the next day. When our critics became ruthless in their reviews, we ended our careers as radio stars. No sense being the fodder for other kids' jokes.

Bounding up the marble steps of Bernard's parents' villa, I noticed that the heavy front door was ajar. I pushed it open.

"Bernard?"

"*Hände hoch!*" (Hands up!)

I couldn't believe my eyes. It was that Gestapo fatso. He sure didn't have to shout. His 9mm automatic staring at my forehead was enough. I raised my hands with only one thought in my head, and it was truly peculiar, considering the severity of the moment. Was that a Luger or Walther? Before I could ask him, he pushed me face first against the wall next to a petrified Bernard. I could tell from the crimson splotches on his face that Bernard had been slapped a few times.

After being frisked by a uniformed Waffen SS corporal, I was ordered to turn around. Fatso was wearing the same tweed suit. There was a Nazi Party button on his lapel.

"It's the gardener who didn't have his I.D. papers," he said smugly. "What are you doing here?"

"I wanted to see why Bernard missed school yesterday."

"Do you have your papers today?"

I nodded and handed them to him. I held my breath. These were the papers that I had hoped they wouldn't find in my father's study. My false identification papers.

"Pierre Berceau. You're Italian and have a French name?"

I slid Bernard a glance. Either he was too preoccupied with his own troubles to take notice of my bogus last name or he had a great poker face.

"My father's French."

"Of course."

I held out my hand for my papers, but Fatso slid them into the breast pocket of his jacket. Not a good sign. He pointed at Bernard's shortwave transmitter that was sitting on the floor.

"Have you seen this before?"

"Sure, my friend has played with it for many years."

"And you didn't report it?"

"Why should I?"

"It's illegal. It's a weapon, not a toy."

Bernard started to turn around.

"*Gerade stehen!*" (Stand straight!) The corporal bounced Bernard's head against the wall. His glasses went flying. Whimpering, Bernard knelt to pick them up. A kick in the rear lifted him into the air.

"He needs them," I protested. "He's almost blind without them."

Fatso crushed the glasses under his heel.

Two SS soldiers pushed an elderly couple into the entryway. They were the housekeepers who had raised Bernard.

"*Was wollen Sie mit den anfangen?*" (What do you want to do with them?), the corporal asked.

"They're Italian nationals. Let them go," Fatso answered. "Have your men take the blind one here and lock him up. I'm sure we can find room on the Paris train for this gardener."

I was in a panic, but I couldn't let on that I knew their language. When they put me in handcuffs I blurted out, "What did I do?" This time it was my head that was bounced off the wall.

What did I do? Well, it was pretty bad luck on my part to have popped up twice in Fatso's presence in the span of a week. From his vantage point I had to be guilty of something. And that was all the excuse a Nazi needed.

They hustled us out of the house. Bernard was between the two soldiers and I was behind the corporal and Fatso, who was carrying the transmitter and a bag of loot from the house. What a dirty thief, I thought. Luigi, the gardener for the estate next door, watched from behind the iron fence that my bicycle was chained to. He had seen me lock up my bike that day and many other times. I managed to get the key for my lock out of my pants' rear pocket and drop it when I passed him. I knew he wasn't a collaborator, so I was pretty sure I could trust him. This was crucial. I was a courier for the French Resistance, and there was a message hidden in the air pump of my bike. That's why I had false I.D. papers. I used them to get past roadblocks when delivering messages.

The gardener gave me a wink. Hopefully he would hide my bike in his tool shed. If the Nazis found that message and connected it to me, it would be certain torture and death.

Bernard and his guards got into one of the two Citroëns parked at the curb. I had noticed the cars when I locked my bike, but hadn't given much thought that they didn't have the cumbersome *gazogene* coal burners that civilian cars dragged behind them to fuel their engines. How stupid of me! Only the cars of Nazis and Vichy officials ran on gasoline. Fatso shoved me into the rear seat of his Citroën.

During the drive to the Nice railroad station, I listened carefully to the conversation between the corporal, who was driving, and Fatso, who was inspecting the confiscated valuables.

"I'll return in a week. Meantime, see if you can get the other little bastard to talk, but keep him alive. Understand? He might be worth a ransom. His family is definitely wealthy and well connected. With his ever-expanding quotas, the one in the back will make Speer happy."

I breathed a little easier. It seemed that Bernard and I would survive for a while. Speer was Albert Speer, the head of Nazi weapon production, and I, it appeared, was going to become one of the millions of sprockets in their war machine. This meant, if I was smart, my involvement in the Maquis would stay a secret and I would be spared any interrogation and torture.

The corporal took back roads to the train station, a shortcut I had volunteered after he pulled out a map in front of Bernard's house. The way I saw it, the shorter the trip, the sooner I would be rid of the handcuffs. During the drive, the only person I saw whom I knew was the coffee merchant who was sweeping the sidewalk in front of his shop. I would tag along with my mother when she went to his shop because I loved the dense, invigorating aroma of the freshly roasted coffee beans. With the war came blocked shipping lanes and the aroma disappeared, replaced by the harsh smell of roasted date pits brought in from the French territories in North Africa.

At the station, a passenger train bound for Paris was waiting for us—waiting for Fatso to board, to be exact. The corporal led me to a passenger car behind the caboose. The windows were wired shut and armed guards stood on the platforms at either end of the car. Once inside, the corporal removed the handcuffs and I was finally able to scratch some very nervous itches. He shoved me into a passenger compartment that had a vacant seat next to a girl a couple years younger than I was. Her freckled, turned-up nose gave her a cocky air, but she greeted me with a shy smile. A feeble "Hello" squeaked from my throat as I sat down. Any other time I would have played the café Don Juan with such a *belle môme*.

I eyed my traveling companions with a mixture of suspicion and curiosity. Any of them could have been a collaborator, a Nazi plant, or desperate enough to sell out a fellow countryman to save his or her own hide. A slip of the tongue could be a noose slipped around my neck. No one talked except for the whispers shared among loved ones. It could have been that we were all leery of a rat in our midst. When the train pulled out of the station it seemed to ease those suspicions and slowly bring home that we shared a common plight. Conversations were struck and soon enough I was acquainted with my fellow prisoners.

Across from me at the window sat Marius, a middle-aged man with a handlebar mustache stained yellow from nicotine. He wore a leather jacket, corduroy pants, work boots, and a cap as dirty as his fingernails. A corncob pipe was stuffed in one jacket pocket while cloves of garlic, which he munched on like bonbons, were stuffed in the other pocket. Marius was a Corsican plumber and a low-level official of the French Communist Party. Next to him sat a beautiful young Honduran with shoulder-length jet-black hair and flawless olive skin. She was a stunning mix of Central American Indian and Conquistador. Her Austrian-Jewish husband, sitting on her other side, was at least twice her age. He was some kind of professor and had a coiffure like Albert Einstein. Every time I looked at him I couldn't help but wonder if there was a correlation between high IQ and crazy hair growth. She constantly fussed over their two-year-old twin daughters sitting between them. They were headed to an enemy civilian internment camp because of their Honduras citizenship.

Sitting at the window on my side was a refined lady who was constantly wiping her nose and dabbing at tears with a lace handkerchief. Her husband I recognized from photos in the newspapers. He had been an official in the French Socialist Front Populaire government, which had been in power from 1936 to 1938. From their conversations I gathered that the girl next to me was their daughter, Stella.

For some reason the monotonous clicking of the car's wheels on the rails reminded me of the metronome my mother used when she rehearsed for a recital. She was a contralto who had performed all over Europe before I was born. After I arrived, my father decreed that there would be no more tours, but she still performed locally. There were times her rehearsals drove me out of the house. I closed my eyes and thought, if only now my homework was being disturbed by her practicing scales.

Stella leaned toward me. Her breath tickled my ear.

"Would you like to step out with me?"

I nodded, welcoming the chance to stretch my legs.

"I can't bear watching my mother cry," she said once we were outside the compartment.

"Why were you and your parents arrested?"

"Because of my father's politics and editorials and my mother being Jewish. My father's internment has been a priority since the Nazis crossed the demarcation line. How about you?"

"Because of pure, irresponsible stupidity."

"What do you mean?"

"It's not important. Never mind."

Oh, Stella was pretty, but she was a pretty stranger. I wasn't about to open up to her. At least not yet.

"How about your parents?" Stella asked.

"They're safe, but I'm worried about them. I'm sure they're going to be frantic when they realize I'm gone."

By giving the Nazis false identification papers I had made it impossible for my parents to trace me. Neither my parents nor any of my friends knew that I was involved in the Resistance, and the only person in the Resistance who I knew was the man who had given me the I.D. papers, Lucien Meffre. He was the man who recruited me and had been my contact.

A German officer came down the hall.

"Maybe we shouldn't be out here." I whispered, touching her arm.

Once we sat down I saw the SS officer stop and peer through the glass window in the sliding door of our compartment. I stiffened. Now we're going to get it, I thought. The *boche* opened the door. With his chest full of medals, he made a perfect poster for the "master race." He smiled and addressed the mother of the twins.

"I have milk for your girls," he told her in perfect Spanish.

She seemed more resigned than happy about the news. Her husband stroked the heads of their daughters as she followed the officer. He looked sad. I believe there were tears in his eyes.

The mother returned a while later with her dress in disarray, her face flushed, and two cans of evaporated milk cradled in her arm. Her husband snatched them from her as she sat back down.

Not a word was uttered between them the rest of the way. Their uneasiness shrouded our compartment. From that moment, all conversation seemed trite. The couple's unsavory predicament brought home to all of us that we were at the Nazis' mercy. But the guards sure made an effort to seem friendly. For our journey they acted as if they had gone to charm school. During our eleven-hour ride, they even managed to get us some food—a piece of bread, some cheese, and some sausage. The professor wondered out loud if the sausage contained pork. I almost laughed. That should have been the least of his worries.

I went out to take a leak. As I walked to the end of the car, I glanced into the other compartments. There wasn't an empty seat in any of them. All my fellow prisoners had been held at the Hotel Excelsior in Nice. Some had been locked up for two weeks, others only a day. While I was pedaling to Bernard's, they had been herded into the street and marched to the train station.

We were all asleep when we reached Paris. The jolt of our car's being detached from the train brought us back to our sad reality. Stella's head had been resting on my shoulder.

"Oh, I am so sorry," she said blushing.

"I didn't mind."

She flashed that shy smile again.

To ensure that none of us had the chance to melt into the crowd of travelers at the Paris station, the Nazis had an engine pull our car to a desolate area of the train yard. There, two green-and-white buses waited to take us to Drancy.

CHAPTER 3

Drancy, November 1943–January 1944: I sat next to Stella's father. Stella sat in front of us with an arm wrapped around her mother. Two SS guards stood on the ticket-taker's platform at the rear of the bus. I decided to memorize the street signs so if I escaped I could make my way back to the station. With Nazi goons checking papers, it would be impossible to slip onto a passenger train, but I might be able to hop a freight train.

The buses rumbled down empty boulevards. Because of the gasoline rationing there were hardly any vehicles in sight. The Parisians we passed were either on foot or on bicycle. I had never been to Paris before, but the people sitting around me remarked on how drab and dark the capital now looked. Many store windows were boarded up and the entrances were protected by stacks of sandbags. Other shops appeared to be abandoned. Some of the streets barely hinted at human life.

"How can you be proud of something that doesn't belong to you anymore?" a man behind me asked.

We traveled alongside a high gray stucco wall. "*Monsieur*, you lived in Paris for some time. What's behind this wall?" I asked.

"*Père Lachaise*. My mother is buried there."

19

We passed the gated entrance to the most famous cemetery in France. Sitting on the steps was a woman breast-feeding her baby. Stella turned around, with tears wetting her cheeks.

"Daddy, I want to visit grandma's grave."

"I'm sure we will soon."

I could see in his eyes that he didn't believe his own words, and that was unnerving. What does he know that's making him lie to his own daughter? I asked myself. I searched for words of comfort to say to Stella. Realizing I would be deluding both of us, I sat silent and stared at her red hair.

Our bus reached Boulevard Gambetta. On the corner was an elderly gentleman relieving himself at a *pissoir*, a green kiosk with a pointed roof, encircled by a three-foot-wide metal band that obscured the user's midriff. Some of the prisoners giggled and waved. The man looked up and raised his hat. As we went down rue de Paris, a couple of kids on roller skates raced after our bus, trying to hitch a ride, but they backed off when they saw the German guards.

The buses turned onto avenue du Parc and we found ourselves at our destination, a horseshoe-shaped housing complex with an expansive cinder-lined courtyard. Barbed wire surrounded the four-story buildings and a large gate sealed the compound's opening, which was manned by *gendarmes* instead of Nazis.

I turned to Stella's father as our bus drove into the courtyard. "Is this a French military brig?"

"This is part of a new agreement between the Vichy and the Occupation administration. Frenchmen doing the Nazi's dirty work," he said. "They're the jailers of many brave men who fought side by side with them when the Germans invaded."

The captain of the *gendarmes* stepped onto the rear platform and was handed a ledger by one of the SS.

"Raise your hand when I call your name," he barked.

When he came to Pierre Berceau, I held up my arm.

"Stella, Ruth, and Emile Binda. . . ."

The captain stared at Mr. Binda, then looked down at his feet. Mr. Binda shook his head.

"He used to stand at attention and salute me when I entered the ministry building," he whispered to his family.

"*Raus!*" The two SS guards waved us off the bus.

As I helped an elderly couple with their luggage, Frenchmen with red armbands directed us to the center of the courtyard, where they had us line up three deep. These red armbands were the camp police, the Nazis' lackeys, mainly well-educated professionals but prisoners just like us. They received certain privileges for administrating the camp. It was the efficient Teutonic way of saving their manpower for the battlefield.

The buses pulled out and the *gendarmes* closed the gates. A red armband, whose mannerisms made me think he had been a schoolteacher, briefed us.

"You'll be housed in the building to your left. The construction of all these buildings hasn't been completed, but for lodgings they are more than adequate. The connecting building at the end of the yard is off limits. It's quarantined. We have a scarlet fever epidemic here in Drancy, but there's no reason to be alarmed by this. All those that have been stricken are quarantined. Now, if you have had scarlet fever, please step out."

Without thinking I stepped forward.

"Only one?" the man asked. "Don't be afraid. We need you because you're immune. You cannot catch it twice."

I started thinking I had been foolish, and then I found Stella standing next to me. Only a handful of us stayed in Drancy. The rest, mostly Jews, gave the Nazis the twelve hundred inmates they needed to fill a train. The Germans would never waste coal on a light load. To Stella's relief, her parents were able to avoid the deportation because of her assignment in the quarantine ward.

Stella and I spent many hours together in that ward. While she attended to the needs of the stricken, I carried the pails that their bedpans filled down to Le Château. Our shithouse got its prestigious name because of the castle-like crenellations at the top of the walls. Every day I emptied one hundred and ten pails, making fifty-five trips up and down four floors. My legs must have thought I was living in the Eiffel Tower. And at the end of every shift I scrubbed the stairs to erase the double yellow line created by the sloshing pails.

I would watch Stella with admiration and warmth as she fed patients whose hands were too shaky to hold a spoon, applied ointment to bedsores, and sponged down bodies that were wracked with fever. There wasn't a single patient who died whom she didn't shed tears for.

"You cannot cry for everyone," I told her.

"Someone should."

"You're going to make yourself sick."

"I can't help that it acts on me this way," she shot back. "Anyway, they said we couldn't catch it again."

"But there are a lot of other things you might catch."

"Don't worry about me. I'll be fine."

I could make her laugh and evaporate some of her tears with my Laurel and Hardy impersonations. I was never sure if she was giggling at the jokes or just found me incredibly silly. Regardless, it seemed to distract her from the sadness that surrounded her.

Stella also enjoyed my recollections of my mother's singing. She felt it was a pity that my father had stopped her from touring, but she thought it must have been magical to grow up in a house echoing with arias. She missed her violin and was overly concerned that she would lose her ability to play.

"If you've been practicing since you were six, there's no chance of that," I reassured her.

Emptying the buckets wasn't my only task. I was in charge of cleaning Le Château, too. Marius, the Corsican plumber, gave me the title *"Roi du Château,"* or "King of the Shithouse." To keep the long row of concrete squat toilets disinfected, twice a day I would sprinkle lime around the funneled holes in the floor. Easy enough, but some prisoners had got into the habit of painting the ceiling with their feces, especially in the women's section. This exercise in frustration and animosity toward the Nazis made my life a stinking hell. It was impossible to escape the brown raindrops as I struggled to unglue their mess with a garden hose and broom. I had only the clothes that I had been arrested in, and the stench on them became unbearable for everyone. When Stella stopped brushing up against me I knew something had to be done. Thankfully, one red armband took me to a storeroom full of suitcases and clothing.

"Take anything that fits. These belonged to the departed."

I didn't ask if "departed" meant dead or deported. The armful of tailor-made suits I quickly chose got me the nickname "the Dandy of the Shithouse."

I was also responsible for emptying the pails of those prisoners in solitary confinement, who were held in the same building those in quarantine. This was where the SS and Gestapo tortured men and women. Many times I would find a mangled corpse instead of the living person I had spoken to the day before. Standing over these corpses, I would ponder if they had died because they refused to reveal their contacts in the Maquis or because they wouldn't disclose the hiding places of their art collections, jewelry, or other coveted valuables. To me, it was foolish to die for a painting or diamond ring, and it was sad that those Resistance members probably knew nothing more than the names of their contacts, which were more than likely false names.

Stella and I quickly found ourselves acting like boyfriend and girlfriend. We never discussed it or announced it to anyone, but we were an item. Hell, the fifty men I shared sleeping quarters knew she was "my Stella." How could we not become involved? It was inevitable. In each other's arms, we forgot for a few sweet moments the gravity of our predicament and dreamt of fairytales futures.

As the weeks went by Stella and I made more time to sneak off into a staircase or the corner of a comatose patient's cell to kiss and caress. As long as we performed our duties nobody paid attention to us. I loved the way she felt, smelled, and tasted. She liked that I had some experience. I didn't tell her that it had been a thirty-six-year-old woman who had initiated me at fourteen. The wine they gave us with our meals was spiked with saltpeter because sex between "undesirables" was *verboten*, but it hardly had any effect on the two of us. Stella could be pretty bashful, though. One time I knelt, raised her dress, and began kissing her thighs. Realizing my intentions, she became embarrassed because she hadn't washed yet, but I didn't care. Afterwards, she wanted to try on me, but I finished before she could start. Tears welled in her eyes. She thought she had done something wrong. Holding her hand, I reassured her that that wasn't the case at all. I brushed my thumb over a pyramid-shaped scar above the knuckle of her left index finger.

"A parrot, a big Macaw, bit me when I was in kindergarten. I thought he was going to bite off my whole hand. Oh, I cried. And I hit that bird so hard that I stunned him. I thought I killed him," she giggled.

One day I came out of my castle and found Mr. Binda standing in the courtyard. I had been avoiding him and his wife so I wouldn't have to answer any questions about my relationship with their daughter. He grabbed me by the arm. "Let's go for a stroll."

We walked in silence and I began to sweat. Had Stella let something slip about our relationship? "I want to thank you for being such a good friend of Stella's. It's been traumatic for her."

"I know. I wish I had met her, all of you, under other circumstances."

We came to the gate. A jovial group of *gendarmes* were standing there.

"Those dirty sons of bitches. Don't they have any shame? I would rather die than be in their boots," I said.

"Don't judge them too harshly. They're professional soldiers trained to take orders from whoever's in charge. Believe me, some of them are working hand in hand with the resistance."

"Yes, I know one in Nice who notified our network and some Jewish families on impending raids."

"I may know him, too."

"One of the *gendarmes* told me that he would close his eyes if I slipped through the wire on his shift."

Mr. Binda shook his head. "You can't chance it. He may be a rotten egg hunting for a promotion."

"That's why I'm still here. There's no sure way to candle the good eggs from the bad ones."

◆ ◆ ◆

On Christmas Eve, I had emptied my first two pails when a red armband approached me.

"Wash your hands and come with me."

"Why? Where to?" I asked.

"To the administration building, but don't ask me why."

My stomach instantly knotted up. Being escorted to the Nazis' offices meant only one thing—trouble. A *gendarme* escorted us out the gate and to a high-rise building across the street. We went down a hallway on the first floor and stopped at a door where a large cardboard box was sitting. After knocking, my two companions entered the office. As I stepped into the doorway an SS officer sitting at one of three desks barked in French.

"Stay there! You're contaminated."

Looking over papers at another desk was that Austrian Gestapo officer wearing the same black leather coat. His black hat was hanging on a coat rack. Now I knew I was in trouble. The question was who squealed on me and for what? Oddly, the Austrian looked up at me puzzled.

"*Warum ist dieser gute Lügener noch hier?*" (Why is this good liar still here?) he asked the officer.

"He's our orderly in the ward. You know him, Herr Brunner*?" The officer asked.

Again the Germans arrogantly assumed I couldn't speak their mother tongue.

---

* SS Captain Alois Brunner was the Commandant of Drancy from June 1943 until August 1944. When the Germans took over the Italian zone of France, he was sent to Nice to oversee the roundup of Jews. Brunner was responsible for deporting 24,000 people from Drancy to the extermination camps.

"He's an accomplished liar." He stared directly at me. "Someone sure did a lousy job burying a box of jewelry and gold watches in the basement of that house."

I kept a blank look on my face. Obviously he hadn't found Claude or the message in my pump, but he had kept his promise and returned to our house. After hearing that the Nazis were emptying every safe and bank in Nice, I took it upon myself to bury my mother's best jewelry along with my father's gold watches in the dirt floor of our basement.

The Austrian went back to his paperwork.

"Ship him out when the crisis is over."

"I was going to send him to Compiègne. The kid is a political. He's not circumcised," the officer replied.

"No. Put him on a transport to Ausch . . . Germany."

The officer nodded, then turned to me.

"Take that box of supplies to the infirmary."

What a Christmas present, I thought as I walked back, a train ticket to a German prison. If only I could figure out a way to infect the incoming prisoners with the fever, then Stella and I could work in the infirmary until the end of the war.

◆ ◆ ◆

Finally the dreaded moment came. All the scarlet fever patients were either cured or dead. The quarantine ward was empty and our deportation date was set. The honeymoon was over.

"Don't drink the wine anymore," Stella instructed.

"Why?"

"I want to do it like it's supposed to be. I want to be a real woman."

I wanted Stella so much, but had never attempted to make love to her and had never brought up the subject because of my fear of losing control, as I did on the staircase. Pregnancy could be a disaster for a female prisoner. There had been two sisters in the camp and one of them had been pregnant. The other wanted to tell the

Germans about her sister's condition, believing it would prevent her from being deported. A red armband quickly straightened her out.

"How can you be so naive? She won't be able to work and she's creating another mouth for them to feed. She will be the first on the train."

So I kept drinking the awful-tasting wine. But Stella became impatient, nearly frantic. There was an urgency in her eyes that puzzled me. I mulled over the possibility that she had had a premonition, but something stopped me from asking.

At the first opportunity, I snuck into the camp's administration office and stole the key to the storeroom. Late the next afternoon, after I had finished my shift, Stella led me down the hall. I turned on the light. We stretched out on a pile of coats among the stacks of suitcases and quickly pulled down our clothes.

"Make love to me."

She was biting her lip and her face was flushed with anticipation. I kissed her as I slid on top of her. I felt a resistance. She whimpered. I couldn't believe that as I entered her my mind drifted. When would we be able to do this again? Where were they shipping us? Would we stay together? How could I face her parents?

Stella started moaning softly. We had to keep quiet. I muffled her mouth with my hand, and suddenly she sounded like Kiki, my pet guinea pig. Stella held me tight, her fingernails digging into my back. She let out a subdued groan, trembled, then relaxed. I pulled out just in time.

Her eyes closed, Stella smiled. "Now I won't die a virgin."

Stunned, I blurted, "Don't be silly. You're going to live a long life."

She stared at me as if she hadn't heard my fairytale words, then she cuddled on my chest. To classmates and friends I had always proclaimed with some bravado that I was a fatalist, and here I was unnerved by the girl whose virginity I had just taken. What she was hinting at was darker than anything I dared to imagine.

♦ ♦ ♦

What was Stella thinking now, I asked myself as our bus arrived at the rain-soaked freight yard in the Paris suburb of Bobigny. I peered out the window. The *boches* weren't spoiling us with comfortable passenger compartments this time around. No, we were going to travel like farm animals. My belly was filled with fear. I was glad Jonny, the circus strongman, hadn't removed his arm from around my shoulder.

As our bus pulled up to the loading ramp, Nazi guards were locking one of the cattle cars. I had foolishly hoped to catch one more glimpse of my Stella before we were loaded. Now I would have to wait until we reached our destination, wherever that was.

CHAPTER 4

"Forty Men or Eight Horses" was stenciled on the side of the cattle car. I followed Jonny up the rain-slicked ramp. We squeezed inside and began jockeying with the others for a spot where we could comfortably sit on our luggage. When the Nazis locked the door, silence fell over us. It was as if we had all stopped to admire how a single action utterly defined our predicament.

They had told us in Drancy that we would be riding for two or three days, so when the train started moving the guessing games of our destination began.

"We're going to stop in Metz for screening."

"What do you mean, screening?"

"Why would they give us food when Metz is less than a one-day ride?"

"It seems that there is a big camp in Saxony."

"Do you think we're going to clear away the rubble in Berlin?"

"I know that we're going to Theresienstadt."

"Theresienstadt is only for old people."

"Let's pray we don't go to a Polish ghetto."

"Shut up, you silly fools," Jonny snapped. "We're going to the spas of 'Pitchi Poi'."

You won't find "Pitchi Poi" on any map. Someone in Drancy, long before I arrived, had dreamt up this fictional destination because it was a big Nazi secret where these transports were bound.

"Let's find a way of getting out of here before this train goes too far," Jonny said.

Hypolite, a weasel-faced little fellow in his early twenties whom I had never crossed paths with in Drancy, stood up.

"Listen. Everybody, listen. I've ridden this line to Alsace more than a hundred times. We left Bobigny at noon, correct? At this speed we should be at the place that I'm thinking of at around six o'clock. There's a steep hill and the track curves at the top. The train will be moving like a snail then." He glanced at his watch. "It's three o'clock now. We have enough time to get the job done."

"Yes, but we need tools to get out of here," someone shot back.

Hypolite smiled.

"I don't do anything without forethought."

Tucked into his socks was a rasp with one end sharpened like a chisel, a saw blade, and a pair of pliers. From inside his hatband he pulled out a drill bit. Many of the men moved closer to the little fellow. He definitely had my attention.

"No sense in trying to force the door open. More than likely it's wired to an alarm. The best thing is to cut an opening in the back wall," he said moving to the rear of the car. "If anyone has a better idea, speak up now."

No one spoke. Hypolite nodded and, using the pliers to turn the drill bit, he began to bore a hole in the back wall. Despite the thickness of the planks, it was a relatively easy task.

"Hey, you could enlarge the hole with the rasp," I suggested. "The saw blade will never cut through."

Hypolite agreed and I began to file. After a few minutes I stopped to catch my breath and Hypolite peered through the hole. He told me to take a look. The next car was the caboose and I could see the silhouette of a sentry standing in the brakeman's shelter. Fortunately the *boche* hadn't noticed anything, but it seemed our chance to escape had vanished. A few went off and sat in despair.

"Why not try the other end?" a Hasidic Jew whispered.

"No. Two or three might jump off, perhaps, then the rest would be shot like pigeons," Jonny said.

"The hell if I'm going to let myself be taken off in a cage like a circus animal," Hypolite spit.

He dropped to the floor and attacked it with his drill. As he slaved away, sweat dripped from his forehead and his shirt stuck to his back. The region we were passing through was white with frost, but it was stifling in the car. The two small windows barely provided any ventilation, and our fifty packed bodies gave off heat like freshly sheared sheep. I was broiling in the three layers of winter clothes that I had piled on the night before.

The floorboards were stronger and twice as thick as the planks of the back wall. Even when his hands began to bleed, fingers ravaged with splinters, Hypolite's determination didn't waver. Realizing the drill wasn't long enough to go all the way through the wood, he wound a handkerchief around the saw blade and went to work on the edges of the hole until it was funnel-shaped. He pounded the rasp with the heel of one of his boots until the sharpened end punctured the floorboard.

"Now we can really begin sawing," he proclaimed.

Jonny looked at his watch. There was only half an hour left—hardly enough time to saw a hole large enough to allow a man to escape, but nothing was going to deter us now. We took turns. Sawing, sawing, sawing, only stopping when the blade burned our hands. Finally we had a hole large enough to allow Jonny and two other men to rip out three planks. The rush of cold air catapulted our excitement. Everyone was smiling.

The train began to slow. We could hear the locomotive straining.

"Here we are, boys. It's time to jump," Hypolite said as he wrapped his knees and elbows with strips torn from his blanket.

No one could argue his right to go first. Hypolite lowered himself slowly through the opening. I could hear his feet dragging on the cinders. He leaned on his elbows for a moment, then ducked his head through the hole. He was going to drop belly first. His hands released their hold. Hypolite was gone. We all wanted to rejoice, but was he a free man or did he get crushed under the wheels? We had no idea, but there were fifteen of us who wanted to find out. The others were too old, too sick, or too afraid.

One after another they dropped through the hole. Suddenly it was down to Jonny and me.

"Go ahead, kid. I'll be the last. The train could derail if I bounced," he laughed, pushing me toward the opening.

I had already made up my mind to be the last one through that hole.

"Go ahead, Jonny. I'm not a kid anymore."

"I won't hear of it. Go on, Pierre, we're running out of time."

Something was holding me back. I kept thinking of what I had promised Stella when we walked down those stairs. I felt foolish. I wanted my freedom, but I didn't want to break my promise. I didn't want to abandon her. She was sitting in another car thinking of me, depending on me. At least that's what I hoped.

"Please, Jonny, I want to be the last one."

Jonny had lost his patience.

"Have it your way."

He dropped his few possessions through the hole and began to lower himself. His bald head turned crimson as he struggled to squeeze his barrel-chested torso through. His boots hit the cinders. That's when I realized that the locomotive wasn't panting and puffing anymore. The harsh, metallic grinding of the wheels left no doubt that our car had reached the curve.

"Jonny, hurry up!"

Nothing was visible except his powerful hands with those short, square fingers. When he let go there was a ripping sound. I threw myself down and looked through the hole. The back of Jonny's tight-fitting leather jacket had snagged on a lantern hook and he was swinging from it like a puppet. He tried to release himself, but his arms couldn't reach the hook. He thrashed about as if he were drowning in the ocean.

"What happened?" I heard someone ask.

"He's caught on something!"

Jonny's heavy body tipped, throwing his head inches from the track. I leaned out the hole. It was pitch black. The rattling and screeching of the steel wheels was deafening. The icy wind stung my face. My eyes watered and my nose began to burn as I fought to unhook him. I pulled with everything I had, but Jonny's jacket held fast.

The train gathered speed. The cars banged together, then jolted apart, threatening to throw me out. I caught hold of Jonny's legs. Someone grabbed an ankle. I took the other, but before we could hoist him up, his body gave a sharp jerk. Jonny shrieked, a cry of agony that faded into a guttural moan. I grabbed his twitching legs. It was a strange and sickening sensation. I pulled with all the strength I had. Someone took hold of his trousers. His suspenders broke. From all directions hands reached out. His legs were in. More hands came. Jonny's jacket and shirt peeled over his head as we finally lifted his upper body through.

Everyone gathered around as we laid Jonny on the cold floor. I stripped off the bloody jacket and shirt that covered his face like a shroud. Once full of laughter, his blue eyes were now fixed and slightly protruding. A thin stream of blood trickled from a deep gash at the base of his skull and disappeared through a gap in the floor. Great brown clots formed in his ears. How did this happen? Someone said that Jonny's head must have struck a switching rail. An old doctor from Toulouse bent over and examined the wound.

"Nothing we can do," he shook his head. "There's a fracture at the base of his skull."

I knelt beside Jonny and carefully dabbed at the wound with his shirt. You're strong, hold on. Fight. That's what I wanted to say as his breathing became increasingly jerky and irregular, but I couldn't utter a word. No one spoke. There were no poetic words or reassuring Bible passages that would give Jonny any solace as he endured the final strangulation of his life. His death rattle brought me to my feet. Consumed with grief and guilt, I let go of his bloody shirt and flopped down by the door.

The smoky kerosene lantern hanging from the ceiling swung in rhythm with the rails, throwing fantastic shadows on the walls. It cast a shifting yellow glow over Jonny's slack face. When the light fell on the living, all I saw was dismay and bewilderment. Everyone had looked up to Jonny. I'm sure we all believed he was the one who could survive anything the Nazi had in store. I closed my eyes.

What had Jonny thought when I refused to go? Did he think I was afraid? Did he perceive it as misplaced politeness, or did he realize Stella was holding me back? His last look at me had been angry, but not scornful. I would have liked to explain to him. I would have liked to ask his pardon, his forgiveness, but even if I had jumped, that hook would have still snagged him.

I opened my eyes. The train was now traveling at a dizzying speed. Wind howled through the hole, swirling straw and sawdust over Jonny's body. I got up and closed the hole with the broken planks.

♦ ♦ ♦

I awoke with my heart racing. I had been dreaming that I was in the middle of a bombing raid. My body relaxed when I realized that the explosions were the train cars passing over a bridge. Painfully I stood up. The stink of unwashed bodies and excrement hung thick in the car. We had been riding for three days.

I went to one of the windows and opened my mouth wide, hoping that a little moisture might condense in it. Dark green clumps of pines enlivened the gray landscape speeding by. Here and there patches of snow clung to the hillsides. From the architecture of the houses and the onion-shaped steeples of the church towers in the distance I could tell we were heading into Poland. We had crossed through Germany, and that meant we weren't being delivered to Dachau, Buchenwald, or Sachsenhausen. Where the hell were we going? What was in Poland other than Jewish ghettos? Maybe we were going even farther. Could we be slave laborers meant for the Eastern Front? Looking at my fellow prisoners I thought, how could any of us survive a Russian winter?

When the train finally stopped at a station, every man, woman, and child in the cattle cars screamed for water. The Nazis hadn't given us anything more to drink or eat. The bucket of water they put in our car in Bobigny had quickly been emptied. How could we have known that they wouldn't refill it? We implored our guards, but to no avail. The civilians on the platform turned a blind eye except for one well-dressed gentleman who approached an adjoining car with a hot beverage. Before he could reach an outstretched arm, a guard slapped the cup out of his hand.

"*Umdrehen, das sind Dreckjuden!*" (Turn around, they're dirty Jews!)

There was a hospital train parked on the other track. Medical corpsmen in white uniforms scurried back and forth in coach cars crammed with wounded men on gurneys stacked on three tiers. Looking out his window, a soldier with a bandaged forehead gave me a friendly wave, no doubt thinking that I was one of his compatriots heading to the front. Oh, how I envied him, all of them. They were suffering physically, but they were being well cared for and they knew where they were going.

I couldn't help but think of Jonny, whose body was now lying miles behind us. An hour after his death, someone said the Kaddish in Hebrew, then Father Tonanti, an old Catholic priest, stepped forward. Though he was a man of the cloth, I respected him greatly. The priest and I had had long philosophical conversations in Drancy, but he couldn't make a believer out of me nor could I convert him to atheism.

"Since we pray to the same God, let me pray for his soul."

As he prayed for Jonny, the priest's accent, full of the sunshine of Provence, warmed me for a moment. With his amen, the planks were lifted and Jonny's body was lowered through the hole.

Father Tonanti was now sitting in a corner. His eyes were closed and his lips moved almost imperceptibly. He was praying, his hands mechanically counting the beads of an imaginary rosary. He was in the cattle car because of his blind devotion to humanity. One of his parishioners, a member of the far-right Croix-de-feu, had gotten wind that he was providing refuge for a handful of Jewish toddlers. The man threatened to turn the priest over to the Gestapo if he didn't surrender the children. He stood to gain a hefty bounty for those Jewish orphans. The enraged priest chased him out of the church, but before the children could be shepherded to a safe haven the man returned with some of his fascist cronies. Father Tonanti's strength of conviction and faith humbled me. As the train started up again, I pondered whether I would have the strength to hold on to my humanity.

PART II
AUSCHWITZ

CHAPTER 5

I leaned my head against the car's rough wood wall and realized that the train wasn't moving. I was perplexed. How long have we been parked here, I asked myself. When did we stop? I hadn't dozed off. I struggled to focus my thoughts, but my head was as thick as jellied consommé. I had lost all perception of time and couldn't say with any certainty how many days we had been traveling. The dying flame of the kerosene lantern lit the dull eyes of the zombies around me. How could these be the same men who sang so defiantly in the courtyard? The lack of food and water had ravaged us to near inertia.

A train rattled by.

"Water," rasped a voice.

Another seconded the plea. Suddenly the familiar chant was echoing through the cars again, but by now no one expected the plea to be answered, and it faded quickly.

I stared at the planks covering the hole in the floor. With the train stopped, why hadn't any of us thought of escaping? Were we that beaten down? I swore to myself that if nothing happened before daybreak I would ask for Stella's forgiveness and lift those planks. If I got shot at least I could scoop a handful of snow into my mouth before I died.

I heard the distant sound of voices and barking dogs. Others heard them, too. Someone got up and looked out the window, but all he could see was darkness. The voices got louder. They were speaking German, no doubt about that, but it was impossible to make out what they were saying. The dogs began to feverishly yap as if on the hunt. The sound of cinders crunching under boots made me stiffen. Someone rattled a chain, then the door slid open. Frigid air burst in.

"*Raus! Wollt ihr raus! Alles raus verfluchte Hunde!*" (Get out! Get out! Everyone out, you goddamn dogs!)

No one moved. None of us wanted to know what waited for us out there. An SS guard brandishing a truncheon climbed into the car and began swinging and kicking to stampede us out. I jumped to my feet and became dizzy, but fought the urge to sit back down.

Rousted from our collective stupor, we surged toward the exit with many belongings lost in our wake. The older men, their joints stiff from sitting, suffered most of the guard's blows. There was a four-foot drop to the tracks, and many tried to lower themselves down, only to have their fingers stepped on by those behind them. I leaped out and tumbled into a small gully.

The train was stretched out like a python with a reddish halo hovering over its head. Human beings were cascading pell-mell out of all the cars. Children shrieked and men and women howled as the stragglers were hurled off. Around me men floundered in the mud like netted fish.

An armed guard took a position near each car. SS guards with German Shepherds moved in and out of the gloom. The dogs' growls kept me away from the patches of snow on the piles of coal and stacks of wooden ties. I overheard some women lamenting the "poor dears" who hadn't survived the journey. Probably corpses in every car, I thought, but I was pretty sure no one had been left behind in ours.

Fog floated past the lights in the yard like wads of cotton batting. Over a loudspeaker, a German snapped orders.

"Women and children to the left! All men to the right! Leave all your belongings on the side of the track. They'll be returned to you after your processing."

Stella. I had to find Stella. As the guards began to separate us, I spotted a head of flowing red hair.

"Stella!" I called to her, but in the tumult she couldn't hear me.

I had to catch her before she got into line. Water splashed into my shoes as I pushed through a swarm of clinging families. Slipping in the mud, I called after her again. She ducked past a guard waving his truncheon. I stopped. The girl was too tall. My heart sank. In the chaos and darkness there was no way I was going find her. It was hopeless, for now.

From the loudspeaker, one order followed another.

"All men over fifty years old will remain with the women. All those who cannot walk will go with the women. They will all ride in the trucks." Why did the speaker's voice seem to quiver as if he were trying to suppress laughter?

"All the doctors who are over fifty years old will remain with the men."

Why must the old doctors walk? That didn't make sense. Moving into line, an elderly man with a matted beard grabbed my forearm.

"What did they say?"

"I'm not sure," I lied, too overwhelmed with foreboding to tell him the truth.

A weary Father Tonanti marched toward the swelling line of women and children.

"See you later," he waved.

I waved back, holding tightly to his words. When he was out of earshot I realized I should have begged him to locate Stella and reassure her that I would find her.

"All men march past with hats off!"

A searchlight was turned on. In its luminous pencil appeared a tall, thin man in a dark green uniform. He climbed onto a small platform near the engine and our line slowly began to move. When each man passed in front of the platform, the officer scrutinized him, then waved his riding crop to the left or to the right. As I got closer I realized that he was triaging us into two groups. The men bunched on the left were either middle-aged or frail.

The officer's profile was like that of a bird of prey. The silver death head on his cap gleamed in the harsh light. Three men in front of me, two, one—it was my turn. I stepped into the light. The officer bent slightly forward to see me better. Instinctively, I stood on my toes and puffed out my chest. With the spotlight shining in my eyes, it was impossible to distinguish his features except for the prominent Adam's apple bobbing up and down. The buzzard studied his carrion carefully. He signaled for me to go to the right, and I joined a group of young and robust fellows on the other side of the tracks. I placed myself next to familiar faces.

"Fall out by fives," commanded a soldier. The screening was finished.

The women, one of them Stella, disappeared into the fog along with their wails and pleas. A five-year-old girl came running toward us. "Poppa, Poppa, Poppa!"

Mordechai, a Turkish butcher from my hometown, barreled through our ranks. A guard grabbed his daughter by the arm before she could reach the tracks and dragged her back to her mother and six sisters. With hands preventing him from going any farther, Mordechai let out a disturbing groan. In Drancy I had asked him why he had fathered so many children. "If I had had a boy I would have stopped on the first one."

With its whistle taunting us, our train began to back out. If I were religious, that would have been a good time to pray. Instead, I lit the cigarette that I had gotten from a new arrival to Drancy and eagerly breathed in the smoke. I hadn't smoked it on the train because I didn't have any to share.

The man beside me was shivering and his teeth were clattering. Another one was beating his arms against his chest to keep warm. I wanted to stomp my feet, but my shoes were stuck in the mud. I moved my toes and thousands of steel needles shot up my stiff legs. What the hell were we waiting for in this arctic dampness? Even with my layers of clothes the cold was penetrating the marrow of my bones. A guard yawned noisily. He looked bored to death. In the distance, the bell in a church tower struck twelve. If I were in Nice, I would probably be leaving the cinema with my pals and on my way home to my soft, warm bed.

A sentry passed by.

"Where are we?" I asked.

"Auschwitz," the soldier said with a smirk.

What was the twisted smile for? Did I miss the joke? Well, it was a funny-sounding name. He was about to continue on his way when he realized I was smoking. He sprang on me, crushing the cigarette against my mouth with his gloved hand. The blow dropped me into the mud.

"*Rauchen verboten!*" (No smoking!), he screeched.

When I got to my feet, icy water ran down my neck and dripped from my sleeves. Despite myself, tears filled my eyes. So this is "Pitchi Poi." I wiped the ashes from my lips. Oh, how I regretted not escaping with the others. What good had it done me to stay in that cattle car? I wasn't reunited with Stella. I didn't even get a glimpse of her. Filthy *boches*. It was obvious now that the Nazis had lied to us. There was never any plan to keep us all together. The whole time in Drancy they had lied, and instead of revolting en masse we had allowed ourselves to be led along like spineless cuckolds. I was standing ankle deep in mud, passively awaiting my fate. I was pissed, angry with myself for being so foolish and gullible. I would have kicked myself, but the way things were going, it seemed certain I would be getting an SS boot in the ass soon enough.

From the shadows appeared ghastly creatures dressed in blue and gray striped uniforms. They shuffled toward us, bent over like hunchbacks. I had to pinch myself. I couldn't believe they were human. They went along the tracks gathering up our scattered luggage and throwing it into a heap. They slithered among our rows without uttering a sound. Their vacant eyes ignored our existence. What horrible secret weighed on those sagging shoulders?

"I bet we'll all look like them pretty soon," predicted a voice behind me.

There's no way that can happen, I thought.

The hunchbacks loaded our belongings onto handcarts and pushed them into the night. Since we had nametags on our bags, some found it reassuring, as if those gaunt fellows were bellhops delivering our bags to our suites. It was amazing how willing we were to delude ourselves with the slightest hint of hope.

A snarling dog on a taut leather leash sniffed at my legs. I curled my hands into a fist, not wanting the beast to mistake my fingers for bratwursts. Another barking German Shepherd, his hot breath steaming, passed by, dragging his handler. For some odd reason it made me think of an anti-Semitic cartoon that I had seen in the Nazi newspaper *Der Stürmer* ten years before, when my family vacationed in Berlin just as "the god with a moustache" was coming to power. The caption read, "Jewish Beggar Bites German Shepherd." The Nazis had sure gone to some length to make sure that would never happen.

A convoy of big dump trucks approached, slipping and sliding in the mud, splashing everything in their path. The tailgates were dropped, and we were ordered to climb onto the coal-dust–covered beds. We were packed so tightly that none of us could move our legs an inch but the warmth produced by our close proximity was welcomed. When the last man was loaded, SS guards took their places on the trucks' running boards and the convoy started out.

Our truck slipped into the ruts in the road, then lurched sharply out of them. The low railing around the bed cut into my flesh. I tightened my muscles to resist the truck's jolting. Someone dug an elbow into my ribs, and then I was thrown against the man next to me. He didn't utter a sound and kept his gaze downward. I could tell he was petrified. So was I. We were all petrified. There was something depraved here. The place reeked of it and none of us were prepared to confront it. We all feared that if we looked, if we stared deeply, if we acknowledged it, our fate would be worse than Lot's wife.

The trucks splashed packs of shadows struggling along the left side of the road. I couldn't believe it. The women and old men—the people who were supposed to be riding—were walking. Now I understood why the man on the loudspeaker had struggled to keep from laughing. I tried to observe each shadow in hopes of spotting Stella, but it was dark and foggy and most of the women were shrouded in their blankets. As the truck hurtled me away from them, I craned my neck to see the lead group being directed off the road and onto a muddy footpath.

The road improved and the convoy gathered speed. We passed through a grove of pine trees. Branches slapped and beat my face. A rosy shimmer on the horizon silhouetted the final string of skeletal pines. What the hell could that be, I wondered? It was too early for dawn. Coming out of the woods I got my answer. Past a sweeping black field stood a foreboding complex of mammoth factory buildings bathed in a sea of light. With monolithic chimneys spitting fire at the stars, it was the largest industrial complex I had ever seen, at least five miles long.

As we got closer, the acrid smell of smoke became unbearable. The road began to run parallel to the plant. We sped by immense factory warehouses, and the strident concerto of the machinery inside drowned out our truck's motor. On the other side of the road sat a cluster of fenced-in barracks. The convoy swooped under a bridge and crossed a web of train tracks, the tires squealing on the wet rails. We went through a metallic gorge of massive tanks reeking of methanol. With the racket of the trucks' motors echoing violently against their walls, the tanks seemed poised to crush us. The molten metal from a blast furnace momentarily created daylight.

At a crossroads we turned right and descended a gentle incline. Ahead was a sea of barracks lit by sweeping searchlights and walled off by a high barbed-wire fence. The trucks passed through the gate, then the brakes squealed and the tires grated on the gravel.

We all pitched forward, then fell back onto one another. The SS guards ordered us off the trucks. Stiffly, I jumped down.

Rubbing my frozen ears, I looked at the rows of barracks, speculating whether the men sleeping inside worked at the factory complex. Since guessing games were pointless, I turned my attention to a broad-shouldered fellow with thick, wavy gray hair staring us down. He was a handsome man who could have been mistaken for a matinee idol, but the folds around his square jaw and his sharp, unblinking eyes left no doubt that he was an unmitigated brute. He wore a black uniform with riding breeches trimmed on the sides with wide red stripes, which were tucked into high black boots. He had a black cap on his head and a riding crop tucked under his arm. It would have been easy to presume that he was an SS officer, but there were no Nazi insignia on his uniform. Instead, sewn on his jacket was a patch with a green triangle and the number 4. The men who gathered our belongings had colored triangles and numbers on their striped uniforms, so I could only assume that he was a fellow prisoner. But why was he dressed so differently?

"*Zu fünf aufstellen!*" (Line up by fives!) His accent was clearly Prussian.

A blond Austrian in his twenties tried to gain favor. He stepped out and shouted in French: "Line up by fives!"

The Prussian stiffened. "*Was bist du?*" (What are you?)

"I'm Max, your interpreter," he answered self-assuredly. Max was a socialist who had spent a few months in a concentration camp when Germany annexed Austria, then fled to France where he had been rearrested.

The Prussian moved slowly toward Max.

"Here is my best translator."

The blows from his whip sent Max rolling into the mud. The callousness of the *boche* startled me. The handful of SS members in Drancy had kept a low profile, and the only time I witnessed a German lash out was to break up an illegal dance we had going in a vacant room. His half-hearted kicks to clear us out sprang from irritation, as when you swat flies. This Prussian's eyes sparkled with sadistic glee as he beat Max. What filled me with dread wasn't the violence, but that this was the action of a fellow inmate. I could only hope that he was the exception.

"*Los marsch!*" commanded the Prussian.

As we started walking, a handful of men dressed in the striped garb approached from between two barracks. I recognized one of them. He had been shipped out of Drancy in December. It was a relief to see that he hadn't become one of those hunchbacks.

"*Comment que c'est ici?*" (How is it here?) the man next to me asked them.

"Awful."

"Worse than you can imagine."

The group scattered when the Prussian approached, waving his "translator."

We were led into a barracks that had the number 36 on the door. The empty, cavernous space smelled of freshly cut wood and varnish.

"*Alles ausziehen!*" a voice barked.

The few of us who understood German began to disrobe; the rest watched like bewildered monkeys, then slowly followed suit. That's when I grasped how difficult Auschwitz would be for those who didn't understand the Nazis' language. I took off my entire "Dandy of the Shithouse" wardrobe—coveralls, plaid flannel shirt, golf knickers, and ski pants. Chills and goose bumps raced over my naked body from the icy wind cutting through the barracks' walls.

Men began moving to the opposite end of the barracks where prisoners armed with clippers were waiting. I carefully folded my clothes and felt the shoulder of my jacket. The ring that I had hidden in the padding before leaving Drancy was still there. A portly man came to retrieve his belt.

"What are you going to do with that?" I asked.

"Those are the orders. We're to keep our belts and our shoes."

I then realized that I would never be wearing my warm winter clothes again. Incensed, I kicked them across the floor. How could I be that stupid to expect to keep them, I asked myself? My ring!

Shit, I had to get my ring! I scooped up my jacket, tore open the lining, and closed my hand over my one and only true possession as prisoners began to gather up our clothes.

I fell into line for the barbers. We were all naked except for the belts around our middles and the shoes on our feet, which seemed to accentuate how vulnerable and powerless we were. Men stood or sat on stools depending on what part of their body was being sheared.

A big sign hung on the wall behind the barbers. Beneath a skull and crossbones was written EINE LAUS DEIN TOD (A Louse Means Your Death). It made me think of Nicole. I was sixteen, she was fourteen, and we had been necking on a street bench in full moonlight. I wish it had been a moonless night because while I was kissing her, a louse trekked beneath her bangs. It was the first time I saw one of those miniature gray scorpions. I was so shocked that I forgot to take my tongue out of her mouth.

I stepped up onto a stool and a moon-faced barber grabbed my genitals and started cutting my pubic hairs. He had a grip that could crack walnuts.

"Hey, you don't have to pull on my balls like that!"

He looked at me with dull eyes and said, "*Nix compris*" (I don't understand French).

I yelled it in German. With his clippers, he pointed to his red triangle that had the letter "P" written inside it. "*Ich Pole, lieber Mann*" (Dear man, I am a Pole), he informed me and kept on clipping.

I winced and gritted my teeth as the clippers pulled out more hair than they cut. I told myself that I would have to learn some Polish swear words fast. After he was through with my armpits, the Pole had me sit so he could assail my head. The hair on my head was less than a half-inch long. What good would it do to cut it any more? I pointed to my head and indicated the measly length with my thumb and forefinger. Grinning broadly, he shook his head and bent over so I could admire his closely shaved skull. I shrugged and submitted. On my arrival in Drancy, I had put up a fight when they tried to cut my hair and I lost a tooth. It was obvious I would lose a lot more here.

The barber finished by slapping disinfectant powder on my body. I tapped him on the shoulder and signaled that I wanted a drink. He shook his head again. *"Nix Wasser"* (No water).

I had to find water. My throat felt like ancient parchment, my glands were swollen, and a crushing headache made each pulse beat a hammer blow. There's plenty of snow, I thought, on the steps outside, and it sure couldn't be any colder out there than in here. I went to the door, but the damn thing was locked.

A number of my fellow "nudists" were grouped around a tall prisoner with gold-rimmed glasses. He had kind eyes and a vigorous voice with a strong Alsatian accent. On the right sleeve of his striped uniform he had an armband with the printed letters HKB. Curious, I joined them. HKB, I learned, stood for Häftlingekranken-bau (inmates' infirmary). He was in charge of it.

"This is Monowitz, a branch of the Auschwitz camp. They will be putting most of you to work in the Buna plant, which I'm sure you noticed on your way here. Helping finish the construction, mostly. Soon you will receive a shower and your striped uniforms. Tomorrow you will be given a medical examination, quarantined for a few days, then all of you will be housed in the same *Block* (barracks)." He began to walk away. "Oh, yes. Be sure to keep your shoes. You will need them to work in. If your feet go bad, you cannot work, and if you cannot work, you will be in a lot of trouble."

"Water?" I interrupted.

"Be patient. You will get some coffee soon. Do not drink any water. It's not fit for human consumption. Believe me, it'll make you sick."

It was heartening to see that there was someone who cared about our well-being. My overwhelming dread returned, though, when the Prussian entered the *Block* with an SS guard.

"Everybody line up with your shoes in your hands," the guard commanded in German.

We lined up and he flung open the door to an adjoining shower room. As men filed in, the guard inspected their shoes, armpits, and mouths. How was I going to get my ring past this *boche*? Tucking it into my belt and flesh was too risky, and I didn't have a tuft of hair left to conceal it in. There was only one solution and it was one I truly didn't savor.

I stepped out of line unnoticed, then leaned my back against the frozen wall and tried to put the ring into my anus. I had never attempted anything like this before. Apprehensively I pushed it up. My muscles, taut from nervousness and the cold, resisted. My legs started trembling as I tried to work it in like a corkscrew. Luckily no one was paying any attention to me. I wasn't shoving my grandfather's heirloom up my ass for sentimental reasons. No, the ring, two crisscrossed snakeheads with a ruby and diamond for their eyes, was currency and could help make my imprisonment more bearable. Finally it slipped in. The muscles tightened around it, and I felt the ring slide up into my colon. With a deep sigh I slowly shuffled back into line.

The SS guard looked me over and waved me in. I hung my shoes on a nail near the shower room door. Most of the others kept theirs on or in their hands, but I wasn't about to be stuck walking around in soggy shoes. It was an odd-looking shower room. There were no showerheads hanging down from the ceiling, just a network of pipes with holes at regular intervals attached to the rafters.

Someone bolted shut the sheet-metal door. Bouncing off the walls, our speculating and bitching dissolved into the hum of a beehive. The heat of our tightly packed bodies quickly warmed the room. Arms, bellies, backs, buttocks, and tufts of bristly hair brushed up against me. Repulsed, I would step away from one only to be more tightly pressed against another. Why didn't they turn on the water? What the hell were they waiting for?

"Water, water!" I roared.

"Water, water!" Others chanted until it was like thunderclaps in a cavern. I don't know how long we shouted, but finally the pipes began to tremble and hiss. A few yellowish drops fell, then a deluge.

To hell with the HKB man's warning, I thought. With eyes closed I swallowed as much of the lukewarm water as I could. It had a rotten, metallic taste and smelled even worse. Oh, well, it's better to get ill than to suffer any longer from this burning thirst.

Without warning, the water shot from pleasantly warm to scalding. Men howled. I clasped my hands over my head and tried to get to a wall, but I kept slamming into solid barriers of flesh. We were all hopping from one foot to the other as if performing some ridiculous native rain dance. I worried if I kept jumping about I would lose my ring. A dense vapor filled the room until I could no longer see.

As quickly as it had gone up, the water temperature plummeted. The steam disappeared. The icy water had me gasping for a breath. It was futile to try to dodge the cascade, so I stood there shivering with my arms wrapped around myself. Thankfully the torrent stopped, then the door opened and we flooded out.

I grabbed my shoes, which were now filled with water. So much for worrying about soggy footwear, I chided myself. As I went through the door, a prisoner tried to snatch my shoes.

"*Loslassen!*" (Let go!), the man ordered.

Thinking of the HKB man's words, I hung on to them. The bastard raised his fist.

"*Meine Schuhen, meine Schuhen!*" (My shoes, my shoes!), I pleaded.

His kick sent me falling backwards. When I dragged my wet body off the floor, my shoes were lying in a growing pile. The same thing was happening to everyone. I was slowly learning that the instructions of the SS guards weren't always followed and that there were prisoners in charge who made life more miserable than was even intended.

I lined up with the others. Since no towels were given out, we were all squeegeeing our shivering bodies with our hands. If they wanted us to work in their factory, why were they grinding us down?

The Prussian yelled, "Everybody take a striped uniform!"

Next to the entrance was a huge pile of bundled striped uniforms—shirt, coat, trousers, and a beret-styled cap. Prisoners pushed us toward the door. I blindly grabbed a bundle and had only enough time to put on the shirt, which was old and came down to my knees, before I was shoved outside. On the way down the steps I was thrown a pair of canvas shoes with wooden soles. I never dressed so quickly as I did getting those rags over my wet body. The pants were short and so tight that I couldn't button them, and my arms were lost in the sleeves of the coat. I put on the shoes. One was too small and I was swimming in the other. My days as the "Shithouse Dandy" were definitely over. Looking about, I found some comfort in the fact that I wasn't the only one with an ill-fitting uniform.

"*Los marsch!*" commanded the Prussian, and two hundred and forty new *Häftlinge* (prisoners) followed him down a cinder path.

Though everyone seemed to be stumbling, not walking, I could barely keep up with the group. The damn shoes were burning my feet. Despite the frozen ground, there were men carrying their shoes to walk faster. Soon I was, too. The cinders cut my feet, but at least I wasn't lagging behind.

A gray dawn was rising behind a range of snow-covered mountains. On one side of us was a long row of *Blocks* and on the other a barbed-wire fence. Hanging from it was a sign with skull and crossbones and a streak of lightning.

In front of one of the *Blocks* a band of *Häftlinge* were loading one of the dump trucks with living skeletons. Half naked, these devastated souls laid on a wooden pushcart waiting their turn to be tossed like trash onto the truck's bed. They possessed a nightmarish serenity that I had never seen before. Their bodies looked as if life had literally been wrung out of them. They had the legs of storks and their pelvic bones protruded like those of a bankrupt coachman's cab-horse. They stared at us with eyes so sunk into dark-rimmed sockets that I wondered what kept them from falling into their skulls. We marched past and not a word was spoken. They weren't being taken to any hospital—that I was sure of. You don't treat a man like that if you want to nurse him back to health.

"Worse than you can imagine." It sure wasn't an exaggeration. What hardships would we have to endure, and for how long, until we were heaved onto the back of a truck? Had I been stripped of a future along with my warm clothes? Thankfully I was distracted from my dread when we were swallowed up by one of the *Blocks*.

CHAPTER 6

The barracks smelled newer than the one we left. We were massed in a large, open area in front of rows of three-tier bunks, which were braced at the rafters. Against the wall to my left was a group of hollowed-faced *Häftlinge* and a couple of tables and some wooden chairs. When the last of us was inside, the Prussian left without a word. A little man in his thirties walked over from the wall and stepped onto a stool in front of the rows of bunks. On his striped uniform were a green triangle and a yellow triangle forming the Star of David. It was a relief to see a man standing in front of us who wasn't reeking of savageness.

"*Halt die Fresse!*" (Shut up!) he yelled in a high-pitched voice. "I have important information for you. My name is Herbert. I am the *Blockälteste* (barracks supervisor). I am the law while you're in quarantine. Do not forget it. I will give you a few minutes to swap your uniforms and shoes for something better fitting. This will be your only chance."

Somebody translated it into French so everyone understood that we were now human clothing racks. We eyed one another up and down, then the grabbing, swapping, pulling, and chasing began. I dashed from one man to another, sometimes trailing a potential fit from one end of the *Block* to the other while they, too, hunted. Somehow I managed to get a uniform that hung comfortably on my body. I even got my hands on a pair of shoes that were only a tad big before Herbert called off the hunt.

"Everybody get a pair of *Fusslappen*" (foot rags), Herbert said, pointing to a tall stack of square rags in a corner. These were to be our socks. Snatching up a pair, I realized it was going to take some practice to fold the rags around my feet before they wouldn't come apart in my shoes.

"Now hear this!" he yelled. "It's time to be processed and registered. You're going to be given a serial number and a color triangle. They will be sewn to your coat and pants, and you will have the numbers tattooed onto your left forearm."

An alarmed murmur shot through the room.

"Don't be sissies. It only hurts a little. Your women are being processed the same way," Herbert added.

I could picture Stella whimpering and biting her upper lip while being tattooed, as she did when we started to make love.

The *Häftlinge* standing against the wall moved the tables and chairs behind Herbert; set stacks of green cards, pens, and inkstands on the tables; then sat behind them. Unlike others, I jumped quickly into one of the assembly lines. At the first table, a son of a Warsaw haberdasher sewed the number 172649 onto my jacket and pants. I sat down at the next table, where a German prisoner wrote my name and serial number on a card. From the corner of my eye I watched, alarmed, as the man next to me got tattooed. The bleeding numbers were taking up his whole forearm. The German processing me grabbed my left arm, dipped his pen into his white porcelain inkstand, and attacked my forearm with fast, little jabs. I clenched my teeth, but the physical pain was less than the realization that the numbers 172649 meant I was now officially the property of the Third Reich.

"Will this ever come off?"

He shook his head. "It's permanent."

It took a few hours to complete our processing. I sat on a bunk across from the *Block's* heating pipe, which ran the length of the barracks. I stared at the steel pipe in a futile attempt to keep my mind off of my predicament.

Herbert climbed up on the stool again.

"Those colored triangles next to your numbers aren't there for decoration. They signify why you are here, because we are all in this camp for a reason. Red triangles are political prisoners, anti-fascists, communists, socialists, what have you. Black is for lazy, drunken bums who were sabotaging 'the fatherland.' Purple means you're here for your religious beliefs. Yellow is for Jews and Jews only, and green signifies German criminals. I am sure you've noticed that I have a yellow and a green triangle. Take a good look, because you probably won't see another one like it in the camp."

The only colored triangles I saw around me were yellow and red; mine was red.

"Oh, and I almost forgot," Herbert smiled. "Pink signifies homosexual, so it would be wise not to bend over when you are next to a 'pinkie' in the shower."

There were a few half-hearted laughs. I wasn't sure if he was joking or not.

"Soon you will be housed in another *Block* and assigned to a *Kommando* (work detail) depending on your aptitude and experience. Follow the orders of your *Kapo* (supervisor) and *Vorarbeiter* (foreman) or you will be punished. If you're caught trying to escape you will be executed, and remember that nobody likes to stand in the cold while you are hanging. Stay in a perfect line when being counted and do not speak. Remove your cap in the presence of a German officer or guard or you will be punished. You will receive a meal in the morning and in the evening. You will also receive one at noon if you work in the factory. If you're sick you may report to the HKB. Do not stay in there too long or you will be shipped to Birkenau and, trust me, that will be the end of you. If you get the crud or ringworm, you will stay at the *Krätzeblock*, where they'll have you sleep in blankets soaked in kerosene. Again, do not stay too long. Every day check the seams of your clothes for lice. They carry typhus. Crack the lice between your thumbnails."

Someone raised his hand. "May I ask a question?"

Herbert wrinkled his forehead. "About what?"

"Are there any bedbugs?"

Herbert managed a grin. "Oh, yes. And these little fellows are fast. Use a bar of soap to catch them on your mattress. Smash it down on them and they'll be stuck to it. You'd better be quick with that soap, because the one you do not kill you'll blow out your nose in the morning."

A few men laughed.

"It's not funny; they bite. All right, keep clean and good luck."

Herbert hopped off the stool and went into his private quarters, pulling the curtain closed behind him. His *Stubendienste* (barracks foremen) lined us up and doled out our mess kits, a spoon, and a new white-enamel bowl. We then received our first meal: a piece of brown bread, a small square of margarine, and a ladle of a warm, dark water they called coffee. Was that all? We hadn't eaten for over forty-eight hours. Were the Nazis experiencing a food shortage? At least that would explain the condition of those skeletons on the truck.

Everyone filtered through the four rows of bunks to stake out a place to eat and sleep. I went back to that bottom bunk and gobbled up my meal without tasting it. The man sitting next to me picked at his bread. He was distressed that the *Stubendienst* who had given him his mess kit snickered when he asked how he could find out where his family was. Silently I climbed up to the top bunk and stretched out on the burlap-covered mattress. I pulled the blanket over me. The mattress's straw stuffing crackled as I tried to make myself comfortable. In spite of myself, I pondered where Stella was and what she was doing, and what would happen if I never saw her again. Thankfully, sleep spared me from torturing myself for long.

◆ ◆ ◆

I awoke in the middle of the night with gut-wrenching cramps. I should have listened to the man from the HKB. That shower water was hellishly potent. The *Häftling* on watch had fallen asleep, so I easily ducked outside unnoticed. There was an outhouse close by, but there was only one way of relieving myself and retrieving my ring. The cramps tore at my belly, and I barely had enough time to take down my pants. Lucky for me, the searchlight didn't sweep where I squatted. Once I was finished I found a twig and after a little digging I had my ring.

The next morning, Herbert had us line up outside. At his side was his interpreter, Max. A severe beating hadn't deterred him. I respected his persistence, but questioned whether it would ultimately pay off. Herbert stared at us with his piercing blue eyes as if to read our minds.

"*Wer hat hinter den Block geschissen?*"(Somebody crapped behind the *Block*. Who was it?)

While Max translated, Herbert's fury drained the color from his face. We all stood in silence. I hadn't breathed a word to anyone about the cramps or my ring, which was now hidden in the shoulder of my jacket.

"Am I to believe that this shit fell from heaven?" Herbert's voice trembled. "Stand at attention!"

We did as he ordered.

"You'll stand here until whoever did it gives himself up!" Herbert stormed back into the *Block*.

I couldn't believe he was making an issue of this. If I had known, I would have buried my mess. Damn it! Shortly afterwards, our soup was delivered and Herbert had them leave the steaming cauldrons in front of the *Block*'s door. I was in a panic. I was hungry and freezing, and I knew the men standing around me were, too. What should I do? I wanted to come forward because of the suffering I was causing, but I was frightened of what was in store for me if I confessed. As time crept by, guilt devoured me. No, I couldn't stand silent any longer. I took a deep breath and stepped out of line. Herbert was standing at the *Block*'s threshold. I climbed the steps as if mounting the hangman's scaffold.

"So it was you!"

As he spoke I wanted to jump back, giving some excuse for having gone up there, but all I could do was stare at my feet. Herbert took my silence for an admission and his fist sent me rolling down the steps. He pounced on me, grabbed me by the neck, and with strength surprising for one that small, dragged me into the *Block*. I hardly had time to realize what was happening when a rubber hose came down on my ass. I gritted my teeth to keep from crying out. Each blow straightened me up. It felt like an electric shock shooting through my body.

"Bend over!" Herbert screamed.

I jerked up again. A blow over the head knocked me unconscious.

I awoke on the cold floor, unsure what had happened to me. I had dreamt that I was sitting on a hot stove, but the searing sensation had followed me into consciousness. How could that be? Hit with a blinding torrent of pain, I remembered. I rolled onto my belly, but that did nothing to alleviate the agony. Hot tears rolled down my face as I bit into the sleeve of my jacket.

Certainly I hadn't deserved such a punishment. I had never beaten my dog when he did his "doodoo" in my room. What gave these men the right to thrash us? They weren't SS. Wasn't it enough to be imprisoned, to have lost one's freedom? Weren't we all comrades in misfortune who should be aiding, not trying to kill each other? I passed my hand over my jacket. The ring was still there in the seam. At least it hadn't been all for nothing, I consoled myself as I crawled to my bunk and slipped into a pain-induced stupor.

"Why did you confess?"

The man from the HKB* was standing over me.

---

* The name of the Man from the HKB is Siegfried Halbreich, a Polish Jew who was incarcerated at Sachsenhausen and Grossrossen before being shipped to Auschwitz. *Before-During-After* (Schor Press) is Mr. Halbreich's autobiography chronicling his Holocaust survival. Mr. Halbreich has lived across the street from me in Beverly Hills, California, for the past thirty years.

"Why did you confess?"

I shrugged. "Somebody had to or we would've been there till doomsday."

"You foolish kid."

He shook his head and smeared a soothing ointment on my ass, which had swollen up like two balloons. He must have repeated my words to Herbert, because from that moment on he treated me kindly, giving me double rations and making a hero of me. Unfortunately those perks lasted only a week, at which point we were all transferred out of the quarantine *Block* and assigned to *Kommando* 136.

CHAPTER 7

I sat with twenty other *Häftlinge* of *Kommando* 136 around an oil-drum brazier inside a shelter of discarded planks and sheet metal somewhere on the Buna plant grounds. It was our lunch break. No one spoke while we ate. The sound of twenty-one famished men slurping up the brownish water the Germans had the audacity to call soup nearly drowned out the snowstorm howling outside. For the last four weeks the weather had been increasingly cruel.

Yes, I had already been in the camp for a whole month. The time had passed quickly, and nothing distinguished one day from the next. Morning roll call, work, work, work, back to camp, evening rations, sleep, wake, repeat. It was as if I had fallen into a well that had no bottom. And day in and day out it was the same food and never enough of it. At least in Drancy we got three meals, with plates that usually consisted of a piece of meat and a few vegetables. I would still be hungry, but compared to the "Buna soup," the food in Drancy was a king's buffet.

Monowitz's repetitive routine and my body's lack of nutrients were erasing all my interests and desires. The only thing I cared about was my stomach's incessant crying. It was the only thing any of us gave a shit about.

I stirred the contents of my rusty mess tin with my wooden spoon, hoping to find even a microbe of soggy, rotten beet. It was a hopeless struggle. The plant's owner, the German chemical company I.G. Farben, provided our lunches, but the *Häftlinge* in the kitchen diverted most of the food to Monowitz's thriving black market. I became aware of the black market after seeing a *Kapo* wearing the plaid flannel shirt I had gotten in Drancy. It's not surprising that *the Kanada Kommando*—the "bellhops" who collected the belongings of the new arrivals—supplied most of these goods. Food, clothing, shoes, blankets, cigarettes, jewelry, gold teeth— anything that had some value to someone could be found on this black market. The problem was that you had to have something to barter with. Only German and Polish *Häftlinge* could receive packages from loved ones on the outside, so many of them prospered on the black market. For the rest of us, only those good at "organizing"—camp slang for stealing—could enjoy an extra bowl of soup or wear a warm sweater.

I slurped up the final drops in my mess tin, licked my spoon clean, then put it back in my pocket. My shoes were soaked from the snow, so I held my feet up to the brazier. The coke's bluish red flame radiated blistering heat. My shoes began to steam. I felt revitalizing warmth on my legs, stomach, and chest, but my backside was still ice. I stood up and backed up to the brazier. Quickly the heat became unbearable and the smell of freshly ironed clothes filled the shelter.

"*Pierre, passauf*" (Pierre, watch out), came a voice from the other side of the brazier.

It was our *Kapo*, Hans, a green triangle who reminded me of the American movie star Spencer Tracy. Growing up, his movie *Captains Courageous* had been one of my favorites.

"If you burn the seat of your pants, the rubber hose of the *Blokowy* will burn your ass."

Blokowy was Polish for "*Blockälteste*." Most non-German *Häftlinge* addressed their barracks' supervisor using this easier-to-pronounce word. When a *Häftling* broke any of the rules, it was the

Blockälteste who doled out the punishment of his choice. If the infraction was severe enough, he would be the one reporting it to the SS. You were always better off with a red triangle *Blockälteste* than a green triangle, whose past incarceration in a German penitentiary usually made him a rabid dog waiting for the slightest excuse to pounce. From what I had seen and had been told by old-timers, red triangle *Blockältesten*, as well as *Kapos*, didn't take advantage of their authority or relish exercising physical discipline.

A siren sounded outside. It was time to go back to raising factory buildings for "the fatherland."

"*Auf geht's!*" (Let's go!)

Hans opened the door and our arctic tormentor blew in, making my nose tingle. "*Los schneller!*" (Faster!)

We went out into the snow in single file, each of us walking in the tracks of the man in front of him. I quickly wrapped my hands with *Fusslappen*. There was an abundance of the rags in my *Block*. Our job on this construction site was to drill holes in the brick walls so windows could be anchored. With my mallet and chisel in one hand, I climbed up a ladder to an opening in the wall. I brushed away the snow that had accumulated and put one leg over the ledge. At least through the afternoon I would be more comfortable straddling the wall because I had "organized" an empty cement sack to sit on. Some *Häftlinge* stuffed sacks inside their clothing for insulation. I put mine under my ass because I wanted to avoid chafed thighs, since I already had enough patches of irritated skin.

On one side of me was a screen of snowflakes, on the other a black void that was the interior of the building. I hugged the wall with my thighs so that a gust couldn't sweep me from my perch. Someone took away the ladder. There was only one ladder for every five windows. If I had to piss, I would have to make yellow icicles over the ledge. I pounded out holes the best I could. When my legs became stiff from the cold, I started to bicycle in the air. The *Häftling* who had tattooed my number had given me one good piece of advice.

"If you want to survive, work only with your eyes."

I stopped pedaling. Yes, I had to expend as little energy as possible to economize the precious few calories I was getting.

My mind wandered to Stella. Had she been lucky enough to be taken under the wing of a camp veteran? Was she getting advice that would help keep her from being sent to the crematoriums of Auschwitz's second camp, Birkenau? The ovens and gas chambers were no secret to us in Monowitz. I had heard plenty of filtered-down accounts from members of the Transportation *Kommando* who delivered our corpses and near dead to Birkenau.

Stella could have been consumed in those flames weeks ago, but until I had proof I had to keep hoping. My survival depended on it. A few days before, I bumped into Mordechai, the butcher from my hometown. He was a shuffling shell of his former self. Somehow he had gotten word that his wife and seven daughters had been exterminated that first night. In camp slang, he had become a *Muselmann*, the German for Muslim. Like many others, Mordechai had become so emotionally and physically broken down that, shrouded in his blanket, he looked like a gaunt pilgrim on the road to Mecca. In Auschwitz, there was only one road and it led straight to the crematoriums. This was a path I was determined not to step onto, and I hoped my Stella had the same resolve. In truth, her will would have to be monumentally stronger than mine. In all likelihood, her father and yellow triangle mother were dead, and Stella was just as aware of that as Mordechai was about the rising smoke of his family.

Back at our *Block* that night, before *das Essen* (our meal), the *Blockälteste* announced that those *Häftlinge* not working at their skilled professions or trades were to report to the *Schreibstube* (Administration Building) in the morning. I had told the *Häftling* who filled out my green card that I was an electrician. It was a lie, but I knew enough of the basics that I figured I could con my way through. The prospect of not working ten, twelve hours in the brutal Siberian blast kept me awake most of the night. Only the *Kommandos* working outside returned to camp carrying corpses. The odds of my survival would definitely rise if I could pass muster as a craftsman.

A few mornings later I lined up in the Appelplatz (roll-call square) with the *Elektriker Kommando*. I marched with them to Buna's main generator, which was housed in a tall red brick building with four metal smokestacks that looked like they belonged on an ocean liner. We entered a warm, brightly lit hall resonating from the hum of four monstrous turbines. The wooden soles of our shoes were like a stampede of jackhammers as we climbed a metal staircase to the tool room and workshop.

The *Häftlinge* went to their workstations. The *Kapo* turned to me.

"*Folge mir*" (Follow me), the green triangle ordered. He handed me a schematic from his desk. "What do you read?"

I nervously looked over the diagram. In my physics class I had learned the equations and symbols for volts, amps, watts, and ohms, so it was easy to point out the capacitors, resistors, switches, and outlets. For some of the more technical items on the print I spit out names with more bluff than knowledge. The *Kapo* smiled.

"Join that detail over there."

I walked over to a *Vorarbeiter* and four *Häftlinge* who were dragging out their toolboxes. They were all German red or green triangles.

"How do you bend conduit?" the stocky Bavarian *Vorarbeiter* asked.

These men weren't in the business of wasting any time with formal introductions. "With a tube bender," I blurted.

"If you don't have one?"

I smiled; this had happened to me at home. "I look for anything with the right radius, I cap one end, fill the conduit with sand so it won't collapse when I bend it, then cap the other end."

"How do you push the wire through?"

The *Vorarbeiter* wasn't going to nail me on this question, either. "I push a snake through the conduit, attach the strands of wire to the snake, then pull it back."

"From the box in the corner get me two transformers, one for two hundred and fifty volts to one hundred and twenty volts and another for eighteen volts."

When I came back with the right transformers, the *Vorarbeiter* seemed satisfied that he could depend on me not to screw up.

As we prepared the wiring for a new building that morning, I was amazed by the jovial mood of my co-workers. On their faces were the first smiles I had seen since my arrival. It was a startling contrast to the gloom that hung over *Kommando* 136. Then, again, it's hard to smile when your face is frozen. At lunch I discovered one reason these slave laborers seemed not to mind their work. Their soup was a much thicker and tastier fare than anything I had eaten so far. They all laughed when I licked my bowl.

"*Speckjäger, haben einen Nachschlag*" (Bacon hunter, have a second helping), grinned the *Kapo*.

"May I really?"

"Have two; there's plenty left."

No wonder there wasn't a sickly skeleton in the bunch. Relatively speaking, I was in paradise.

At the end of the day, the *Kapo* handed me a small industrial fuse the likes of which I had never seen before.

"Is it any good?" he asked.

I looked through the glass of the porcelain fuse.

"Sure," I said confidently.

"Check it again. You see those little black specks? This fuse has a manufacturing defect. It blew the moment we screwed it in the socket. You're not very observant. We would've wasted a day searching for an open line."

That damn fuse sank me. The next day I was back shivering my nuts off with *Kommando* 136.

◆ ◆ ◆

It was early evening. The north wind had frozen everything that the pale winter sun had thawed, making our usual path back to camp a sheet of ice. By threes, we walked on one of the many tentacles of train track criss-crossing the Buna plant. Ice splinters falling from the electric wires overhead stung my face. The wind cut through my "pajamas"—camp slang for our striped uniforms—chilling my bones, which hardly had any meat left on them. As usual my stomach was throbbing with hunger, but it had been such an exceptionally exhausting day of fitting panels of cement and seaweed up onto the skeletal frame of another warehouse building that all I wanted was my infested straw mattress. I hoped they wouldn't make us take a shower when we returned to our *Block*. There was no way my feeble legs could carry my wet, naked body fast enough across the one hundred yards of frozen cinders that lay between the showers and our *Block*. It would be a sure way of catching pneumonia.

I heard bells, and turned to see two Polish peasants, bundled in warm furs and smoking pipes, passing by on a sleigh. They were probably on their way back from picking up the garbage at the civilian kitchen. The short longhaired horses pulling them trotted with heads down, noses steaming, and tails whipping in the wind. It reminded me of the illustrations in my mother's copy of Dickens's *A Christmas Carol*. I looked at the *Häftlinge* ahead of me. No holiday picture here. The dragging gray line of misery was more akin to the painting of Napoleon's retreat across the Berezina River. Our *Kapo* Hans strutted in his high polished boots with his new *Piepel* ("errand boy") by his side. It had been no surprise that Hans had dumped his former *Piepel*, a deformed little beggar, when this fourteen-year-old Dutch kid with big green eyes arrived in the camp.

Hans held the boy by the arm as we took a shortcut along a cluster of butane tanks and twisting pipelines with safety valves that let off jets of steam that smelled like cider. He then put his hand on the boy's shoulder and let it slip down his back, affectionately squeezing his waist. The *Piepel* stepped away, glancing at Hans with guileless eyes and a smile. What innocence, I thought. You don't understand at all, do you, kid? Yes, Hans is fond of you, but not in the way you think. I'm sure you feel lucky that you don't have to work like the rest of us, but soon enough you'll learn the price. Hans will take you to a secluded spot while we work. The *Vorarbeiter* will ensure that his *Kapo* isn't interrupted.

Like a father, Hans will sit you tenderly on his lap. Panting with excitement, he'll whisper in your ear all that he can do for you. His hands will press your body. Your few carelessly sewn buttons will pop off. While he holds you with one strong arm, he'll wet your bottom with his saliva, and before you realize what's happening, you'll feel your intestines being pushed through your stomach. I would like to open your eyes, you beardless boy, but truly—what business is it of mine? Don't I have enough troubles of my own? Perhaps this will be the only way you will get out of here alive. I stumble, almost crashing to the frozen ground. I mind other people's business, but I can barely stand on my own two feet, I scolded myself.

Of course, things turned out a little differently from what I had imagined. On the day of our shower, Hans joined us instead of taking a shower on Sunday morning with the other *Kapos* and *Blockälstesters*. He stood beside his *Piepel*, devouring him with his eyes. The couple was given a wide berth. Hans didn't even try to cover his excitement. He had brought along a blue-and-white checked towel, a luxury unknown to any ordinary *Häftling*, and handed it to the boy while the rest of us returned to the *Block*, wet and naked.

That night I was awakened by a low voice. I was sleeping on the second tier. Above me was a Russian snoring like a sawmill, and below me was the *Piepel*. I peeked down. Hans was crouching next to the bunk.

"Shh!" he ordered his *Piepel*.

The bunk creaked when Hans crawled in. I closed my eyes and tried not to care. The boy started sobbing softly. I thought, don't worry, kid, it will stretch. All three tiers began to sway. Hans was doing him from the side. The SS really needed to switch the color of his triangle.

The Russian's snoring became irregular as the bunks quaked and Hans panted. I looked at the bunk above me and hoped that the Russian wasn't prone to seasickness. If he is, he's going to vomit all over me.

The boy's eyes were deadened from that morning on, and soon after he contracted pneumonia. Hans went on the hunt for a new *Piepel* and the fourteen-year-old died alone in the HKB.

Not long after, I found myself with a suitor.

My *Kommando* was doing odd jobs, laying bricks, hammering spikes into train track tie plates, and tightening track bolts. I was crouched on what would be the base for a railroad track switch, chiseling a gully in the cement for the rod that connected the switch handle to track that hadn't yet been laid. It was lucky for me that the cement hadn't completely cured.

A *Kapo*, whose *Kommando* was laying electrical cable in freshly dug trenches, had been staring at me for a while. I told myself that he was just suspicious, since I was so far from the other members of my *Kommando*. But didn't he have enough "pajamas" of his own to watch over? Suddenly he was standing next to me. With chisel in hand, I got up on tingling legs.

"Boy, look at your shirt. It's filthy," he said.

How observant. I had worked and slept in it for over a month.

"I'll give you a new one." Give me? I knew it wasn't my lucky day. What did he want?

"Let's get out of the wind."

The *Kapo* grabbed me by the arm and led me to a secluded area between two buildings. "Take that off."

He indicated to the scrap of cement bag I had wrapped around my left hand to prevent my skin from sticking to the steel chisel. I did as I was told. The *Kapo* held my hands.

"Young man, rub your hands before you get frostbite."

Again, I did as I was told. A moment later he held my hands again.

"That's better," he said, and opened his coat, revealing an erection poking out of his unbuttoned fly.

I had seen this coming, but I was surprised that in this weather he could get his battery charged just by looking at me. He pulled me close and had me touch his erection. I had no choice if I wanted to walk back to that slab of concrete.

I stroked his stubby prick with a droopy foreskin while he moved his ass rhythmically. He was breathing heavily, and I could hear his heart dancing the conga. I hoped to get it over with before the *Kapo* decided he wanted to be satisfied in a different manner. Finally his knees buckled, he grunted, and ejaculated.

With a grin and a kick he buried the evidence in the sandy soil, turned on his heels, and returned to his *Kommando*. There goes my shirt, I thought as I picked up my chisel. Well, I wasn't really expecting one anyhow.

That asshole Hans. Being too old for his taste, Hans had pimped me. It was no accident that he put me on that slab of concrete. Maybe he got the shirt. Then again, it could have all just been shithouse luck.

I went back to work and made sure the job was finished before they lined us up for the march back to camp. I wasn't going to make a second "date" easy for that *Kapo*. I didn't see him the next day or the day after that. When I finally did spot him he seemed just as uninterested in me as I was in him, but it still took me weeks to stop looking over my shoulder for him while I worked. It was a pittance compared to the price Han's fourteen-year-old paid.

♦ ♦ ♦

One of the nice things about my life in Drancy, other than Stella, was the fact that I could get cigarettes regularly. This was a big deal for an eighteen-year-old who had started smoking at age ten by making cigarettes with the tobacco from his father's cigar butts. Unfortunately, cigarettes were nearly impossible to get in Monowitz, so I joined up with four other *Häftlinge* from my *Block* who also had a strong need for tobacco smoke in their lungs. Every morning one of us would make a trade with a Russian black triangle: the margarine that we received with our bread and coffee for a pinch of coarse Russian *makhorka* (tobacco stems). Since the stems pierced newspaper, we rolled it in squares cut from the middle layer of the triple-lined cement bags that we "organized" from the plant's construction sites.

Once rolled, the five of us hurried behind the *Blocks* before morning assembly. The one who traded his margarine got the first puff. He would then exhale the smoke into the mouth of the next man, who would exhale into the mouth next to him. Once the fifth man got his, the cigarette would be passed to the second man and he would inhale and the smoke was passed around again. The cigarette lasted long enough for everyone to get one drag from it.

Exhaling into one another's mouth was about the unhealthiest thing we could be doing in the middle of winter. When the yellow triangle Czech and red triangle Serb showed up with nasty coughs, we just took our one drag from the cigarette. Still the third, fourth, and fifth men were taking in a lot of germs. Twenty-one days and twenty-one cigarettes later, we wisely dissolved our smoking circle after we all started hacking up phlegm.

In March, I befriended a new arrival, a nineteen-year-old yellow triangle from Holland who was in my *Block* and *Kommando*. Peter was tall and unusually skinny for a new arrival. He was lucky that I.G. Farben was demanding more manpower for the Buna plant. He would have been directed to the left if he had arrived with me. Peter had been shipped in with his father, whom he missed terribly. During our lunch break one frosty day I asked him where he had learned to speak fluent German, and without a Dutch accent.

"I'm a German Catholic from Cologne."

"Then how come you wear a yellow triangle?"

"My father is Jewish. Eight years ago we fled to Holland by hiding on a barge."

"How about your mother?"

"She's Catholic. She stayed in Cologne because everything we own is now in her name."

"Do you miss her?" I pried.

"Before the war she visited us a few times, but I haven't heard from her since the Germans came into Holland. I worry about her because Cologne has been bombed many times."

I mumbled matter-of-factly, "I guess you were starving in Holland, too. You don't look good."

"No, we were doing okay in Groningen, but when we were discovered by the Gestapo I got a bad infection. My father told them that I'm not Jewish, but the agent screamed that a leopard doesn't change his spots."

Peter bragged to me constantly about his father. It seemed that he was the owner of a prosperous factory that produced women's corsets, and Peter believed that he had landed a good job in Auschwitz.

"I'm sure they're taking advantage of his excellent bookkeeping skills," he would say time and time again.

I didn't have the heart to inform Peter that he was living in a dream world. I assumed he used this feeble thread of hope the way I did with my thoughts of Stella, to keep the will to live strong. But amid the stories of camping trips and his father's keen business mind, I could sense that Peter was becoming more and more distraught. Against my advice, he went to the *Schreibstube* and asked to be reunited with his father in the main camp.

A few days later I openly cried when he waved to me from the back of a truckful of *Muselmänner*. You fool, I wanted to scream. Was he that delusional that he couldn't see that no one his father's age ever escaped the gas chambers? Or was he crazy like a fox, committing suicide without offending his faith? I would never know. The answer disappeared in smoke.

My memory was failing. It was as if someone had wiped my eighteen-year-old mind with a blackboard eraser, leaving me with only the faint outlines of my family, friends, and classmates. Stella was slowly becoming a phantom. I had difficulty seeing her spirited eyes, hearing her voice, smelling her scent, and feeling her touch. There was only one image that had become more vivid, and it savagely haunted me: food. In my mind, I could conjure up the most complicated recipes. Delicious and appetizing smells would fill my nostrils, and my mouth would water until my salivary glands were close to cramping, but it did nothing for my belly. I couldn't survive for much longer on the meager pittance of food they gave us.

Every week I was becoming noticeably thinner. I had to find some means of supplementing my rations, but it wasn't time to trade my one and only possession on the black market. Not when there was a pyramid of cabbages behind the camp's kitchen guarded by only one green triangle armed with a stick, and not when there were two French yellow triangles in my *Block* willing to help me "organize" a few heads.

On a moonless night, when the chain of searchlights was providing the only illumination, Antoine, Jules, and I eased out of our bunks. We met next to the red triangle Pole working a shift as night watchman. With the promise of a fistful of cabbage, he didn't see us walk out. Antoine was our goat; he had drawn the short straw. Jules and I laid in wait behind one of the *Blocks* as he crept toward the kitchen. Suddenly, he jumped out from the shadows. The guard went after him, and Jules and I threw ourselves onto the pile of cabbages. Antoine took a few knocks, but we were victorious. Behind our *Block*, we munched away like rabbits. Though the insides of the cabbages were frozen and we had no salt for seasoning, it was an amazingly delicious salad.

◆ ◆ ◆

"*Links, zwei, drei, vier, links!*" (Left, two, three, four, left!) Hans commanded. As we did every night, we goose-stepped in rows of five through the camp's gate. My feet felt like bricks as I kicked them into the air. As always the *Lagerälteste* (camp administrator) and *Lagerkapo* (head of camp) were standing side by side inside the gate. The *Lagerälteste* was the Prussian with the riding-crop "interpreter." He ensured that the affairs of the camp were to the *boches'* liking and dealt out the punishment when they weren't. The *Lagerkapo*, who I figured for some Berlin garbageman, had a red triangle with the number 1 and was in charge of the *Kommandos* working inside the camp, which included the kitchen and HKB.

These two senior *Häftlinge* were like night and day. Where the *Lagerälteste* was a sharply dressed, sadistic matinee idol, the *Lagerkapo* looked like a wallowing pig with his big, upturned nose and sloppy uniform. Where the *Lagerälteste*'s eyes seemed focused on every detail in front of him, the *Lagerkapo*'s eyes were listless. I believed he held no pride for his position, doing only the minimum necessary to keep his privileges. That made him sympathetic in my eyes.

"*Kommando* one hundred and thirty-six. Forty-four *Häftlinge*, one dead!" Hans announced as we passed the guard station.

Roster in hand, the SS guard counted our lines. The last row was made up of the dead man who had collapsed while mixing cement and his four pallbearers. The dead had to be returned to the camp or we would have hell to pay. Being so consumed with preventing us from breaking out, I questioned why the Nazis didn't hang the dead for escaping.

Like birds on a wire, fifty of us sat on the *Block*'s heating pipe with our bowls of soup and began to thaw out. The bell for assembly rang.

"*Alles raus!*" (Everybody out!) the *Blockälteste* shouted.

Armed with a stick, the *Stubendienste* hustled men toward the door. I hadn't finished my soup. I took a quick swallow, then hid my bowl on a rafter above my bunk.

Thick clouds blanketed the moon on this damp night and searchlights lit up the Appelplatz where *Blocks* were already lined up in rows of five. The beam of a single searchlight enveloped three gibbets. Rumors of who was to hang circulated, but no one had any real idea. A group of SS guards with bayoneted rifles formed a semicircle in front of the gibbets. Three *Häftlinge* were marched across the Appelplatz. This was my third hanging, but the first time witnessing a multiple execution.

It was about three weeks after my arrival that I witnessed my first hanging. I looked down at my torn shoes when the condemned

Dutchman stepped up to the scaffold. As an SS officer rattled off some Nazi legal crap that frequently mentioned the *Führer* and the greater glory of Germany, I closed my eyes and considered what the Dutchman's last thoughts were. The trapdoor's dropping made my body jerk to attention, but I kept my eyes shut. As they marched us past the scaffold, I stared at the blue stripes of the fellow in front of me. It was only a few weeks later that I witnessed my second hanging. By then I was hardened enough by our daily misery that I didn't bother to close my eyes.

The execution orders for these three men were ridiculously longwinded. Two of the condemned men were Poles who had been caught trying to escape. The third was a young Greek, not much older than I, who had stolen some bread during an air raid alert.

"*Im Namen des Reichsführer Heinrich Himmler!*" (In the name of Reich führer Heinrich Himmler!) The *Lagerführer* finished and shoved the orders into his SS coat pocket.

A group of green triangle *Kapos* laughed. For these career criminals the hangings were a Grand Guignol attraction, an entertaining diversion from their monotony. As if betting on racehorses, they put money and cigarettes on which of the three would live the longest.

Resigned to their fate, the two Poles stepped up to their nooses without uttering a word. The Greek fell to the ground with tears rolling down his face.

"*Nichts klepsi, klepsi!*" (No stealing, no stealing!)

I looked over at my cabbage-stealing cohorts. Their blank stares told me that we all had the same thought—it could easily have been our necks. Two green triangles had to carry the Greek up to his gibbet. The *Lagerkapo* put the noose around his neck. The boy's legs buckled, tightening the noose. There doesn't seem to be much reason to drop the trapdoor now, I thought.

The trapdoors were sprung, the bodies fell, and the ropes went taut. The three men swung in slow circles. The Poles' bound hands convulsively opened and closed as their shoulders jerked and their legs kicked furiously in the air. One of them lost his trousers. His white, sweaty legs and buttocks glistened in the searchlight's beam. The Greek hung lifeless like an empty sack. The *Kapos* who had bet on him spat curses.

"The dirty dog cheated us."

"Tickle him to make him move."

Other *Kapos* chimed in.

"Give the Poles some gum so they can chew on something more than their tongues."

"Look how that one runs along."

"Let's hope he doesn't escape altogether."

When the only things moving were the ropes, the *Lagerkapo* yanked on each man's legs, and we heard the last cracking of their tendons. It was then that I realized that there was more than one way to die from hanging. The two Poles were pale and their tongues weren't protruding from their half-open mouths. The drop had broken their necks and their thrashing about had been only reflex spasms. The young Greek had turned purple and his tongue jutted from his swollen face. This was my first death by strangulation.

"It's perfectly justifiable to hang a thief," said a *Kapo*.

The others chortled in agreement. Assholes, I cursed to myself. How can these bona fide criminals sit in judgment of one whose only offense was being hungry? If the Greek lost his life because of a few crumbs of bread, how many times had they deserved to die?

"*Links, zwei, drei, vier!*" We filed past the gibbets.

At my second hanging, the *Kapo* in charge of the gallows pulled me out of line as we marched past. "*Komm mit mir*" (Come with me), he ordered.

I was in a panic. What did he want with me? Was he going to practice with my neck? I relaxed when I saw that he had already cut the rope. The stocky green triangle opened a small door at the base of the gibbet.

"Get him out."

Inside lay the crumpled body of a young red triangle Pole whose failed escape had earned him the rope. He had stood erect on that platform and died without a whimper. I pulled him through the small opening by his legs. His coat slid over his head, straightening his arms in a gesture of surrender. I took the noose off his broken neck, curled the rope on his chest, and waited for the *Kapo* to return with a flat dolly. Staring at the Pole's face, I decided that a broken neck was far easier than facing a trip to Birkenau.

When the *Kapo* arrived with the dolly, he pointed at the corpse.

"Switch shoes. They're better than yours."

I had noticed them, too, but didn't dare take them on my own. They were still warm.

"*Abtreten*! (Fall out!)" the *Blockälteste* commanded, and we all rushed toward the *Block*'s door as the bodies of our three comrades gently swung in the cold wind. I elbowed my way to the front of the herd. I had to get to my soup before someone else did. Minutes later, ribs bruised and out of breath, I sat on my bed and greedily wiped out the last cold drops with my fingers. In Nice, seeing a dog run over would have taken away my appetite for a whole day, but here the sight of those three men had hardly moved me. I was still relatively new to the camp, but many of my civilized attitudes and emotional endowments were muted or gone.

I couldn't condone the *Kapos*, but I was beginning to understand why they were so cold-blooded and cruel. Auschwitz was a world where brutality and inhumanity were rewarded with privilege and preferential treatment, and compassion and empathy only hastened death. The SS sure knew what they were doing when they assigned convicts—hardened criminals—to run things. The cold truth was that the *Kapos*, like the rest of us in the camp, were just doing whatever they had to do to survive. The only difference was that some of those bastards truly enjoyed doing it.

CHAPTER 8

New arrivals assigned to our *Block* forced us to double up in the bunks. My sleeping companion was Olaf, a twenty-one-year-old college student and soldier from Oslo, Norway. We quickly became friends. I was ecstatic to be able to converse in German with someone well educated. When the lights were turned off we carried on long conversations in low voices. He had been taken prisoner in the first days of the blitzkrieg on Norway. Whole battalions had been surprised and encircled, and the German paratroopers left few survivors. I asked him why he had been sent to Monowitz since he was a POW.

"After my second escape attempt from the Stalag (POW camp) they shipped me here," he answered with a smile.

Our principal topic of conversation, of course, was the war. "We wouldn't be sitting here if the French army had gone after the Nazis when they marched into the Rhineland," I proclaimed. "They had a chance to stop Hitler cold, but they fell for his bullshit."

"Every prime minister, president, and monarch in Europe was a gullible idiot. 'Peace in our time,'" Olaf spit sarcastically.

"And how can you fight when you have traitors stabbing you in the back at every step? It makes me sick to think how many good Frenchmen are rotting in here because of those Vichy bastards."

"Yes, you have Laval* in bed with the Nazis and we have that bastard Quisling**. The best day of my life will be when I see him hanging from a flag pole."

Ultimately, our empty stomachs steered our discussions to food.

"How can you French eat frogs and those slimy snails?" Olaf asked with a disgusted face.

"Snails are delicious. You just need to know how to prepare them. Someday soon I'll be serving you escargot fattened on grape leaves."

"You eat them raw?"

"Oh, no. You have to fry them first with some garlic and parsley butter. Oysters we slurp raw."

"Well, we finally have something in common." Olaf's eyes lit up. "You know, when a girl likes oysters, it's a good indicator that it'll be a successful date."

I muffled a laugh.

"That's been my experience, too."

Returning from his work detail one night, Olaf seemed changed. He was cheerful like a lottery winner. There was a gleam in his eyes as if the future no longer worried him, which was abnormal for any *Häftling*. Despite my curiosity, I didn't ask the reason for the sudden shift in his demeanor and Olaf didn't volunteer an

---

* Once the Nazis occupied France in 1940, Pierre Laval used his media empire of newspapers and radio stations to support Philippe Pétain and the Vichy government. For his effort, Laval became the head of the French government. He enabled the Gestapo to hunt down members of the French Resistance in unoccupied France (southern France). He also created the Vichy Milice, a paramilitary force, which in conjunction with the French police rounded up many French Jews and left-wing activists and had them shipped to concentration camps.

** Vidkun Quisling was the leader of Norway's Nasjonal Samling (National Socialist) Party, which the Nazis declared the only legal party after their invasion in 1940. In 1942, Quisling was installed as prime minister.

explanation. In the nights that followed I realized that his bony frame was poking me less and less as we tried to sleep, and many times he would say his belly was full and give me his leftover soup.

One evening, as Olaf poured his soup into my bowl, I asked whether he wasn't depriving himself with his generosity. I leaned in close, figuring that at last he would reveal his culinary benefactor. Olaf raised his eyebrows in overstated surprise. "Are we not allies?"

I left it at that, realizing that the reasons Olaf gave me his soup were unimportant. What was important was that my benefactor held onto his benefactor as long as possible.

Weeks passed, and Olaf became more confident and stout. I was beginning to gain back a few pounds, too. As we were sleeping head to foot one night, Olaf anxiously tossed and turned, waking me up every few minutes. He even picked my nose with his little toe. The next morning when the *Blocks* separated into *Kommandos*, Olaf stared at me, then shook my hand instead of waving as he normally did. He didn't utter a word, but I knew in my gut that I was seeing him in the camp for the last time. A good friend was leaving me.

That evening, before all the *Kommandos* had returned to camp, the bell for assembly was rung. When the rumor reached me that a *Häftling* had escaped, I knew it was Olaf and I silently wished him luck. After a half an hour of standing at attention, the *Lagerkapo* hurried along the ranks.

"172649!" he called out.

My heart began to dance a polka. What did he want with me?

"*Hier,*" I replied.

"*Los schnell, zur Schreibstube.*" (Come along quickly to the administration office.)

"Why?"

"I don't know," he said pulling me by my sleeve.

Like a basset hound chasing a greyhound, I tried to keep up with the *Lagerkapo*'s long strides as he led me across the Appelplatz.

Gentle warmth greeted us as we entered the administration barracks. I took off my cap. The *Häftlinge* typing at desks didn't dare look up at us. There was a contingent of SS mulling about, which made me extremely apprehensive. As a *Häftling*, one did everything possible to stay far away from the men in green uniforms. The *Lagerkapo* knocked at a door, then opened it a crack.

"*Herr Arbeitseinsatzführer, der Häftling 172649 ist da.*" (Labor Deployment Officer, prisoner 172649 is here.)

"*Rein mit ihm.*" (Get him in.)

As the *Lagerkapo* led me into the office, a *Häftling* brushed against me on his way out. Even with his face covered with blood, I recognized him—Olaf's *Kapo*. Olaf had repeatedly told me he was a mean *Schweinehund* (pig dog). In escaping, the Norwegian had managed to kill two birds with one stone. The prick's red *Kapo* armband was gone. He was now just another nobody.

The *Lagerkapo* closed the door behind me, and it sank in that the *Kapo*'s battered face was not a good omen.

The *Arbeitseinsatzführer's* office was small and his enormous mahogany desk made it seem even smaller. The officer was sitting behind it with his shirt unbuttoned and his forehead glistening with sweat. His baby-pink bald head was at odds with his deeply tanned face. I had seen him duck into my *Block* for perfunctory inspections and speed by in a motorcycle sidecar, but I had seen the officer this close only once before, and that was on my first day in the quarantine *Block*.

He leaned forward, his hairy chest touching the desk, and fixed his blue eyes on me. Like a mouse hypnotized by a snake, I stood motionless by the door. I was afraid to look into those transparent eyes, but I didn't want to look down either, for fear of its being misconstrued as an admission of guilt. He grimaced, which was evidently intended as a smile, and waved me to a chair. I had never heard of a *Häftling* sitting down in the presence of an SS officer—or any SS, for that matter. He spoke to me in excellent French, but with a harsh German accent.

"I have been to France, in Bordeaux, to be precise. I love French wine and have the highest respect for French culture," he cordially told me.

Why the niceties from this member of the "Master Race," I

mused? I played meek, not uttering a word. One false move could cost me my life.

"How's the food in the camp? I hope the work isn't too rough."

No reason to respond to that, since he knew as well as I did that the lice in the bunks were better off than we were.

"What would you think of becoming a *Kapo*?"

The *Arbeitseinsatzführer* was underestimating me.

"Well, there are prisoners who've been here longer. Wouldn't they be more entitled?"

"It isn't seniority, but aptitude that counts. Besides, I'm the one who appoints these positions. Think what it would be like to have better food and a warm *Block* to sleep in. But to become a *Kapo* you'll have to tell me where Olaf went."

This was why Olaf never shared his plans with me. It wasn't that he distrusted me; he had no idea how well I would hold up under interrogation and possible torture. Hell, the Norwegian did me a favor. Having knowledge of a planned escape and not reporting it would have been as damning as making the escape. I continued to play the fool that the *boche* believed I was.

"Which Olaf?"

"You know very well, the Norwegian who shared your bunk. Where was he planning to go?"

"I don't speak Norwegian."

The Nazi's face hardened, but he restrained his anger.

"Olaf speaks perfect German and so do you. The job of *Kapo* doesn't interest you?"

"Yes, it does, but I honestly do not know anything."

"You cannot sleep in the same bed with someone for a month without knowing something," he shot back.

The *Arbeitseinsatzführer* got up and began to twirl a braided leather whip that had been lying on his desk. I jumped to my feet, but he pushed me back into the chair with the handle of his whip. He paced silently. My eyes followed him like a cornered rabbit. What now? He sat down in front of me on the edge of the desk and glared.

"And what would you think of a trip to the *Stehbunker*?"

The *Stehbunker* was a solitary confinement cell no bigger than a coffin.

"That wouldn't bring Olaf back because I don't know anything."

The veins in his forehead swelled. "I don't know! I don't know! All the bastard can say is 'I don't know!'"

He swung the whip down on the edge of my chair. I felt as if I had received an electric shock. My right hand began to burn terribly. The blow had crushed my middle finger. Drops of blood oozed from under the nail. Instinctively, I closed my other hand over the injured finger to ease the pain.

The *boche* went around his massive desk and picked up a lavishly framed photograph that had overturned. He handled it like a sacred heirloom. I figured it must be a photograph of his family, but it was a portrait of "the god with the mustache." The officer looked at me with fixed, dull eyes. He seemed to be deep in thought. Was he thinking up some refined torture or a better trick to make me squeal? I'll never know, because the telephone rang. He snatched the receiver. I felt like a boxer momentarily saved by the bell.

"Hello? Yes, it's me. Where? Krakow? What? Dressed in civilian clothes. But the description and identification number correspond? Good. Tried to escape. Dead? Shot on the railway platform. Excellent. Do I want to see the body? Certainly. Get it here as quickly as possible before it can stink up the place."

With a little smile on his lips, the *Arbeitseinsatzführer* dialed three numbers. "August, you can stop the search."

He hung up the phone, lit a cigar, and puffed on it with smug satisfaction.

I couldn't hold back my tears for Olaf. I hoped that he hadn't suffered, that he wasn't lying on that platform realizing that his carcass would be dragged back for the SS to spit on. His family, like countless others, would never know that he died a proud man. I would never have the pleasure of making him escargot, and I felt foolish believing that I ever could. It was painfully obvious how dependent I had become on his friendship, a commodity as scarce as food and almost as vital. I was again alone with thirteen thousand men in a place where a bowl of soup could turn a pacifist into a cold-blooded murderer. And in this place where men spoke only curtly and swore at one another, it could be months before I would share a laugh with another human being again.

The *Arbeitseinsatzführer* looked at me with surprise. In his jubilation he must have forgotten me.

"*Raus!*"

He didn't have to tell me twice.

CHAPTER 9

It was Sunday, Easter Sunday, 1944, to be exact. We were supposed to stay in camp. Sundays were usually free days, but at the last minute a train arrived with a shipment of steel rails and concrete reinforcements. To help expedite the unloading, *Häftlinge* and *Kapos* from all the *Blocks* were randomly drafted into *Kommando* 15. In spite of my bandaged, smashed finger, I was among those given the glorious opportunity to work on a holiday for the Third Reich. Hell, it wasn't that I cared that it was a holiday. We worked on every holiday—Christian, Jewish, Muslim, and pagan. It was just too miserable a day to be breaking my back outdoors.

We marched to the Buna plant in rain swept horizontal by an icy gale coming down from the Carpathian Mountains. There were times I wondered if Mother Nature herself wasn't a Nazi stooge. Past an array of buildings under construction was a rail spur with two boxcars and a flatcar parked on it. In gangs of ten, lined up by height, we carried the rails on our shoulders and stacked them about a hundred yards from the track. Because the ground wasn't level, the full weight of the rails would crush my shoulder one moment, then hover over my head only to come crashing back down. After two hours of this punishment, and despite the cement bag I was using as a shoulder pad, I was battered and exhausted, and scheming for a way to get a little rest.

"*Austreten*" (I have to piss), I told the *Vorarbeiter*, a German red triangle with the crooked nose of a boxer.

"*Nur fünf Minuten*" (Only five minutes), he grumbled.

The downpour had turned the ground into a quagmire, making my trek to the *Scheisshaus* a ridiculously daunting task. Mud threatened to steal my shoes at every step as I circled past a red brick warehouse. The rain came down harder and rusty brown water rolled down my jacket, obscuring my triangle and number.

Finally reaching the latrine, which looked more like a hunting blind than an outhouse, I sat down on one of the three holes, twice as tired as when I had set off. My drenched clothes were steaming from the heat of my spent body. The old boards making up the shelter were pitiful protection from the wind and rain, and the stench of shit, mold, and disinfectant were overwhelming. I would have been better off staying in line and lugging those rails. At least there I could keep my circulation stimulated.

I looked down at my throbbing finger. Puss was oozing through the bandages. I had gone to the HKB the day after my visit with the *Arbeitseinsatzführer* and had my finger dressed, but the fingernail still turned black. On my return visit to the HKB, they yanked it off. The pain had yet to subside and it had definitely become infected. Sometimes the rotten finger would be under my nose when I ate my morning piece of bread, and I would swear I was enjoying a Limburger cheese sandwich.

I decided to play things smart and use the loading platform encircling the red brick warehouse on my return trip to the train yard. Then, at least, I would have firm ground for half my jaunt back. I climbed up the steps and made my way slowly along the platform. The wind pushed me from behind. I heard a door banging. Turning around, I asked myself what could be inside the warehouse. Something I could eat? I shuffled toward the flapping door. At least on the other side was a true reprieve from the wind and rain.

I peeked in. The vast warehouse was filled with sheets of glass. I looked over my shoulder. There were no eyes, so I stepped inside and closed the door.

The warehouse was a labyrinth of crated and uncrated shipments of glass. The floor was littered with straw and packing material, and sheets of glass leaned against the walls. Not far from the entrance was a stack of tall, unpolished glass with a gap large enough for me to crawl behind. It won't piss off the *Vorarbeiter* if I dry out here for a few minutes, I thought as I made myself comfortable.

A slamming door startled me awake. What time is it, I thought? My clothes are nearly dry. Shit, I must have slept for hours! By now the *Vorarbeiter* had surely noticed that I was missing. I heard footsteps. Someone had come in. Had the *Vorarbeiter* reported me to the SS already? Were they searching for me?

I glanced out from behind the glass. Under the only light stood a man in a brown leather jacket, thumbing through an inventory. He wasn't SS, but that was hardly comforting. I had no way out. The I.G. Farben employee was between me and the door. He looked around, apparently searching for some particular item. Frowning, he looked in my direction. I froze. Did he see me? He moved slowly toward my hiding place. I heard him unroll a tape measure. No, he hadn't seen me.

He grabbed the first sheet of glass and leaned it against another pile. He measured the next sheet, counted, then swore in German. He moved that sheet, scraping it along the concrete floor. My only salvation would be if he found his desired specs before I became visible through the unpolished glass. He kept searching, swearing, and stripping the stack.

Suddenly I could see his legs through the glass. He would have spotted me if he had glanced down, but he was busy measuring the tops of the sheets. The man measured the second to last sheet, then took it away. I pressed my body against the wall in a desperate attempt to make myself as small as possible. He unrolled his tape measure along the final sheet.

"*Na, endlich doch*" (Well, finally anyhow), he sighed.

I watched terrified as his two big hands lifted the glass. It was then that he discovered me. Startled, he let go of the glass and took a quick step backwards. The sheet balanced for a second, then fell against the wall. With the sound of a plucked harp string, the glass shivered into a thousand pieces. The civilian stood as if rooted to the floor as the shards rained down on me.

As fast as my wooden-soled shoes would allow, I shot for the door. I opened it as his hand fell on my shoulder. He swung me around. The *boche* was in his fifties and wore thick-lens glasses that he pushed back up his nose with one hand as the other kept me anchored to the floor.

"What are you doing here?" he screamed.

"Just drying out a little," I said.

He pushed me outside. The rain was still unrelenting.

"Where's your *Kommando*?"

I pointed, and without a word he dragged me toward the railroad tracks. The swastika button on his jacket told me that begging for mercy was pointless. I tried to break away, but he was strong, lifting me off the ground with one hand. We rounded the corner of the warehouse.

The columns of *Häftlinge* were still working, but the train cars were almost empty. I must have slept for a damn long time. A *Kapo* spotted us and rushed over with my group's *Vorarbeiter*. I was going to get it good.

"I found him in the glass warehouse," my captor informed them.

There was nothing I could say to this *Kapo* that would save my hide. Since I wasn't in his regular *Kommando*, I was worthless to him. No excuse would appease him. In fact, it would only make matters worse. A well-placed uppercut blasted me off my feet, and I went sliding into the mud. To impress the civilian, the *Kapo* and *Vorarbeiter* punished me with soccer kicks. I slipped in and out of consciousness. When their fury died down, the *Kapo* profusely thanked the *Meister* for bringing me back.

The civilian left and the *Kapo* said to the *Vorarbeiter*, "Since they've been notified, we'll have to make a report."

I played possum as the *Vorarbeiter* bent over me with a notepad in his hand. "It's so dirty I can't read it."

"Get it from his arm," the *Kapo* said impatiently.

The *Vorarbeiter* yanked on my left arm, pulling up the sleeve. He wrote down my number, then gave the notepad to the *Kapo*, who talked out loud as he began to write.

"The *Kapo* of *Kommando* 15 reports to the *Lagerführer* that the prisoner . . ."

I watched through my eyelashes as he made a few flourishes over the paper as if he was unsure what to write next.

"Bruno, wake up the scumbag. I'm going to write up the report when we're back in camp."

By the seat of my pants, the *Vorarbeiter* dragged me through a sea of cold, muddy water, then shoved me toward the railroad cars.

"Where the hell have you been?" someone hissed as I groggily found my place back in line.

Cloudbursts came in welcoming waves, reviving me and washing away the muck my clothes had collected during my beating. I struggled to stay focused on the task at hand, but all I could think about was the thin line I was now walking between the *Stehbunker* and the rope. Would my Easter nap be considered an escape attempt, even though I hadn't left the plant grounds? That would all depend on how the *Kapo* wrote his report and who in the *Schreibstube* read it. Every one of us had a foot in the grave, and now it felt like my other foot was on the way down. I fought back tears and reminded myself I had to be a fatalist. When your time is up, it's up. A rail banged against the side of my head as if in agreement.

Apprehension and the pain of a battered jaw and infected finger tormented my sleep. The next morning I awoke with a fever and swollen glands under my arms. After a torturous day of digging a ditch, I arrived back at camp with my face on fire and my whole body trembling with chills. I dragged myself to the end of a long line of sick men waiting outside the HKB. An epidemic of ring-worm had spread through the camp, and it was being treated with a tarry ointment that left the infected *Häftling* looking like a spotted leopard. When I stepped inside someone took hold of me, and before I could utter a word, my whole face was smeared with the black goo.

"Next!" called the orderly.

"But I have a fever," I said.

"Then what are you doing here?"

"Well, I saw the line . . ."

"Go through that door," he interrupted, pointing over his shoulder.

The sign above the door he pointed to read SCHUHE VERBOTEN. So with my shoes in my hands, I entered a big white room. From the distinct smell I could tell the floor had been cleaned with kerosene. A green triangle orderly wrote my number and the date on a card, handed it to me, then pointed to a bench that ran the length of the room. There were at least fifty other "pajamas" waiting. The doctor was conducting examinations in an adjoining room. Those who came in after me had to stand or sit on the floor. The line scooted slowly along the bench, and I found some comfort in having a warm spot for my bony ass.

A Polish orderly came around taking temperatures. I pressed my tongue as hard as I could against the thermometer in hopes of getting a higher reading. There was no need—it was high enough: 102°F. Now, I began to worry. Walking over I relished a stay in the HKB, a chance for some needed rest and relief from the awful weather. Realizing that I was truly sick, I started to view my situation with dread. There was no medicine for flu, blood poisoning, or whatever it was that I was infected with. The HKB stocked only aspirin and charcoal for diarrhea. I was now running a real risk of becoming a *Muselmann* and getting thrown onto the back of a truck.

The doctor waved me in. He was a yellow triangle in his sixties who wore thick horn-rimmed glasses. His medical expertise was the only thing keeping him alive. He glanced at my card. Seeing that I had a fever, he gave me two aspirin tablets, told me to come back the next morning, and handed me a card to give to my *Blockälteste*. I was now an *Arztvormelder*, which meant I wasn't officially sick, but was exempt from work detail for one day.

Heading back to my *Block*, I realized I would have to find a new hiding place for my ring because, if I was admitted to the HKB, they would issue me new clothing on my release. My rectum was not an option this time. I would surely shit it out in there, and I couldn't hide it in my pillow or mattress because there was no guarantee I would get my bunk back. After everyone had fallen asleep, I hunted for a hiding place. I found a board in the rear wall with a deep knothole. My ring disappeared into it nicely. I slid back into my bunk with chills that made my teeth chatter.

I awoke with the need to urinate. The soup made everyone get up once or twice a night. In some *Blocks* it was the night watchman's duty to empty the piss pail while in others the *Häftling* who topped off the bucket had to dump it outside. The latter was the law in my *Block*. With ice on the windowpanes and my body on fire, this wasn't the time to go outside. Leaning on my elbow, I listened to the streams of urine going into the pail. I had heard that bucket fill up enough times to know the level by the sound. It was full. The pail's handle squeaked, a door slammed, and a gust of cold air swept through the *Block*. Now was the time. I jumped out of my bunk and dragged myself to the other side of the *Block*. A line had already formed. We all used the same method. Shit, I thought, I might be the one topping off the pail after all.

Standing there, I regretted not wrapping myself in my blanket. I was so wracked by chills that by the time it was my turn, I could barely keep a steady hand. To my great relief my bladder wasn't holding much. As I made my way back to my bunk, I heard the next man swear as he began to piss.

In the morning, the doctor declared me sick and I was officially admitted to the HKB. I took a shower, was given a clean shirt to wear but no pants, then led into the sick room—a dormitory of the usual three rows of three-tiered bunks. The fetor of shit, puke, and rubbing alcohol made me shiver. If I hadn't been so ill I would have dashed out of there without looking back.

"*Bist du aus Frankreich?*" (Are you from France?) an orderly asked.

I answered in German, and he asked if I was fluent in other languages.

"German, Spanish, and Italian."

"Are you able to climb?"

"Yes."

"Then take the upper tier over there."

I climbed up and found all three of my bedmates asleep. The second *Häftling* over caught my attention. He was close to my age, with red hair and a puffy, jaundiced face that made him look Asian. He seemed to look familiar, but his swollen face made it difficult to say for sure. I crawled in with my head at the stinking feet of the man next to me and attended to a more urgent matter—sleep.

The orderly in my section woke me. I couldn't believe my eyes. It was the Pole who had shaved me on my arrival. He was distributing the evening soup. The bastard hadn't changed. Hell, he looked a little fatter. He remembered me and was surprisingly friendly. He told me his name, Janec, and promised me an extra helping if I did translating for him.

"What a luxury, young man, to be able to sleep through the whole day," he winked. I nodded as I sat up; it certainly was. My joints weren't as stiff and my fever had subsided some.

Only my jaundiced bedmate was awake and he was greedily slurping his soup. I knew that I had seen him before, but I had no idea where. He glared at me, with soup dripping down his chin.

"*Pourquoi tu me regardé?*" (Why are you staring at me?) he muttered with a familiar Mediterranean accent.

I stared at him, dumbfounded. No, it couldn't be.

"Hubert? Is it you?" Hubert was a school chum whom I hadn't seen since our graduation twelve months ago.

"Do I know you?" he asked.

"Of course, you do. It's me, *Pierrot le Moustachu.*"

That was my nickname. In my senior class I had been the only one able to grow a full mustache. Hubert's yellowed eyes studied me. He had a hard time recognizing me, and that's when I realized how severely my body had withered. His eyes began to fill with tears.

"Yes, yes, it's you, old buddy," he choked.

Hubert had been the captain of our volleyball team and was a real Casanova. His loyalty to friends could never be questioned except when it came to the opposite sex. Nobody's girlfriend was safe when he was around. I had known Hubert since we entered high school. His parents grew carnations on the outskirts of Nice. Hubert got his red hair from his mother, who had the prettiest freckles. He didn't volunteer, and I didn't dare ask about his parents, because Hubert was a yellow triangle.

That night, after the lights were doused, we lay next to each other and reminisced about school and our neighborhood. Remembering escapades and pranks had us giggling like the normal teenagers we should have been.

"You know, Hubert, actually we were mean kids. All those dirty tricks we played on the teachers."

Hubert's eyes lit up. "Yes, that math teacher with the bad ticker, Mr. Thiriad. He sure turned blue when we exploded that cherry bomb against the blackboard."

"Remember how I would weave chewing gum across the aisles when we had that little substitute teacher with the thick glasses who dictated while walking up and down the room?"

"Yes, yes," Hubert nodded, "he would have that whole sticky web wrapped all over him before he noticed. I think the idiot only had one suit."

"I pulled that on him three times."

"Do you remember Leggs?" Hubert asked.

"How could anyone forget?" I said. "Leggs" was the nickname we had given our history professor, Miss Galand. She had been a beauty-contest winner and I used to drop my pencil to admire her thighs from the correct angle. After class one day someone inflated a condom in her inkstand, then filled it with ink. The next morning when Miss Galand dipped her pen, ink sprayed all over her new dress.

"She was so angry she was demented."

"I've never heard someone scream that loud and for that long."

"When she transferred to another school I thought my goose was cooked," Hubert admitted.

"But Charles told me he did it. He always had a couple of condoms in his pocket."

"Well, yes, it was him, but it was my idea."

"How was that girl with the big tits?" I asked. "Marcelle. You used to date her."

"Yes, yes."

"Was she a good lay?"

Hubert hesitated, then snickered. "That was only a front."

"What are you talking about?"

"I was really screwing her mother. For two wonderful years."

"Her mother?"

"She's only thirty-eight."

We both burst out laughing, and for a brief second I thought I was back home.

◆ ◆ ◆

It quickly became apparent that the HKB wasn't a hospital or an infirmary, but a way station to the crematoriums. The unsanitary conditions along with the garbage they fed us made our weakened bodies unfettered feasts for parasites and viruses. The stink of human decay hung like incense. The bunks were full of men who had no hope for anything except the end of everything. I had seen enough corpses in the camp, but I had never been a fixed spectator to the slow, ugly transition. Every couple of hours someone died, and most of the bodies just lay in the bunks, their bedmates too weak to call out. The bodies would finally be discovered by the orderlies passing out the rations, then they would lay there until a couple of orderlies felt like dragging them away. I was thankful for Hubert's presence. Our conversations between sleep kept my heart light and my mind far from the nightmares around me. Our shared laughter must have seemed like the mark of insanity among the coughs, moans, and death rattles.

On my third day, the orderlies collected corpses after morning rations, and when they were finished, the bottom tier of our bunk was empty. Hubert and I climbed down and made it our bed. Janec informed us that we better not get comfortable.

"You guys are going to get company. I have a French Jew who's driving his Polish bedmate crazy."

Minutes later Janec returned with a hunched-over *Muselmann* who was hacking and spitting. He appeared to be in his sixties, but was probably no older than thirty. His shirt, which reached only to his belly button, was soaking wet. I greeted him in French, but he answered me in Greek. I tried Spanish and again he babbled in Greek.

"This man's Greek, not French."

Janec shrugged. I guessed that to an untrained Slavic ear all the Mediterranean languages sounded alike.

"What's wrong with him? Is it something catching?" Hubert asked.

"Pleurisis is pressing on his lungs. He won't last," Janec said matter-of-factly and walked away.

The Greek kept tugging at my sleeve, muttering indecipherable sentences between moans and coughing fits. He was desperate to discuss something of importance. I turned to Hubert, who was sitting at the other end of the bunk. He wanted no part of this.

"Talk to him in Hebrew. Find out what he wants. The poor fellow is desperate to tell us something. Maybe he's going to divulge where a treasure is buried," I winked.

"Buried, my ass. I can't speak Hebrew."

"But didn't you learn the language for your Bar Mitzvah?"

Hubert informed me that he had learned the prayers phonetically.

"That way I wouldn't embarrass my parents in front of all my relatives."

Janec came back with a large needle that he unceremoniously shoved between the Greek's ribs. A greenish fluid gushed out onto the floor. I was fascinated. Hubert got up and headed toward the piss pails. The procedure seemed to give the Greek some relief, but he gave up trying to speak to any of us. By the time evening rations arrived I realized that the man had fallen into a coma.

With his back turned to the Greek, Hubert giggled.

"What's funny?" I asked.

"You thought that all of us can speak Hebrew, didn't you?"

"I guess," I shrugged.

"The only thing we Jews have in common are a few traditions, snipped foreskin, and these yellow triangles."

After rations the next morning the Greek's body was carried away along with his treasures.

Since Hubert had been in the HKB for more than a week, his odds of being "selected" for the ovens were in the Nazis' favor. To the *boches*, if you were too weak and sickly to be a productive slave, then you were a useless mouth to feed and had to go. At irregular intervals and always without warning, the SS would conduct a "selection"—a weeding out of the *Muselmänner*, in all the *Blocks*. They made more frequent visits to the HKB because they hated to waste aspirin. Recovered or not, Hubert knew he would have to leave. He prayed that, when discharged, he would end up in a different *Kommando*. The *Kommando* he had been in mixed concrete for the ever-expanding plant complex, and the dust from the mixers was ruining his lungs. Many from his *Kommando* had already been stricken with emphysema. Two days later, and still edematous and yellow, Hubert got a release from a reluctant doctor.

"Listen, *mon ami*." I grabbed his arm. "We have to stay in contact. Together we've got a better chance of getting back home." Hubert agreed, but with about 10,000 inmates in the camp, we both knew this wasn't going to be an easy task. You could go for months without laying eyes on someone if that person wasn't in your *Block* or *Kommando*. And the Nazis made contact more difficult by regularly shifting us around, depending on their labor needs and to prevent gangs of resistance from being formed. Hubert promised that through Janec he would get word to me of his *Block* number and *Kommando*.

CHAPTER 10

I had fully recovered. I was amazed what a few days' rest could accomplish. Janec kept telling me that my saving grace was the resilience of my eighteen-year-old body. By rubbing the thermometer, I was able to make it register high enough to allow me to remain in the HKB. Because of my numerous childhood illnesses, I was barely out of bed until the age of five, and thus I lulled myself into believing I was immune to the epidemics raging around me and could pass any "selection." I managed to switch to a bottom bunk near a window, figuring I would breathe in fewer germs from those coughing and spitting up blood. I would also have a reminder that there was a world, no matter how unsavory, outside this sideshow of unraveling mortal coils.

For some lucky reason I shared my bunk with only one other man, and though sometimes I woke up chewing his toes, there was enough room for me to roll over. Mario was an anti-fascist Italian who barely uttered a word to me. He was extremely sick and slipping fast. Every night, he would implore some saint or ancestor while his feet kicked my face. Every day the doctor would come by and ask Mario where it hurt. He would point at his whole body,

and the doctor would walk away shaking his head. One time I overheard him mention to an orderly that Mario must be a hypochon-
driac, but I knew better. No one could fake the cramps and
convulsions that wracked his body. I was sure that worms were
chewing through his guts. A medicine man in the Amazon could
have cured Mario with a few herbs, but unfortunately our circumstances were more primitive.

One night I awoke to find Mario trembling and pressing his
abdomen with both hands. He was crying silently, his moist, black
eyes staring out the window. I felt uneasy, as if I had blundered into
a private moment. I wanted to comfort him, but how? Words were
impotent—lies, actually—and although I was lying next to the man,
I couldn't bring myself to wrap my arm around him in solace. I
didn't have the courage.

His face taut with pain, Mario slowly sat up at the edge of the
bunk. I figured he had to take a leak. He dropped to all fours and
crawled to the window. Curious, I sat up. Grabbing hold of the
window ledge, Mario pulled himself to his feet. He tried to open
the window, but he was too weak.

"What are you doing?" I asked in Italian. "Mario, stop."

He shook his head defiantly and kept struggling. Not wanting
any trouble for either of us from the night watchman, I jumped to
my feet.

"*Alto!*" (Stop!) I hissed.

Breathing heavily, Mario pressed his face against the glass.
Coming up behind him, I realized he was staring at the barbed-wire
fence only a few feet away. A searchlight's beam swept across it. In
the nearby watchtower I could see the reddish glow of a guard's
pipe. Mario tried to open the window again, but it wouldn't budge.
He turned to me with imploring eyes.

"*Ajuto, amico*" (Help, friend), he whispered.

How could I ask him to go back to that bunk and continue his
senseless suffering? I studied his eyes to reassure myself that this
was the best and only way. I pried open the window. My muscles
tightened against the rush of cold air.

Mario grasped my hand. "*Gracie, tante.*" (Thanks a lot.)

At least it's on his terms, I consoled myself.

Mario slid over the sill, dropped three feet to the ground, and began crawling toward the wire. The searchlight found him.

"*Halt, halt, oder ich schiesse!*" (Stop, stop, or I'll shoot!)

Mario didn't stop. He reached out. A flash of blue light enveloped him, then a thunderclap rattled the window.

As I shrunk back into bed, a burst of machine gun fire echoed. I guess the guard wanted to leave evidence that he wasn't sleeping on duty. I had seen many bodies lying next to the fences on my way to work detail, but I had never before seen a person electrocuted. It was hard to fall back asleep. Finally, I got up and closed the window. The smell of Mario's burnt flesh was just too much.

In the morning, an Austrian named Pressburger became my bedmate. He was a man of forty, relatively old for the camp. I knew at first glance that he wasn't going to leave the HKB alive. His breathing was labored, and there was a wet gurgling coming from the depths of his lungs. I had to feed him like a baby because he couldn't hold a spoon in his trembling hands. I wondered if Janec was bunking me with the most critical cases because he knew I would nurse them. Or was it just his way of scaring my ass out of the HKB?

The second night after Mario's death I was awakened by the sound of gunfire and guards shouting. The barbed wire glowed red with the reflection of huge flames. One of the *Blocks* was on fire. I anxiously called to the *Häftlinge* outside my window, asking if they knew what *Block* was burning. They shook their heads, no. I flopped down beside Pressburger. With my shithouse luck it's probably my *Block* that's burning, I thought, and my only possession is melting into oblivion. The fire burned through the night because the camp's poorly equipped fire squad could protect only the adjoining *Blocks*.

The next day I got the confirmation. Sixty *Blocks* in the camp, and it was mine that was charred. Fate is so perverted. How many times had I laid in my bunk with a growling stomach, dreaming about the loaf of bread and cauldron of soup I would buy with my ring? How many mornings, standing in the freezing rain, had I schemed how I would buy myself the position of *Vorarbeiter* in a *Kommando* working inside the factory? How many ruses had I concocted? How many risks had I taken during searches? And there was that beating I took after I recovered my ring. It had all been for nothing. My only insurance against becoming a *Muselmann* was gone.

◆ ◆ ◆

Every time I had to take a piss I would pass by a section of bunks being tended by an orderly who seemed to be highly competent and compassionate when treating patients. He could have passed for the twin of that Nazi officer on the train from Nice who had the cans of milk, except that the orderly wore a yellow triangle. The day after the fire he came and sat on the edge of my bunk.

"*Mein Name ist Paul. Kannst du Deutsch sprechen?*" (My name is Paul. Do you speak German?)

"*Je parle le français.*" (I speak French.)

He frowned. "*Mon Français nest pas très bon*" (My French isn't very good), he told me.

"That's okay, I was only kidding," I told him in German.

His face brightened. "Did you know any German Jews in France? Two cousins of mine emigrated there in '33. I haven't heard from them since the war started."

"Only German Jews I met were a few elderly couples while I was in a camp in Paris."

"I'm sure those couples didn't make it past the first day here. My parents didn't."

"I'm sorry. Why didn't you leave Germany with your cousins?"

"My father was a decorated veteran. He thought that the Nazis wouldn't touch him, and I was in my fourth year of medical school."

I asked a question that I had been eager to ask a German Jew for some time.

"Why do you think Hitler hates you people?"

"I don't know, but he sure needed us—blaming us for losing the war and causing the depression. He would've been a nobody without us. He got rich off us, too."

"What do you mean?"

"The gangsters confiscated everything we owned. Affluent Jews were jailed, and when they managed to secure a visa to another country, the Nazis turned them loose and legally took everything they had."

"Legally?"

"Oh, yes. Hitler imposed a penalty for fleeing Germany, a *Reichsfluchtsteuer*, which was only a lawful way for him to steal everything a man owned."

"There were many wealthy Jews?"

He shrugged. "Wealthy, I don't know. Understand that many were forced to start their own businesses or be self-employed because the German guilds and unions didn't accept us."

I told him that I never knew that. "I always heard that Jews didn't want to get their hands dirty."

He laughed at my ignorance and bid me good luck. My heart grew heavy, realizing how horrible it must have been for Stella and Hubert to grow up stigmatized and then witness that intolerance turn into ovens.

On a rainy Tuesday night the assembly bell rang as the *Kommandos* returned from the plant. I pitied my fellow *Häftlinge* for having to stand out there, soaked and shivering, after toiling for twelve hours. A gaggle of bitching SS passed by. I went to the window. The wind carried the echoes of the *Lagerführer*'s pronouncement. They were hanging another man for trying to escape. The execution was over quickly; the *boches* were in a hurry to get back to their warm quarters.

I slipped back into the bunk. For the first time, Pressburger was sleeping soundly. I mulled over why the SS hadn't postponed the hanging. Was the man's demise that urgent? Were the *boches* that rigid with their protocol? Of course, they were. They probably kept records of every man, woman, and child they slaughtered. Maybe they didn't want to wait one day because then the condemned man would have enjoyed the double ration of bread and spoonful of jam we received every Wednesday morning. For a doomed *Häftling* that jam would be a royal delicacy, but as the White Queen told Alice, "The rule is, jam to-morrow and jam yesterday—but never jam to-day."

The Nazi jam, like their margarine, was made from coal. I didn't believe it when I was first told, figuring it was a dirty trick to sucker me into giving my portion to an "old timer." Then I overheard some *Häftlinge* mention that they worked in the factory labs that used coal to make synthetic food products and other materials used in the camp. There wasn't any nutritional value whatsoever in the ersatz jam, but it did help quiet the hunger pangs for a while.

I awoke as a searchlight beam skimmed across the icy windowpane, making it sparkle like crystal. The footsteps outside told me the sentries were being relieved. I had to relieve myself, so I ran for the pail. My bare feet stuck to the cold, oiled floor. I passed the *Häftling* who was on night watch. He was asleep in a chair, snuggly wrapped in a blanket. Nice to see that one of us was momentarily having it better than the Nazis outside.

When I got back under the covers, Pressburger's feet were on my side of the bunk. Irritated, I pushed them away. His legs were rigid and cold. He was dead. Pressburger was gone.

Having slept next to a man while he gasped his final breaths gave me the creeps. My instinct was to run, but since there was nowhere to go I just laid there and got goose bumps. It's a depressing revelation how easy and unceremoniously life can vanish. I couldn't help thinking that if life had any value at all, then Pressburger's death wouldn't seem so completely meaningless. I thought about waking the night watchman, but he would have to wake the *Stubendienst*, who would have to wake a couple of the orderlies. I felt foolish that Pressburger had that much sway over me. Why rouse the whole *Block* for one corpse? It could wait till morning.

I took Pressburger's blanket, and was about to shove his body out so I could have the whole bed to myself, when a better idea popped into my head. In a few hours Janec would arrive with the morning rations, and if he saw that Pressburger was dead he would keep his share. Why should he get it instead of me? The big Pole didn't need the bread and jam; he got packages from home. I was the one who had taken care of Pressburger, made things easier for him in his last hours. I deserved his ration.

I dragged Pressburger to the other side of the bunk, away from the light of the corridor. The body had stiffened, and it took all my strength to move the limbs into the semblance of a normal sleeping position. I turned his face toward me. The features were contorted into a horrible scowl. I pushed on his jaw, but his mouth wouldn't close. His eyes were rolled back and his eyelids kept sliding up every time I tried to close them. I pulled the blanket so that only the top of his head showed. I went to the spot where Janec would stand while distributing the food and inspected my stage setting. It seemed perfect.

As I tried to go back to sleep, I considered what Pressburger would have done if he had known that he was going to die so forsaken. Would he have confided in me about his life, his dreams, his failures, his loves? Would he have prayed to God or cursed him for such a foul-smelling fate? Here was another man whose family, if he had one and if they were still alive, would never know where and how he died. This man suffered, laughed, thought of the future. . . . No, I had to stop. I wasn't strong enough. There were too many dying for me to grieve for any of them. And was Pressburger the one to be pitied? His suffering was over, but what was still in store for me? What would I have to go through till my forsaken death?

The camp's reveille brought me to consciousness with a jolt. I kept my back turned to my bunkmate and dozed back off. A little while later the *Kommandos* marched out as the camp's band played "Beer Barrel Polka." Every morning the band, which was made up of some of Europe's finest musicians and composers, played moronic German marching songs as we left for the plant. In my first couple of months, goose-stepping past those SS guards I wondered whether the music was for their entertainment or whether they were seriously trying to rouse us to give our all to the Reich. What I figured now is that they decorated this human slaughterhouse with the trappings of normal society so they wouldn't see the butcher in the mirror. The only music playing in the HKB was the symphonic coughing and spitting of awakening *Muselmänner*.

I heard baskets scraping along the floor. The orderlies were beginning to distribute the rations. My heart began to beat faster. I slipped my foot under Pressburger's body and made it move up and down to the rhythm of my own breathing. He sure seemed alive. I looked over to Janec, who was chatting away with one of the Polish patients. What are you doing? Why the morning chat? Don't keep me waiting, Janec, my leg is cramping! Finally he came over and gave me my food.

"Sleep well?"

"Oh, yes."

"Why did you change places?"

"He was falling out of bed," I said, making a gesture toward the corpse.

"Hey, Pressburger," Janec patted him on the shoulder.

I raised the body up a little, like somebody who was stirring, then let it fall back.

"Oh, let Pressburger alone," I said. "He didn't get any sleep last night."

The coughing fit of a patient on the next tier distracted Janec. He took a second ration out of the basket and handed it to me. "Promise me that you'll give it to him."

"You know that I look after him," I said.

Janec nodded and continued on his rounds.

After I had eaten my fill, I feared what the Pole would do when he discovered my trick, but Janec was in good humor. He had a voucher to soak his biscuit at the camp's bordello that he had obtained with the contents of a package sent by his family. That's how he had landed the privileged post of orderly—by paying for it. Many German and Polish *Häftlinge* were able to buy a hell of a lot of favors with the packages they received. I smiled at the irony of the peasant woman who toiled and denied herself so she could send food to her imprisoned husband, which gave him the opportunity to be unfaithful to her.

After Janec left that afternoon I alerted the orderlies that Pressburger was dead. Unceremoniously, they dragged his body out to a nearby shed. The following morning a *Häftling* threw his body onto the bed of a truck loaded down with the camp's dead, and by that evening the only testimony to Pressburger's existence was smoke and ashes.

CHAPTER 11

I walked out of the HKB two days after Pressburger's death by no means the picture of health, but feeling damn good for a *Häftling*. I might even have put on a couple of pounds. Since no one in the HKB remembered that my *Block* had gone up in flames, and the *Kommandos* had already marched off to the plant, I wound up wandering aimlessly about the camp's grounds. Except for the Maintenance *Kommando*, Monowitz was empty. It felt strange to be alone in the camp, but it felt stranger not to have some menial task to perform. I expected at any moment a *Kapo* or *Vorarbeiter* to rush up, eager to beat me into the ground since an idle *Häftling* was a sin to "the god with a moustache."

I considered how long it would take me to locate Hubert. He had never gotten word to me of his new *Block* number or *Kommando*, and I had stopped pestering Janec after the Pole brought up the possibility that my schoolmate was dead. Yes, it was a definite possibility, but one that I wasn't about to entertain. As far as I was concerned Hubert was sleeping in one of the *Blocks*, and it was in my best interest to find out which one as quickly as possible.

I went to where my old *Block* stood to see if the rubble had been removed. Not only had they cleared the debris, construction on a new barracks was well under way.

The gallows still stood at the edge of the Appelplatz. It was unlike the *boches* not to cart it away after an execution. Without the rope the wooden structure looked benign and comically unfunctional. If only I could wipe away those strangled faces.

Lost in my thoughts, I didn't hear the green triangle *Kapo* walk up behind me. *"Arbeitest du im Lager?"* (Are you working in the camp?)

With some apprehension, I handed him my release paper from the HKB and explained my situation. By the number on his *Kapo* armband I knew that he was in charge of the Transportation *Kommando*.

"You'll work for me," he said. "Two of my men were hurt in an accident."

What luck, I thought, but I wasn't so sure after he told me that one of the injured men had lost his foot when the *Kipp Lore* (tilt lorry) he was pushing rolled back over him.

"Come, I'll straighten it out with the *Schreibstube*."

Since I preferred never to set eyes on the *Arbeitseinsatzführer* again, I was relieved that the *Kapo* had me wait at the steps of the administration barracks. It took only a few minutes for him to straighten things out. "You're mine for a couple of days, 'til I get some new arrivals from quarantine."

The Transportation *Kommando* was responsible for moving supplies from the rail yard to the warehouses, factory buildings, and construction sites. This was all done with two-wheel carts that six to eight men pulled by a long rope while two or three others kept the load balanced. The *Kommando* also collected the camp's dead and shepherded them to Birkenau's crematoriums some five miles away.

As we lined up in our *Kommandos* the following morning, the *Kapo* informed me that I would be working on the *Leichenwagen* (hearse) with him. I was overjoyed to be able to leave Monowitz for the day. I might get lucky and speak with a *Häftling* from the main

camp or Birkenau who would have information on the fate of the
women from my transport. But when the bed of the truck was half
full of dead *Muselmänner*, I began to question my eagerness. I had
had my fill of dead bodies in the HKB. Was a day outside the
barbed wire worth staring at all those distorted faces? The *Kapo*
must have seen it in my face. "Look without seeing, boy," he
laughed, slapping me on the back.

Making my way along a row of *Blocks* with a pushcart saddled
with two corpses, the *Blokowa* (female barracks supervisor) of the
Puff, the camp's bordello, waved me over. This green triangle, a
buxom, butch blonde, had the habit of hurling obscenities at us
from the whorehouse doorway as we marched to work in the mornings. The Puff was located in the middle of the camp. It was a
regular barracks encircled by a barbed-wired fence with an SS guard
on duty around the clock. Once in a while I would see a woman's
face at one of the windows, but none of them ever came outside.
Every evening, *Häftlinge*, mainly *Kapos*, were lined up at the entrance. Since their time was limited, the guard would always be seen
pushing out half-dressed laggards with the butt of his gun.

I had been in the Puff once before, months earlier, not for pleasure but to deliver towels from the camp's laundry facility. When I
approached the *Block* that Sunday afternoon, I was scared. If I found
Stella inside it would have broken me, dooming me for a ride on
the back of a truck. With the *Blokowa's* quarters at the far end of the
barracks, I had to pass a honeycomb of makeshift cubicles with no
doors or curtains, and I couldn't stop myself from peering into each
one. I didn't see Stella, but I did get a quick lesson on how cold and
mechanical sex can be. Most of the couples seemed as detached as
stray dogs humping on a street corner, except for one happy fellow,
who, without missing a stroke, gave me a wave and a big smile as I
went by.

Heading back to my *Block* that day, I realized that if Stella had
been in one of those cubicles, it shouldn't shatter my hopes. It
would be ridiculous to be jealous and forlorn if it meant her survival. But as I walked down the hall this time, to retrieve the body

of a young woman who had slashed her wrists, my heart pounded again. When I saw the blonde stubble on the head of the teenage girl on the bed, I let out a silent sigh of relief.

The girl's naked body was curled up on her side and her arms were drawn against her chest. Her mouth was slightly opened as if she were thinking about something to say. Most of the burlap mattress was black from her blood. Someone had strewn sawdust on the floor to soak up the blood that had pooled around the bed. A slight breeze drew my attention to the window that she had shattered. I didn't want to imagine the pain she must have endured to slice open her wrists.

Easing her stiffening body prone, I noticed bite marks and hickeys on her neck and rashes from ringworm under her small breasts. With her fixed green eyes staring at the ceiling, her pale, near transparent face seemed oddly serene. I kicked a bloody shard of glass under the bed as I began to roll her in a blanket. My hands became sticky with her blood. She had welts on her back and buttocks, no doubt the *Blokowa*'s signature.

Two women in their early twenties dressed in baggy "pajamas" stood at the entrance of the cubicle, whispering in French.

"How long have you two been in this *Block*?" I asked.

"We came here from the main camp two weeks ago."

"Did you see any other French girls over there?"

"No. But the day we arrived they sent a bunch of them to work at a camp with a textile mill."

I finished wrapping the corpse. With her body covered and the five o'clock shadow on her head, she could have easily been mistaken for a boy.

"She must've desperately wanted to die," I mumbled.

The more talkative of the two answered. "She was praying and preaching constantly to us and our dates. The *Blokowa* kept beating her bloody, and she still wouldn't shut up. I guess God finally got pounded out of her. First she tried to hang herself."

"Get out my way, you stupid bitches!" the *Blokowa* yelled.

The women scattered.

"What a bloody mess." The *Blokowa* was boiling mad. "I'll never have another one of those *Bibelforscher* in here. Lousy fanatic, I should have let her hang."

German *Bibelforscher* (Jehovah's Witnesses) were turned into purple triangle *Häftlinge* because of their singular devotion to Jesus, which left "the god with a moustache" in the cold. Any of them could easily have regained freedom by pledging allegiance to the Nazi Party. As a non-believer, I had difficulty comprehending their beliefs and their dedication, but I admired their resoluteness. With suicide being an affront to her God, how that girl must have agonized before she broke that window.

"Don't steal the blanket or it will be your ass. The *Krätzeblock* can use it," the *Blokowa* growled. "Not that those crud-infested pricks would care, but blood won't show in kerosene."

"Don't worry. I'll return it," I promised.

I didn't need the blanket, but why expose the girl's naked body to the catcalls of the onlookers I knew were assembled outside? I had been raised to respect and look after the "weaker sex." I cradled her body in my arms and headed for the door. None of the women in the cubicles gave even a passing glance as I walked by. The *Blokowa* stayed on my heels, spitting out obscenities about Jehovah's Witnesses and other "Bible nuts."

The jackals outside scattered once they saw that I had closed the curtain on their main attraction. I laid the girl's body on my pushcart. Three corpses were more than enough for one *Häftling* to haul, so I took them to the truck. To blend with the rest of the load, I placed the girl on her belly. I was relieved that the *Kapo* wasn't around. He would get a good laugh, seeing how protective I was of a whore's bag of bones.

The *Blokowa* was in a more pleasant mood when I returned with the blanket. "You're a good kid. If you ever feel the urge, I'll let you tear off a piece without a voucher," she promised.

After our 100-plus load was counted at the gate, we started on our way to the crematoriums. The *Kapo* was in the cab with the SS driver, and I bounced around in the back with the corpses. First, we passed by a Stalag* housing prisoners of the British Common-wealth. Many of them worked at the plant. Then we drove past a camp for female forced laborers. A group of kids waved to me from behind the barbed wire. I waved back. I had almost forgotten that children still existed on this planet.

I was surprised and somewhat confused when the truck veered off the paved road and ground to a halt below a bridge spanning a small river. The driver and *Kapo* jumped out. I took a deep breath, inhaling the musty smell of the water. It was intoxicating. Gone was the overwhelming, acrid stench of the plant. I almost felt free. Almost . . .

"Unload that girl!" the *Kapo* barked.

I did as I was told. With her slung over my shoulder, I followed the *Kapo* and the driver, who had a gunnysack and length of rope squeezed under his arm, down to the river. Where the hell are we going with this girl, I wondered but didn't dare ask. The driver stopped at the river's edge and looked around. He pointed at a rope in the water that was tied to a tree. When the *Kapo* reeled in the rope, pulling out a bulging, muddy gunnysack that had been sub-merged in the reeds, I knew exactly what was going on. I had done something similar as a child to catch crayfish in the Brague River, but I had used a dead cat in a flour sack.

The driver hefted the heavy sack upright, and the *Kapo* lifted out the bluish white legs of a corpse. The bottom of the gunnysack was squirming with eels. The *Kapo* shook the man's body, then dropped it onto the bank. His belly was sliced open and a couple of lucky eels sprang out of the guts and slithered back into the river. The SS driver swore in Czech, and I realized that he was a *Sudeten-deutscher*, the ethnic German minority in Czechoslovakia. They had complained about discrimination in 1938, which gave "the god with a moustache" his excuse to invade the country.

---

* The camp referred to, E715, wasn't a Stalag but a subcamp of Stalag VIIB, the largest POW camp in Germany. E715 housed British and British Commonwealth soldiers.

The *Kapo* yanked the girl off my shoulder. After they stuffed her into the fresh gunnysack, the driver reached in with his bayonet and gave her a cesarean. "You didn't have to cut her open. Her hole is stretched out enough," the *Kapo* chuckled.

"And let the eels catch the clap?"

The two men howled as they heaved the gunnysack into the water. I turned away, fighting back the urge to throw up. With dinner a long way off, I couldn't afford to lose my breakfast. As the *Kapo* and I threw the man's corpse onto the truck, a question occurred to me. Would I have to drag her body up the trail tomorrow?

The driver was now in such a rush to get to the crematoriums that he didn't bother to avoid the numerous potholes, and I was certain I was going to find myself face-down in one of them. Was the asshole trying to make up for lost time? Or did he want to ensure that his precious eels were delivered alive and squirming? Each jolt momentarily animated the corpses, sending arms and legs flailing, sometimes tapping me on the back. A few more bumps, I daydreamed, and the driver will raise the dead and be marched in front of a firing squad for letting his load escape the ovens.

The truck came to jarring halt right outside one of the gates of Birkenau. SS guards screamed at me to move away from the vehicle and not to talk to any of the *Häftlinge*. What *Häftlinge*, I thought? There wasn't a soul about except the guards. I put a wide berth between me and the truck as the *Kapo* and the driver stayed in the cab, chatting and smoking.

A significant distance past the barbed wire stood two large red brick structures with black plumes streaming from their chimneys. I had never laid eyes on them before, but I knew exactly what those buildings were. They were why the air reeked of grease burning in a skillet.

As if on cue, members of the *Sonderkommando* (Special Detail) came out of one the buildings, pushing flatbed handcars. The *Sonderkommando* was responsible for the disposal of all the dead—those that were delivered to them like our load and those murdered in the "showers." I had never seen such a strange and disturbing group of men. Even though they were walking and breathing, and seemingly well fed, there was no life in them. Their eyes, their faces, had less expression than the corpses that they hauled off the truck. They all moved—no, glided—with shoulders hunched and arms hanging limply at their sides. They worked fast, silently, and without a wasted gesture. It was as if I were watching a ballet of Dante's Inferno. On how many corpses had they rehearsed this gruesome choreography? *Birkenau* is German for "birch groves," and when I first heard the name I imagined a peaceful sanitarium where the truckloads of *Muselmänner* were nursed back to human beings. What wishful thinking!

On the way back to camp we stopped in the Auschwitz main camp and picked up a load of men's clothing. There was a shortage of the striped uniforms in our camp, and the SS were supplementing with civilian clothes that had a square piece of striped material stitched on the back. We then made a detour to the Buna plant's civilian kitchen, where the driver delivered his eels and a bag of unaltered clothes. He came back with a smile and a few packs of Navy Cut, a British brand of cigarettes that an English POW had traded with the cook.

"Gee, they smell delicious," I told the *Kapo*.

"You're too young to smoke," he said.

"But not too young to burn."

He laughed and handed me one.

Loading the truck the next morning, all I could think about was the Jehovah's Witness. My sleep had been wracked with images of her naked body shivering as hundreds of eels burrowed through her. Feigning sick had crossed my mind, but I feared the *Kapo*'s fury more than watching her be poured out of that sack. I could definitely survive seeing another dead body; another beating was a different story.

My stomach was twisted in knots by the time the truck pulled under the bridge. I carried the smallest corpse I could find down to their fishing spot. The SS driver was in a jolly mood, certain that "the whore" had brought him a prize catch. I closed my eyes as he and the *Kapo* extracted her. When I heard her body drop on the bank I couldn't keep my eyes shut any longer. Her mud-streaked corpse glistened in the sun. The ugly welts on her body had receded in the cold water. She sure had put a spell on me, because by the time I heard him, the *Kapo* was screaming in my face.

"Hey shithead, get moving!"

I struggled to carry her up the embankment. I didn't care that my "pajamas" got dirty and wet. She deserved better than being dragged by her bluish white ankles, but how I wished that the cold water had closed her milky eyes. Not wanting to stare at her ripped-open belly, I laid her on her stomach. I felt guilty, but I couldn't help admiring her still firm buttocks. Doubtless she had been a virgin until they dragged her kicking and screaming into that whorehouse. As a final act of desecration, an eel slowly slithered out from under her. I stomped on its head with my heel and ground it to gelatin. The SS driver came up the embankment yodeling. A fat catfish had erred into his sack.

"This one I will keep for myself," he announced.

I looked at the dead eel at my feet and thought, I'll do the same. On the way to Birkenau, I hid the eel in the tube that reinforced the side panel of the truck, then sat down next to the girl's corpse.

"Thanks," I mumbled.

I didn't even know the name of this decent, fervently religious human being whose God had forsaken her. It was no wonder that I was an atheist. In this place, God validated my choice every day.

Again, the SS ordered me to stand away from the truck as the *Sonderkommando* shuffled through their dance. When two of them turned the girl over, exposing her eviscerated belly, they froze for a second, shook their heads, then resumed their roles. After all the corpses had been removed, the *Sonderkommando* loaded the truck with over forty old cement bags filled with human ashes. They stacked the bags in neat, tight rows to prevent them from spilling.

Once the tailgate was closed I climbed into the bed. When I was eight, an elementary school pal showed me the urn that held the ashes of his grandmother. I had a hard time believing that a canister no bigger than a small coffee can could hold a whole adult. There had to be at least twenty to twenty-five men, women, and children in each of the cement bags, which meant I was staring at all that was left of one train load of human beings.

As we drove away I peered inside one of them. I had never seen human ashes before. The ashes were grayish brown and coarse like sand, and peppered with blackened pieces of bone. I looked back. The smoke from the red brick chimneys was beginning to eclipse the sun. Goodbye, you innocent, devout creature. I am sure I'll see you again in my nightmares.

The truck turned onto a dirt road leading to vast fields of cabbages. We stopped at a patch being tilled by a *Kommando*. The driver blew his horn and yelled at them to unload the truck. As they approached, I realized that the *Häftlinge* were women—black triangles from the Ukraine. I handed the bags down to them, and a few immediately started spreading the ashes along the rows of cabbages. The Nazis made sure nothing went to waste, and from the looks of those bulging, green heads, we made excellent fertilizer.

I wanted to see if one of the women would circulate a message for Stella through the women's camps, but none of them spoke any of the languages I spoke. At least seeing that the SS had a use for them bolstered my optimism that I would see Stella again. Yet I couldn't help thinking that there was a father, perhaps even a boyfriend, who was confident he would see that Jehovah Witness again.

After the women loaded our truck with cabbages meant for our camp's kitchen, the driver once again stopped at the plant's civilian kitchen to trade his morning catch, along with a large number of the cabbages. When we arrived at our kitchen I helped unload. While no one was looking I retrieved my catch. I swapped the eel for a ladle of soup with no questions asked, but I could tell by the way that he eyed me that the cook knew how I got it.

CHAPTER 12

The next day, it was a new *Block*, a new *Kommando*, and new companions. I now was part of a work detail that was digging trenches for the plant's sewer, water, and heating pipelines. Most of these trenches had to accommodate several pipelines. The digging would go like this: Four to five *Häftlinge* abreast would swing pickaxes to break up the topsoil as another crew shoveled the dirt out. After having dug about one hundred yards in length and a half-yard in depth, we would take our pickaxes and go back where we started and take off another layer. This procedure would be repeated until we reached the Nazis' specified depth of two to three yards, depending on the diameter of the pipes. At that depth, platforms were erected to facilitate the extraction of the loose earth.

It was a backbreaking *Kommando*. Every evening there were corpses to carry back to the camp. There was one advantage, however. Since we were digging along the road that led to the civilian factory workers' kitchen, all the wagons delivering provisions passed right in front of our noses—right above our heads, to be exact. They were loaded with potatoes, a long-forgotten delicacy, or beets or cabbages. Hearing the rattle of the wagons' ironbound wheels and the clatter of the horses' hooves, we would first make sure we weren't under the watchful eyes of a *Kapo* or SS guard, then ready ourselves for attack. We would let the wagon pass a short distance, then a chosen *Häftling* would jump onto the rear and toss to us whatever he could grab.

We did our work on those trenches as slowly as possible. There wouldn't be any rolling food markets to "organize" from at our next job site. Before heading back to camp in the evening, a few of us would chop at the sides of the trench, and with the help of the night frost and morning thaw, it would be caved in when we returned. Our *Vorarbeiter*, Emile, closed his eyes to all this and naturally got the lion's share of our bounties, but soon the drivers got wise and passed by us at a gallop. We then started attacking en masse, with our mess tins over our heads to protect ourselves from their whips.

Twice a week, a local peasant came to pick up the "pig pot," an enormous receptacle kept behind the plant's kitchen in which the spoiled remnants of the day's soup were poured. The pig pot was always infested with drowned flies, but it took more than that to turn the stomach of a starving man. The peasant drove his wagon slowly in order not to spill any of the foul liquid. That made it easy for us to fill our mess tins as he passed, but left us unprotected from his whip. The lash marked us all, and one *Häftling* even lost an eye from a well-aimed blow. Inevitably one of the drivers complained and Emile was demoted, and we were assigned to a different work detail. Probably for the best, I thought. A few more rancid bowls from the pig pot and we would all have dropped dead from diarrhea or hepatitis.

♦ ♦ ♦

Many times while I dug those ditches, standing ankle-deep in cold mud, I would think about my brief stint in the Resistance. I would chide myself for never seeing action in a raid and for having landed in Auschwitz because of lousy luck and not for my efforts in the Maquis.

My involvement in the underground started in 1941, when I was fifteen years old. At that time, Southern France was under the rule of the Vichy government, a puppet regime of the Germans.

Nazi troops occupied only the northern half of France. Menard, my neighborhood's black marketeer, was the one who steered me to the Maquis. He had made a king's ransom after the Nazi's blitzkrieg by collecting the abandoned cars of those who fled and selling them for parts. I would always give him an earful of my anti-fascist rants when he came over to have a coffee with my father. After seeing the split lip and black eye a school bully gave me for cheering the sinking of the Nazi battleship *Bismarck*, Menard pulled me aside. He told me to meet an elderly gentleman who was interested in talking to me at a bench on the Promenade des Anglais, which ran along the Mediterranean coast.

Adrenaline pumped through my heart when I spotted an old man in a well-tailored suit and fedora feeding the gulls. It wasn't the suit, the hat, or the bird feeding that identified my contact, but his *gueule cassée*, a facial disfigurement that was a souvenir from the WW I Battle of Verdun.

"Bonjour, mon capitaine."

"Drop the title, it attracts attention. Call me Mr. Meffre," he said as we shook hands.

I sat down next to him as he resumed feeding the gulls. "We need a messenger with strong legs and a bicycle."

"I have both." I was working after school at a bicycle shop a few blocks from my house.

"When I need you, we will meet here. You'll meet nobody else. Understand?"

"Yes."

"I'll tell you where to hide or deliver the messages. Don't bother trying to decipher these messages. You won't be able to, and the less you know the better off you will be. Do not tell a soul, not even your family, what you're doing. The Germans and Italians are easy to fool, son; it's our traitors and collaborators you have to worry about." Mr. Meffre got up and shook my hand. "If we win this war you might get a medal, but if we lose they will hunt you down as a saboteur and a traitor."

On my first few trips I tied my fishing tackle to the bike and hid the messages in a double-bottomed can of worms. Then I realized the merits of my tire pump. When I had a girlfriend with strong legs, I would borrow a tandem bike from the shop. We would pedal off on an outing, a movie, or a picnic that included wine and fooling around, and I would deliver a message. I had a good idea that most of these messages pertained to the organizing of different cells around southern France.

In 1943, when Nazi troops occupied all of France, Meffre called a meeting. "Are you circumcised?" he asked me, as he tossed stale bread to impatient gulls. He was happy to hear I wasn't. In the Germans' hunt for Jews, they were forcing males to drop their pants at checkpoints and roadblocks outside Nice.

Now when I pedaled I wondered if the message I was carrying was the arrival time of a military convoy to be sabotaged or the orders to assassinate some Nazi official or collaborator. Every time I met with Mr. Meffre I hoped it would be the moment he would tell me where to pick up a weapon. If I had had the right gun I could have cut down a hell of a lot of *boches*. My bedroom balcony overlooked a road along a cliff, and every day platoons of German soldiers marched along there fully exposed, a perfect target for a sniper or someone armed with a machine gun. I reported this to Meffre.

"I'm glad to see that you're this observant, but don't underestimate them. They're baiting us. At another location outside town they've hidden a machine gun nest aimed at a spot where we could easily ambush a patrol. Shooting a couple soldiers would only give them an excuse to burn down the whole city, like they did in Czechoslovakia."

"Are we cowards? What good are we doing?" I asked.

"Our orders are to lay low until an Allied landing on our coast."

I continued to dutifully deliver my messages and patiently waited for the Allies so Mr. Meffre could give me a more vital mission. Shithouse luck saw to it that I never got the chance.

◆ ◆ ◆

I was at the bottom of a nearly completed trench on the plant's perimeter, shoveling dirt onto a wooden platform, when I noticed a big German Shepherd sniffing the leather toecaps of my canvas boots. Since the *boches* didn't waste anything, I wondered if the dog was smelling the skin of his parents. He squatted in front of me and blessed the trench with a long, steaming turd. With strong kicks of his hind legs, the shepherd began to cover it, but quit when he heard the shrill whistle of his master. I picked the shit up with my shovel and deposited it next to a French *Häftling* on the platform.

"*Merci pour le cadeau*" (Thank you for the present), he muttered.

My laughter was cut short when I spotted a group of SS officers passing by, pointing at buildings and jotting down notes. Standing at the rim of the trench, our jittery *Kapo* and *Vorarbeiter* pushed us harder. As we chopped away at the earth, we nervously watched the strutting, high-ranking Nazis. Their presence was highly unusual, and from a *Häftling*'s perspective, any deviance from the daily routine was a bad omen. These *boches* though seemed preoccupied with something more pressing than the labor of a filthy bunch of *Untermenschen (subhumans)*.

The following morning I found myself behind Joseph, the oldest member of our *Kommando*, as we goose-stepped through the camp's gate. He was a frail, middle-aged Dutch Jew who wasn't very bright. Many *Häftlinge* addressed one another by their first three numbers, which indicated one's transport. Joseph's first three numbers were 175, and that made him the butt of many jokes in our *Kommando*.

"*Bist du ein Hundertfünfundsiebziger?*" (Are you a 175?) they would teasingly ask him.

"*Ja, ich bin ein Hundertfünfundsiebziger,*" he would answer with a grin that always caused fits of laughter. Joseph never caught on to the joke. One hundred seventy-five was the number of the paragraph in the Nazi penal code that outlawed homosexuality, and as far as I could tell, Joseph was a simpleton but he wasn't a "pinkie."

This particular morning Joseph had diarrhea, and the brownish yellow liquid was streaming down his pant legs as we marched. I was splashed and sprayed with every step, as were the men goose-stepping in front of him. As a matter of fact, they were getting it worse. Humiliated, poor Joseph weeped, wiping his tears and nose with his sleeve. When we arrived at our work site, the *Kapo* ordered Joseph to wash his pants at a faucet at one of the factory buildings across the road. Sniveling and bent over from cramps, "175" did as he was told.

The *Vorarbeiter* had us digging double-time on a new section of trench as the *Kapo* paced anxiously, continually looking down the road as if he were expecting an arrival. I noticed that there were German soldiers with binoculars positioned on the roofs of the factory buildings. This had to have something to do with the officers who were surveying the area the day before.

Joseph returned bare ass, his wet pants in his hands. Incensed, the *Kapo* ordered him to put his pants back on and dig in an area of the trench away from the rest of us. When the *Kapo* saw a shivering Joseph leaning on his shovel, he pointed at him and barked at the *Vorarbeiter*. "Helmut, let's make a good impression!"

The *Vorarbeiter* jumped into the trench and snatched the shovel from Joseph's hands. Crying, Joseph sank to his knees. He didn't see the *Vorarbeiter* raise the shovel, and he didn't even moan as he slumped to the ground with his head caved in. None of us stopped digging. None of us even hesitated. We all knew it was coming. The *Kapo* screamed at us to hide the *Drecksack* (dirt bag), and a quick thinking *Häftling* covered Joseph's body with an overturned wheelbarrow.

A few minutes later the *Kapo* and the *Vorarbeiter* took off their caps and stood at attention as a black Mercedes convertible led by two motorcycles slowly passed by. I recognized Reichsführer Himmler*, the boss of the SS, sitting in the backseat. Flanked by two of the plant's engineers, he had come to inspect the fruits of his slaves' labor. That was what all the fuss had been about. That was why 175's body was under a wheelbarrow.

---

* There is no official record of Reichsführer Heinrich Himmler visiting the I.G. Farben plant or Auschwitz in the spring of 1944; it is possible this was one of his doubles.

CHAPTER 13

Every morning, once the *Kommandos* were counted and through the gate, the goose-stepping stopped and we became our true selves—a haggard, shuffling horde of slaves. A half-mile later, the *Kapos* would halt us at the Buna gate, where we would wait for the arrival of the British POWs. For some unknown reason, they and their Wehrmacht (German Army) guards had to enter the plant first. Always whistling some popular tune, these well-dressed and well-fed POWs marched by us like strutting roosters. I would watch them go by with a twinge of envy and resentment, thinking that they wouldn't be whistling such a happy tune if they were in my ill-fitting wooden shoes.

These strong fellows didn't seem to mind working, mainly delivering supplies to the multitude of buildings that made up the plant. Pushing flatbed pushcarts, they would buzz back and forth, laughing and joking among themselves. It was probably a welcome relief from the idle monotony of their Stalag. They definitely enjoyed the opportunity for some contact with the civilians—the female civilians, to be precise. The POWs received chocolate in their Red Cross packages, and some of them bartered the sweets for "romance" with the local Polish girls working in the plant. With thousands of niches and dark corners, and not enough guards to cover the twenty square miles of plant grounds, it was easy for a hungry couple to duck away for a quickie. Hell, I would be whistling in the morning if I could soak my biscuit once in a while, but I would bust a lung singing if I could get my hands on one of those chocolate bars.

Häftlinge weren't allowed to mingle with the POWs, but there were always opportunities to have a quick, furtive conversation. In the winter that usually happened around a barrel with a fire blazing inside, where we warmed ourselves during lunch breaks. From time to time POWs would stop to thaw out, and they would always discreetly pass out a few cigarettes to us "stripees." With the coming of spring, the pace of everyone's toiling outdoors slowed, and that brought more opportunities to chat with our allies.

In halting English I asked a blond, well-tanned sergeant pushing a cart of steel pipes, "What new, mate?" Having overheard fragments of their conversations, I thought "mate" was a common first name for Aussies and "bloke" was a first name for most of the British POWs.

The sergeant gave me a smile and said, "We've landed in Normandy, and Jerry is running back to the 'fatherland.' We'll all be going home soon." No wonder they marched as if they were in front of Buckingham Palace.

"Take it easy," the Aussie said, winking as he left. With his drawl, "easy" sounded like "dizzy," so I thought he expected me to be dizzy with delight about the landing.

A few days later we were digging a deep trench between two warehouses. The sergeant sauntered by with a few of his "mates."

"Is this a mass grave?" the sergeant joked.

I didn't find it funny because it could easily have become one.

"Is war over?" I shot back.

He told me a few battles had stalled the whole campaign, emphasizing "battles" with a swear word that with his accent I took to mean as "foggy," which explained to me why they were held up. It sure would be difficult to shoot those Nazis in that thick Normandy fog.

The news of the Allies' landing quickly filtered through the camp, reviving our hopes and strength. The talk in the *Blocks* was that the end of the war was only a few weeks away. But D-Day also brought the war closer to us. Hardly a day passed without an air raid alert. When the sirens sounded, the civilian workers and guards scrambled into their concrete bunkers, where *Häftlinge* weren't welcomed. We had to crawl into one of the pipeline trenches or roam blindly in the artificial fog that the Nazis pumped out to obscure the plant. In June and July they were all false alarms, the Allied bombers thankfully going after other targets in Poland.

The summer of 1944 was a brutal one, and it seemed that the SS had a "no shade" policy for *Häftlinge*. We were all baked crimson digging those trenches under the sun's unblinking eye. I barely perspired because my body didn't have enough water and oil. After toiling for twelve hours, my skin would be scorched and blistered. Sunstroke and heat exhaustion now took the place of frostbite and influenza. Thirst now superseded hunger, but the heat made the water undrinkable. Cases of typhoid fever ravaged our ranks. I had never seen new arrivals—who were now mainly Hungarian Jews—convert so quickly to *Muselmänner*.

"Follow me. Today is your lucky day," my *Kapo* informed me one morning as we entered Buna.

Apprehensive, I trotted after him toward a gray building. When a green triangle was being nice, there was reason to be suspicious. We entered a well-lit, cavernous machine shop where the hissing of lathes, the clattering of mills, the whistling of grinders, and the pounding of shapers were skull-rattling. A *Häftling* was operating every noisy tool. A sergeant of the Wehrmacht in his late twenties greeted us. The cuff of his empty right shirtsleeve was pinned to his shoulder.

"Herr Kies, here is your man. I hope that he'll work out for you. I'll pick him up at the end of our shift."

Herr Kies directed me to a workbench. "This will be your station. Take good care of the tools and don't lose any. We have an inventory."

All I could think was, Why me? How did I land this job? I wasn't a machinist and I would never think of masquerading as one.

"Look around for a while and get familiar with the shop. Can you read a blueprint?"

"Yes, sure."

Herr Kies nodded, then climbed the steps to a glass-walled loft.

What I had told him was more truth than bluff. I had become pretty comfortable with the basic language of blueprints. One of our neighbors in Nice was an architect who had designed my parents' house and four others on the cul-de-sac. While we both waited for plates of his wife's homemade ravioli, I would look over his shoulder as he worked and ask questions when he put his pencil down. I also studied the blueprints of the Tour de France bikes built in the bicycle shop where I worked. By no means was I an expert, but I was confident that they wouldn't boot me back outdoors, as they had at the electrical shop.

Herr Kies returned and spread a large blueprint on my bench. "What is this?"

I looked at the blueprint's measurements. I had seen something similar in a Nice plumbing store. "Yikes, this is colossal."

"But what is it?"

"Oh, it's a hydraulic gate valve. I was just surprised by the huge specifications."

"Nothing is small in this plant."

Herr Kies introduced me to the machinists and tool and die makers. Like every *Kommando*, they were a multinational group of yellow, red, black, and green triangles, every one of them an experienced craftsman.

"Why me?" I finally asked.

"Because I was told you speak four languages, and I need someone to translate to this bunch. I've had enough misunderstandings and mistakes."

My *Kapo* was right, it was my lucky day. My duty of translating Herr Kies's German directives into French, English, Spanish, and Italian was a wonderful reprieve from what I had endured the last six months. I felt like a human being again. Herr Kies was a good boss, treating us all with an even hand. Once in a while he would even sneak part of his lunch into my tool drawer. He had lost his arm in the battle of Stalingrad, but he wasn't bitter about it. He considered himself fortunate because his wound had brought him home before his battalion was decimated.

The shop was responsible for assembling valves and fittings for pipes, and for repairing equipment for other shops, but its main duty was to line and glue plastic sleeves into five-meter-long pipes. With Germany cut off from the supply of many raw materials, the pipes used in the Buna plant were made of rolled steel or cast iron. Because they lacked any stainless alloys, it was our job to line the insides of the pipes with plastic to protect them from the corrosive fluids that would flow through. We would coat the insides with an adhesive, using a sponge attached to the end of a long wooden rod, then insert a long sleeve of soft plastic, pressing it against the pipes with a spreader. We would stretch the plastic over the face of the pipes' flanges, which another shop had welded on. If the flanges were warped from the welding, we would resurface them on a lathe. Pipes would then be placed in the shop's kiln to fuse the plastic. It took a half-hour to bake a dozen pipes. Once cooled, we would use drills to clear the plastic out of the flanges' four assembly holes. With the plastic covering the flanges there was no need for a gasket when the pipes were bolted together. Many times, once the trenches were dug, we would be the ones to assemble and bury the pipes.

Near my workbench I found a page from a magazine that must have been used as packing material. I figured I could use it as cigarette paper until I saw that it was from a French magazine. There was an ad, a picture of two people, and the last half of an article. I put it under my shirt, and back in my *Block* that night I hid it under my pillow. I must have read that page more than a dozen times that week before it disappeared. It was the first thing I had read in six months. In Drancy, I was able to at least read the newspapers the *gendarmes* had left. Hell, there I had a semblance of a social life. At night we played cards, cracked jokes, listened to someone blowing Glenn Miller's "Don't Sit Under the Apple Tree" on the harmonica, or a few voices singing the Yiddish tune "*Bei Mir Bist Du Schön*" that the Andrews Sisters made popular. It all helped to keep my mind off the fact that I was a prisoner. The only things that kept me from dwelling on my plight in Monowitz were physical exhaustion and unbearable hunger.

One evening, a group of us watched through a window in our *Block* as the orange halo of an immense fire bloomed in the direction of the main camp. Its unusual intensity puzzled us. This was no ordinary blaze. We speculated that a methanol pipeline or tank had ignited. Whatever it was, it burned through the night. At the plant the next morning, I spotted an English POW who had been friendly with me in the past. I asked him if one of their *Blocks* had burned down.

"Oh, no. It was on the other side of our camp. One of our guards told me that the SS had wiped out forty-four thousand Gypsies in one night. The Jerry said they were bragging how efficiently they had done it."

"Forty-four thousand? Are you sure it wasn't forty-four hundred?" I asked in my shaky English.

"No, you got it right, chap."

We parted without another word.

Forty-four thousand? I knew of the existence of the brown triangle Gypsies, but I had never crossed paths with a single one.

That day I was acutely aware of every SS guard I passed at the plant. They had been so secretive about their slaughters for so long, and now they were brazenly bragging. Was mass murder that easy? I guess if you can kill one in cold blood, what's another four or a thousand or forty thousand?

I had become numb to their savagery, and I hated them for doing that to me. I knew I would remember the girl from the Puff, maybe Mario and Pressburger, but my other fellow *Muselmänner* were just faceless cattle in the slaughterhouse.

Rumors circulated for a week about what had happened that night. One was that the Gypsies had been exterminated to make room for skilled *Häftlinge* from the camps near the Eastern Front. True or not, it was sobering reminder that there was nothing preventing the SS from processing all of us the same way once they had no use for us. Another was that the crematoriums had broken down that night, and after the Gypsies had been gassed their bodies were torched in open pits along with many arriving Jews.*

The "prominent" *Häftlinge* arriving from the abandoned Eastern Front camps found themselves stripped of their status and privileges. For some this was as good as being sent to the gas chambers. One morning before roll call I noticed fifteen "pajamas" standing in a circle, yelling obscenities. In the center was a bloodied *Häftling* screaming for help. He was being pushed and punched from all sides. Grinning and laughing, the guards watched from the fence. I was sure they were taking bets. The man finally collapsed to the ground, and the infuriated "pajamas" kicked him until he was just a bloody mess of broken bones. He was dead or in a coma. Either way, the Transportation *Kommando* would make sure he was on the back of their truck. Out of curiosity, I asked a yellow triangle standing at the circle's perimeter why they had done him in. He told me the man had been a Jewish policeman in one of the ghettos.

"He was the worst of the bunch. A son of a bitch."

Well, if that many guys have decided that he had it coming, he must have deserved it, I thought as I lined up in my *Kommando*.

---

* On August 2, 1944, 2,897 Roma (Gypsy) men, women, and children were taken from their camp in Birkenau and gassed. Their bodies were incinerated in pits because the crematoriums weren't functioning at the time.

CHAPTER 14

After so many false alarms, our first Allied bombardment finally came on an idle August Sunday when we stayed in the camp. I thought that the distant explosions in the plant were butane tanks erupting. Forty English POWs were killed in that raid and a woman's camp was laid in ruins. An untold number of female *Häftlinge* had perished, and I couldn't stop wondering if Stella was among them.

I was cleaning out a new methanol tank that we had just buried and connected to our pipes when the air raid sirens started shrieking once again. As I climbed out of the tank, an Aussie came running over, dragging a pretty young woman dressed in factory coveralls.

"Speak English?"

"Enough."

He handed me a half pack of cigarettes. "Mate, have some fags and keep an eye open. I need some privacy."

The girl nervously fidgeted with her blond locks as she scanned the clouds for any indication of American bombers. Grayish puffs of exploding anti-aircraft shells were dotting the sky.

"My name is Pierre," I told the Aussie.

"A hell of a time for introductions, mate," he said as he herded the girl into the tank.

I sat down to enjoy one of the "fags" when I realized I needed matches. From the sounds inside the tank, it would have been rude to ask the POW for a light. Bombs began to explode in the distance as I calculated how many cigarettes I could smoke and still have enough for an extra ladle of soup. It wasn't that I was blasé about the bombing raid, it just wasn't the first time I was on the receiving end of an aerial attack.

My baptism under fire was on a sunny day in June 1940. When the German army occupied Paris and the senile Marshal Philippe Pétain was ready to sign an armistice, Mussolini, the bold vulture of Rome, wanted to share in the spoils. Proclaiming *"Niza nostra"* (Nice is ours), he declared war. The French and Italian armies watched one another from their mountaintop fortresses, pondering who would fire the first shot while I went fishing for eels to supplement my family's meager rations.

I pedaled my bike to the Brague River, which is on the way to Cannes, armed with a darning needle, a nine-foot-long bamboo pole, nightcrawlers, and an umbrella. With the darning needle I strung the bait on three-feet of fishing line, then wrapped it into a ball with another three-feet of thread. When the eels went for the juicy worms they would snag their crooked teeth on the thread. They were hungry that day, and my upturned umbrella was almost filled with the slithering, slimy fish when I noticed an Italian Caproni bomber leisurely circling above me. A French Morane fighter burst out of the clouds with machine guns blazing. I watched with awe and fascination until the fighter's stray bullets whizzed by me, churning up the water. I dropped my pole and hugged a tree, which was raked by rounds. When the planes disappeared behind a hill, I went to retrieve my pole, only to find it shattered. Just as well, I figured, since I was shaking too badly to hold it anyhow.

So, when I saw a squadron of B-17s in a V-formation closing in on the plant from the northwest, I knew hugging a tree wouldn't do me any good. With the explosion of bombs closing in on me, I slid down the tank's ladder. The Aussie was in full action and took no notice of me, but the woman, with her coveralls at her knees, was horrified and tried to hide her face. The tank began to quake from the bombs' shock waves.

"Baby, don't worry, it's only friendly fire. I've got you covered. I'm on top," he joked.

The girl's unease seemed evenly divided between my intrusion and the nearness of the bombs. How could he keep his erection through all this? I asked myself. I like tearing off a piece more than most, at least that was what my eighteen-year-old mind thought, but there was no way I could stand at attention during such a deadly hail. The Aussie had to have been a veteran of the siege of Torbruk. While in school, I had read about the vicious, month-long beating Rommel gave the British in Libya. Hell, he didn't even stop when a near miss shoveled mud through the tank's hatch. No bomb was going to prevent him from getting his candy bar's worth.

As soon as the raid was over, I gave them back their privacy and went looking for something on fire so I could enjoy one of my cigarettes. Unfortunately, the sight of the rubble of Herr Kies's workshop ruined the taste of that tobacco. It was back to digging trenches under the sun.

♦ ♦ ♦

They assigned me to a *Kommando* working close to the cement kiln where Hubert had worked before his stint in the HKB. The kiln had a towering smokestack the likes of which I had never seen before, easily over 300 feet high. All winter most of the smokestack had been hidden by fog. Now it glistened and shone red. It was constructed of concrete castings and the seams of the individual blocks made it look like a patchwork quilt.

"Do you see the second segment from the top?" a Polish yellow triangle asked as we were shoveling dirt out of a trench.

I nodded yes. The reek of kerosene told me that the Pole was spending his nights in the *Krätzeblock*.

"There's a man's body inside it. While we were pouring the cement, he slipped and fell into the mold. He pleaded for us to lower a nearby ladder, but the SS wouldn't let us. Fresh cement was beginning to pile up. I'll never forget his screams and terrified face as that mold filled."

A ribbon of blue carbide fumes weaved from the top of the monstrous smokestack and was swept away by the morning breeze. The red and orange basket that hung from the smokestack was at its lowest position. When the basket was raised to the top of the smokestack, it signaled that Allied bombers had crossed into German territory. Because we were working in such close proximity, the squeaking of the basket's pulleys was our initial warning. The first time I heard it, I thought it was a flock of birds gathering on the smokestack. The blast of the air raid sirens was our last warning, and by that time the bombers would be almost overhead.

A few *Häftlinge* had left to fetch our barrels of soup when I heard the birdcalls. The artificial fog began to blanket the trench, stinging our eyes and burning our lungs. We heard shrill sirens in the distance, then those in the factory began to wail. We watched civilian workers race to their air raid shelters or cling to fleeing trucks. None of us was in a rush. For a *Häftling*, an air raid was a game of roulette. Pick an open space away from the plant buildings or lie down in the hole you were digging and wait and see if the bombs fall on top of you. So I gathered a few dandelions as the fog thickened.

"What are you doing, picking flowers for your funeral?" someone laughed.

"No one else will."

The truth was that I was munching my bouquet in hopes the vitamins in the weeds would strengthen my bleeding gums. I plopped down with the others in the dirt between the kiln and some nearby warehouses. *Häftlinge* working in the factory buildings joined us. If it weren't for those lying on their stomachs with their arms over their heads, and those who had placed discarded planks on top of themselves, it would have looked like we were waiting for an afternoon concert in the park. Someone near me mumbled a drawn-out prayer in Yiddish. We lay there in the Nazi fog for a half-hour. Some of the men even dosed off. There weren't many chances for a slave to enjoy a siesta.

A squadron of fighter planes buzzed by—Messerschmitts, from the sound of their motors—then the sudden cacophony of an intense air battle. A violent opera of screaming planes, barking machine guns, and thundering anti-aircraft batteries played behind the curtain of fog. All at once everything became quiet. The silence was oddly oppressive. The planes were gone. Why hadn't they bombed the plant? They had been directly overhead. Did they have some other objective?

My ears began to buzz strangely. I sat up and saw a man looking toward the sky as he placed an empty cement bag over his head. Shit, how could I have forgotten about the splinters of anti-aircraft shells and the planes' errant machine gun bullets? Someone cried out and crumpled to the ground, holding his head in his hands. The lethal shower fell thick and fast. Not far away was a section of cement sewer pipe. With my mess tin as a helmet, I sprinted and dove inside. Fragments peppered the pipe. Outside, *Häftlinge* were running, screaming, and dropping. The fog machines were depleted and the wind had swept away any remnants of the plant's cover. I peeked out. The sky was sprinkled with little silvery stars, a second wave of Allied bombers out of reach of the anti-aircraft cannons.

All at once the earth trembled and heaved, and the air filled with a terrible roar. My shelter began to roll and skip. I felt myself lifted into the air and savagely dashed to the ground. In a panic, I pressed my arms against the pipe to prevent myself from slipping out. I caught glimpses of buildings erupting in flames. The air was choked with dust and smoke. A bomb exploded next to me and gravel cut into my face as the pipe spun like a top, then rolled into the bomb's crater. My body twitched from the concussion of the blast. My hands, arms, and face were covered with blood, but I felt no pain. Because everything sounded muted, I thought the crater was incredibly deep. When the tinkle of anti-aircraft shrapnel stopped, I dragged myself out of the pipe and discovered that the crater wasn't that deep at all—thirteen feet at the most. Everything sounded muted because the blast had ruptured my eardrums.

Crawling out of the crater, I found myself in a new world. A firestorm was sweeping through a complex of warehouses. Thick clouds of black smoke rose from the butane reservoirs. Steam from the boilers hissed from broken pipes. Train tracks were flayed from their ties, and the remains of boxcars were scattered along them. The sight of all this destruction filled me with joy. I knew that soon much of Germany would look like this.

You would have thought that everyone lounging in grass around me perished during such devastation, but only two *Häftlinge* didn't get back up. It was the hardships in the days that followed that dropped us like flies. The camp's kitchen ran on steam produced by the factory, and with the pipes broken we received neither soup nor coffee for three days. No bread, either, since the trains couldn't run. Seventy-two hours without anything to eat. We were starving, but nevertheless they made us work, clearing away the rubble. Every night we carried back scores of dead *Muselmänner*, and each morning the pyramids for Birkenau grew higher. The camp's band should have been playing Chopin's "Funeral March" as we went out the gate. I was sure that the Allied raids were helping to bring a quicker end to the war, but with all the added misery, I couldn't help but wonder how many of us would be left to see it.

◆ ◆ ◆

I stabbed the earth with my spade, being careful of the heels of the *Häftling* in front of me. Tossed the dirt, took a step, and stabbed where he had just dug. The man behind me did the same just as the man behind him did and the man behind him and the man behind him. I felt like an oarsman on a Roman galley. Ten of us in single file moving in unison; one full shovel, one step forward. We moved very smoothly, digging a narrow, shallow ditch for a single pipe.

We were digging not far from our entrance into the plant. I wasn't sure but it seemed like our ditch was going to be part of a pipeline running to either our camp or the British P.O.W. camp.

The rest of the *Kommando*, ninety men and our *Kapo*, were excavating for a larger project. A red triangle *Vorarbeiter* followed us with half-hearted demands to put our backs into it. If his voice rose, it wasn't because we weren't working hard enough, but because there was an SS guard in earshot. When one of us had the urge for number one or number two the *Vorarbeiter* grabbed the shovel and joined our chorus line. We had no *Scheisshaus*, just a *Scheiss* trench, a six foot pit with a wooden plank laid across it that you could hang your ass over.

The *Vorarbeiter* stepped in for the man in front of me. Lunch would be coming soon, I thought. A smart *Häftling* made sure to empty his bowels before the Buna soup arrived, never after. You wanted to give you body enough time to absorb everything it could from the gruel before saying *adieu*. That's if your bowels were stout enough to have a say in the matter.

A shriek and a loud splash jammed a cog in our motion. The *Vorarbeiter* stopped and looked over his shoulder. So did I. So did everyone in the work party. The *Häftling* who should have been sitting over the shit trench wasn't there and neither was the plank. The *Vorarbeiter* went over and we all followed. The flimsy board had broken at a knothole. Our comrade was treading in the ooze. I didn't remember the stench being so offensive when my ass hung over the plank. His thrashing had churned the brown pond too well.

"Idiots! Don't stand there! Get him out of there!" the *Voribieter* ordered.

A couple of recent *Häftlinge* lowered their shovels but the shit covered figure couldn't get a good grip. No matter how much the *Voribieter* screamed and threatened, none of us were going to reach our arm down to help pull him up. He tried to claw his way up the side of the pit, but it was just too slimy. Shovels were lowered again.

"Back to work, you dirtbags. The creep is not worth cleaning."

We were so engrossed and repulsed by our comrade's predicament that none of us had noticed the SS guard who had walked up. He stared at us with pistol in hand. We stepped back as one.

"You heard him!" the *Vorarbeiter* yelled. "Back to work."

POP! One shot. We moved, fast. Some of the newcomers were flabbergasted. Old timers like myself weren't fazed. He could have just as well shot into the air instead of the trench. Maybe the *Boche* thought he was doing us a favor. Maybe he hadn't fired his pistol in a few days. Whatever his reason, he had just made our day shittier. Alive or dead, dripping in human waste or not, that man had to come back to camp with us to be counted.

When the *Vorarbeiter* was confident the SS brute wouldn't be strolling back, he ordered two of the new arrivals to get pickaxes and retrieve the body. It was not an easy task. We must have dug for thirty minutes before the two men reported that they had snagged him. The *Vorarbeiter* promised *Nachschlag*, an extra ladle of Buna soup, to whoever cleaned up the mess. My workmates were ready to throw up their meager breakfasts. I raised my arm. After my coronation as *Roi du Chateau* in Drancy no sight or smell fazed me.

There was no water faucet with a hose, but luckily for me there was an abundance of steam valves all over the plant. With some doing, I got the body into a wheelbarrow and pushed it over to a valve, which was to a steam pipe that provided heat to our camp. I draped the body over the wheelbarrow's handles, which were resting on the pipe. I turned the body as if roasting a side of beef. As I cleaned him, the steam warmed up the shit and the stench almost overwhelmed a *Scheissmeister* like me.

Trying to clean him with his pajamas on wasn't working, so I stripped them off. He was a yellow triangle. I was sure he was one of the recently arrived Hungarians. He was still in good shape for a *Häftling*.

The *Vorarbeiter*, a red triangle Prussian, looked over my shoulder.

"Throw his pajamas back into the pit," he said in German, then grinned. "Although, it would be fun to dump it at the doorstep of the SS barracks."

I chuckled in agreement. "What a waste. He was worth three *Muselmänner*."

"And now I've got to write an accident report." the *Voribeiter* said as he left.

By the time I shoved the body into two cement bags it was bleached and well done.

When the *Kommando* arrived at the camp's gate that evening, the *Kapo* announced to the guards, "Ninety-nine and one dead." The man's body was on a warped plank shouldered by four *Häftlinge*. I wasn't one of them. I had gotten my extra ladle of soup.

As luck would have it, on a late summer Sunday I was again assigned to *Kommando* 15. Because of my screw-up that rainy Easter, I tried to wiggle my way out of it, but my *Blockästester* wasn't passing out favors that day. It was four months ago, a near lifetime in Auschwitz, I consoled myself. *Kommando* 15's *Kapo* and *Vorarbeiter* could easily have been demoted or died. Lining up in the Appelplatz, I saw that was not the case. I hoped that they wouldn't remember me. My ribs couldn't withstand another round of their soccer kicks.

Again, a pathetic parade marched to waiting freight cars in the plant. We passed the glass warehouse, which was now nothing more than a heap of splinters and shattered glass. I felt a hand on my shoulder, and I nearly jumped out of my skin.

"*Bonjour*, Pierre," whispered a familiar voice.

Hubert was grinning from ear to ear and looking fit without the jaundice. I could have hugged him.

"I've been looking for you."

"And I've been looking for you."

"Never at the same spot at the same time, I guess," Hubert laughed.

Mon ami told me his *Block* and *Kommando* number and how his survival had been going. "I've got a janitor job in one of the buildings that's still standing."

"You're lucky. Mine went poof."

We lined up for a count next to the train cars. After giving his instructions to the *Vorarbeiter*, the *Kapo* retreated to the crudely assembled shack that was his office. The *Vorarbeiter* moved along the line, writing down our identification numbers. He stepped up to me. Gazing at my feet, I rattled off my numbers. He began to write them down, then suddenly stopped. I looked up to find him staring at me, nonplussed. His reaction puzzled me, but I kept a blank face. He quickly regained his composure and continued down the line. What the hell was going on? He looked scared, as if he saw me as a threat. Did he believe I had been punished for my Easter nap and was looking for vengeance? I sure wasn't a physical threat to him. He was well fed. When he divided the *Kommando* into work gangs and left me out, I became concerned. Had he been punished for allowing me to wander into the warehouse and was now planning to even the score?

As Hubert and the others started working, the *Vorarbeiter* grabbed me by my jacket. "The number on this jacket isn't yours!" His face was flushed red as he shook me, and his breath was pungent with garlic.

"And who do you suppose it belongs to?"

His behavior frightened me, but strangely I felt I had the upper hand.

"Roll up your sleeve."

"Why?"

"Do what I say, *Drecksack!*"

I pulled my sleeve up. I remembered that he had copied my number from my arm. What was the big deal?

"You have a nine on your coat and a three on your arm."

"I beg your pardon, but I have a nine on my arm."

He grabbed my forearm and examined it closely.

"Goddamn! What cretin tattooed you?"

"He didn't bother to sign his masterpiece," I chuckled nervously.

"You dare laugh?" He shook me. "Don't you know that someone was hung in your place?"

I was staggered.

"What do you mean?"

"Because a three was written in the report. A three instead of a nine."

"Are you sure?"

I had assumed that either he or the *Kapo* had failed to turn in a report or that it had been lost. "Go to the latrine and be quick about it!" he ordered.

"Why?"

"Move before I bash in your skull!" He hissed, raining blows on my back. "If the *Kapo* sees you, we'll both dangle from a rope."

The latrine was deserted, but I took down my pants in case of an inspection. With my cap, I kept a swarm of big blue flies at bay. The stink was nauseating, but I barely noticed. The *Vorarbeiter*'s words kept ringing in my ears: "Someone died in your place." It was my neck that was supposed to be stretched. I was the one who should have been fertilizing the cabbages, but I was alive, and all because of one wrong number. A three instead of a nine. What shithouse luck.

I could imagine how he must have screamed his innocence and the sinister smirks and savage beatings he received in return. Had he been a young man, middle-aged, a father, a good man, a fair man? I squeezed my eyes shut. My temples pounded. No, I couldn't allow myself to ponder who he was! This wasn't the place to burden one's self with such questions. Suddenly I saw Jonny. I hadn't thought about him for a long, long time. I fought back tears. Was I cursed? Did my life depend on the blood of others?

I looked up to find the *Vorarbeiter* walking slowly toward me. What now? Was he going to drown me in this stinkhole? He sat next to me without dropping his pants.

"Weren't you there for the execution? A man hung for trying to escape on Easter Sunday? They rushed it because of the lousy weather."

"I was in the HKB."

"I missed the whole thing, too. Never got a good look at the man's face." He turned to me with a smile. "I must've had a really silly look on my face when I saw you. Thought I was staring at a ghost."

"I wish I could disappear like a ghost."

"Why did you try to escape?"

"I didn't."

I recited the answer I had prepared that miserable Sunday. "I didn't try to escape. I was being nosey, and when I looked into the warehouse, the wind slammed the door and I was locked in."

"To be honest, you were so muddy I'm not sure now what I wrote and God knows what that illiterate *Kapo* put in his report. It's no wonder Hans screws up all the time; he's been in jail almost all his life."

"How do you know?" I asked.

"Like most communists I was arrested when Hitler came to power. I met Hans in prison."

"Why is he such a prick?"

"Because he's a thief and murderer. How did you come to speak such fluent German?"

I couldn't believe that I was having a social hour with this man.

"I spent a few vacations in Berlin."

This really interested him. "Which area?"

"Charlottenburg at the Litzensee."

"Your father must be a rich bastard."

"Some of his friends are."

"I'm from Wedding."

The Wedding district of Berlin was a working-poor ghetto and a hot bed of communism. There had been years of vicious street-fighting and gun battles between the communists and the brown shirts of the fledgling Nazi Party.

"How many languages do you speak?" he asked.

"Four, and I understand a few more."

"You're lucky. I can barely speak mine." He stood up. "Get to work, and stay away from Hans or we'll both be swinging."

I pulled up my pants and followed the *Vorarbeiter*. He eyed me.

"Kid, nothing is going to unhang that poor bastard now. Understand?"

I nodded. I understood. In the life I had known before I might have confessed and restored that poor man's name, but in this world that would have served no purpose.

CHAPTER 15

Reestablishing contact with Hubert came when life in Monowitz was threatening to bury me. I had been there for nine months and there was nothing I looked forward to anymore. When I was digging a trench not a thought entered my mind. I was an automaton. I had succumbed to the Nazis' desired condition of a slave, a brain-dead machine working without question, detached from all needs except for those that would raise me from bed and send me goose-stepping out the gate. I was aware what was happening to me and didn't like it; there was nothing I could do about it.

I was a voyeur in my own nightmare. The only thing reminding me that I was still human was Hubert—his wave as we lined up in the morning, his nod as he shuffled back into his *Block* at night, his occasional smile. It's amazing how the smallest gestures of camaraderie can resuscitate a depleted soul. There would be times—few and far between—after evening rations that we would meet behind the *Blocks* to ensure that the other wasn't ready for a ride to Birkenau. We would share rumors on the Allied push, discuss SS activity in the camps, and bitch about what scumbags our *Kapos* were. We'd always finish with speculations on the welfare and whereabouts of friends and inflated tales of past female conquests. Those nights I would have the most wonderful sleep.

There were a handful of Orthodox Jews in my *Block*. Since their beards and *payos* (side curls) were long gone, the only reason I knew they were Orthodox was that they would sneak away to pray each morning and nearly every evening during the chaotic distribution of rations. Out of sight of the *Stubendienst*, they would sway back and forth facing the eastern corner of the *Block*. I was certain it was an abridged version of their prayers because they didn't last more than a couple minutes. If caught practicing their religion, they would all be whipped—a high price to pay for a few words to a God who had apparently fallen asleep at the helm.

The Jehovah's Witnesses held prayer meetings behind the *Blocks* at night. When I first stumbled on one of their meetings, I was baffled and curious. What were these men whispering about in the shadows? Planning an escape, organizing a resistance group? The *Häftling* who explained to me that it was only *die Bibelforscher* had a good laugh when I told him what I thought they were up to. A few weeks after the young woman's suicide, I was emptying a piss pail on a moonless night when I spotted a prayer meeting. I felt guilty that I hadn't memorized her number, but I was pretty certain that they had heard what had happened and didn't need any of my ugly details.

One September morning the Orthodox Jews in my *Block* stayed in prayer a little longer and didn't get in line for bread after they were finished. During our lunch break at the plant, two Jews in my *Kommando* refused their soup, explaining that it was their High Holy Day, Yom Kippur. Amazed, I stared at them. It's foolhardy and counterproductive to your survival is what I wanted to say, but I kept my mouth shut. What was the point? I thought about the Orthodox Jews in my *Block*. Why the hell couldn't they have observed their holy day by giving their unwanted bread to a starving atheist like me?

Once the evening count was over I hurried to Hubert's *Block* to make sure he wasn't refusing his soup.

"I don't give a shit," he told me. "I've been starving long enough. The way I figure it, I have credit coming for the rest of my life."

I was thankful that Hubert was smart enough not to be a slave to his religion. Why? The next morning a couple of yellow triangles in my *Block* didn't get out of their bunks, and that evening we carried an unusually high number of corpses back.

Since I was among those in my *Block* who had survived the longest, I was often able to nab the choice chores. This had very little to do with seniority. We "old timers" knew how things in the camp were run and what was expected from us, and no screw ups meant the *Stubendienst* and *Blockälteste* were secure in their posts.

The morning chores were mopping and sweeping the *Block* and ensuring that the beds were properly made. Each *Häftling* was responsible for making his bed, but one *Häftling* was in charge of seeing that the bunks would pass the sporadic SS inspections. The SS had ludicrously stringent rules on how the beds should appear. The *Häftling* assigned to create these masterpieces would use two wooden planks that looked like oversized trowels to iron the wrinkles or creases from the blankets. Then he would have to position all the pillows so the SS officer could look down the row of bunks and see that all the pillows were aligned. If our beds couldn't make "the god with a moustache" happy, everyone in the *Block* would go hungry that night.

Evening chores included washing the *Block*'s three or four thirteen-gallon soup containers. This was the most treasured task. Where most other chores paid with an extra half ladle of soup, the *Häftlinge* who washed the soup containers had the right to whatever remained in the bottoms and clung to the sides. Up to four ladles of soup would be left in those barrels, and there was an unquenchable demand for it on the camp's black market.

Another evening chore was doing a stint as night watchman. It took a good deal of fortitude and endurance to stay awake for that two-hour shift after twelve hours of labor, but the loss of sleep got you a full ladle of soup.

When I was the night watchman, I sat underneath the night-light, where I had a good view of the door and the night watchman's clock hanging on a bedpost. I was also within earshot of the men filling the piss pail. In our *Block* there had been many fights over who would be the one to empty that pail. Many times I took it out myself to ensure quiet during my shift. Peace would be a better word—the *Block* was never quiet. When everyone was awake, there was coughing and spitting and swearing and arguments, and snoring and pitiful moans when they slept.

One night I heard men swearing in French outside the *Block*. I went to investigate and found two men scratching, biting, and clawing each other by the latrine. They were enraged beasts, and I had difficulty separating them. One brawler was a Parisian and the other had a southern French accent. They were real *Muselmänner* and had spent what little strength they had in their fight. On hands and knees, their chests heaving for air, they sobbed like children. The fight had been ignited by a culinary difference of opinion. The Parisian preferred to cook with butter while the southerner swore by olive oil. I stared at the sad fools and wondered if they realized that they would never taste food cooked in either fat ever again.

Another evening, I noticed that the night watchman's clock was gone. My heart stopped. How did it disappear right from under my nose? Did someone steal it when I emptied the piss pail? Had I fallen asleep? Regardless, I absolutely had to find it before the *Block-älteste* woke. The clock was his prized possession. Every morning he locked it up in his makeshift quarters. If I didn't find it, I might as well count my bones.

Like a man possessed, I scurried from one end of the *Block* to the other. I tiptoed up and down the rows of bunks, hoping to hear it. It had to be in the *Block* since no one had gone outside. Finally, my ears caught a muffled ticking. I was ecstatic and at the same time boiling mad. The thief was going to pay for this. I stole up, then unclenched my fists. The clock was in the *Stubendienst's* bunk. There was nothing I could do to that snoring pig. He must have taken it to show the *Blockälteste* that I was incompetent, so that one of his buddies could have my job. You're not going to make me look like a fool. Gingerly I lifted his pillow, retrieved the clock, and hung it back in its place.

While I was in line for my bread the next morning, the *Stubendienst* smugly asked if I had slept well.

"Oh, very well, thank you," I smiled.

"Slept during your watch?"

"Oh, I never sleep then."

"Then how could I've taken the clock?"

I pretended to be astonished. "What clock? Nobody could've taken it since it was there this morning."

"You took it out from under my pillow."

"Pillow? I would never dare do that. You must have dreamt it," I said, staring at him innocently. He threw me an incredulous look and walked away.

After that episode I applied for a different chore, washing the *Blockälteste*'s laundry. I had a cordial relationship with Wilhelm, whose dignified air clashed with the green color of his triangle. He had been imprisoned for embezzling funds to pay for his mistress's lavish lifestyle. He was still grieving for his only son, who had died in the battle of Stalingrad and hadn't ever visited his father in prison. Wilhelm enjoyed practicing his knowledge of foreign languages with me and seemed to treat me better than most. Washing his laundry got me access to soap and warm water in the shower room, some extra food, and a bed of my own whenever possible.

◆ ◆ ◆

As I was licking my bowl clean of the tasteless evening soup, I noticed a bored SS officer standing just inside the doorway. Wilhelm yelled orders for us to undress. It was a "selection." We were hustled into one corner, and the *boche* handed out the green cards that we had filled out on our arrival. One by one we filed past the Nazi. He took my card, looked me up and down, then examined my backside. Why was he dragging this out? I'm no *Muselmann*. I just turned nineteen. On September twenty-sixth, to be exact.

"*Der Bengel ist noch ganz kräftig*" (The rascal is still strong), Wilhelm said.

I turned around. The SS officer gave me another look, then shrugged indifferently. He took my card out of his pocket and put it on the table with the others. "We'll wait until next time," he told Wilhelm.

I rejoined my companions on rubbery legs. I ducked the reaper again. But did I have any real reason to be thankful? With a frigid winter almost on top of us, there was no possibility of putting on weight and regaining strength before the next SS officer looked me over. I was a condemned man who had been given only a short reprieve. If my "selection" was inevitable, then wouldn't it be better to get it over with than endure another month or two of pain and suffering before they pulled my card?

A few days later they rounded up the "selected." Dressed only in their tattered shirts, the chosen from the *Blocks* piled into the back of a truck. They had been told the same old lie—"You're being taken to a rest camp to recover"—even though the Nazis knew that every "selected" *Häftlinge* was well aware of the truck's destination. They weren't going to take a chance of anything disrupting the steady flow of traffic into their gas chambers. Sitting on the truck bed, silent and shivering, most of the men didn't care anymore what was going to happen to them.

"Don't worry!" a *Kapo* yelled as the truck pulled away. "Soon you'll be warm, even too warm!"

From that moment I was determined to do whatever I had to do to make sure my card wouldn't end up in that officer's pocket again. My bones weren't going to stoke their fires. And, I fantasized, if my goose was cooked, then I would make sure one of those SS pricks joined me.

♦ ♦ ♦

In the bunk below me slept Moishe, a yellow triangle from Yugoslavia who had been scooped up by the fascist Croatian militia. He was in his twenties with the face of an adolescent and was a big shot in the camp's black market, thanks to his connections with *Häftlinge* in the Canada *Kommando*. His cohorts called him Moi. Because of his salesmen in *Kommandos* that worked inside the plant buildings, Moi was profiting handsomely from the civilian employees. He was also the *Stubendienst*'s assistant. The *Stubendienst*'s cut insured his eyes were closed to the steady flow of visitors Moi had every night, since *Häftlinge* weren't supposed to enter other *Blocks*.

Word passed that we would be receiving new shirts. We were supposed to exchange shirts every month, but were lucky if we got fresh ones every three months. My *Block* was in a mild state of excitement. The exchange was a lottery. This late in the year, those trading in their heavy wool shirts stood to lose badly and those with light, cotton shirts had everything to gain. The unfortunate *Häftling* who had had his shirt stolen would simply be passed over. Shirts were a much sought after commodity on the camp's black market. One could exchange a good shirt for an old, mended one and a loaf of bread with a Polish civilian factory worker because they had difficulty getting any clothing.

After receiving my new shirt, a wool one, I went to my bed to put my cap under my pillow, as I did every evening before eating. To my astonishment, I found a roll of bills lying there. Someone must have put it there thinking it was Moishe's bed. My heart pounded with excitement. I looked about. No one was paying any attention to me. I thrust the wad into my shoe. Not wanting any evidence that I had been to my bed, I stuffed my cap into my pocket and slipped into the soup line. Ordinarily I would have checked the levels of the barrels. You wanted to step up when the barrel was almost empty because you stood a greater chance of getting a potato or chunk of cabbage. That night I had only one thought—getting out of the barracks as fast as possible so I could count my loot. Somebody's god continued to send good fortune the wrong way because I ended up with a full ladle of thick soup as well.

After eating, I ducked behind the *Block* and counted the money. I was holding 580 marks, a treasure that could change my fate. But there were problems. How was I going to change five one-hundred mark bills? Where would I hide the money? If caught with such a large sum, it was the *Stehbunker* for sure, and possibly the rope. I couldn't keep the money with me. Moi or one of his cronies would surely search me.

I ran to Hubert's *Block*. He nearly fell over when he saw the bills. Hubert knew a pot-washer who was selling a ladle of thick soup for ten marks. I decided that for the next fifty-eight days Hubert and I were going to have full bellies. For the first time, I could truly envision a return trip to Nice.

Moi was sitting on his bed buttering slices of bread when I returned. Obviously, he wasn't aware of the screw-up yet. I stretched out on my bed, letting my legs hang down on either side. For 580 marks, Moi must have sold an overcoat—and one in fine condition, at that. What would he do when he found out that the money had disappeared? I mused. No question he would come at me, but how? Like a sly fox or an enraged bear? I knew there was a chance he would send a crony to beat a confession out of me, but that would be his last resort. With no tracks leading to Hubert, if I played it right I could deflect all suspicion.

A string of Moi's furtive traders streamed in and out. "Moi?" a reedy voice called out in Yiddish from the *Block* entrance. "*Wie bist do?*" (Where are you?)

"*Komm hier,*" Moishe ordered.

A little Jewish fellow, slightly humpbacked and with the type of face the Nazis venomously caricaturized in *Der Stürmer*, hurried over. He sat down on the edge of Moishe's bed. They began to talk in soft whispers, but their conversation was quickly punctured with Yiddish curses. The visitor got up and stared at my bed as I pretended to sleep. It was hard to keep a smile off my face. He started to slip his hand under my pillow when the curfew bell sounded, which gave me an excuse to wake. The little fellow scurried out of our *Block*.

That night I visited the piss pail three times, and each time I returned I could tell my mattress had been searched. Moishe had been thorough. I don't think he slept at all that night.

Returning from the plant the next evening I discovered a neatly folded, red-and-white checkered shirt under my pillow. The shirt looked brand new and would have fetched a hefty sum from a civilian. Moi, that sly fox, sure set his trap with delicious bait. Obviously he figured I would store the shirt in the same spot I had hid the money. I left the shirt under my pillow and nonchalantly went to get my soup.

While I ate I kept an eye on my bed, but no one approached it. Where was Moi? When my bowl was licked clean, I went looking for him. He was sitting on the steps of the *Block*, diligently cleaning his comfortable leather shoes. Why not have some fun with this *schmuck*, I thought, and headed into the latrine. Moishe followed at a distance. He sure figured me for an idiot. I sat in there as if I were constipated, and even pretended to sleep. It must have driven him crazy. I was struck with a masterstroke of an idea and quickly returned to the *Block*.

Grabbing the shirt, I went to Wilhelm's quarters. I pushed back the curtain that hung in his doorway. He was in the midst of playing cards with the *Kapos*. I swallowed hard. This wasn't the most opportune moment to disturb my *Blockälteste*.

"*Was willst du, Speckjäger?*" (What do you want, bacon hunter?)

"I have a present for you."

"Show me!"

I unfolded the shirt.

"How much?" he demanded suspiciously. In Auschwitz everything had a price.

"I said it's a present."

I tossed the shirt onto the table and turned heels. A livid Moishe was standing by our bunk. It was an expensive backfire for him, and it got me clean off the hook.

An hour later, Wilhelm gave me half a loaf of bread.

"*Hier, Muselmann, du brauchst mir nicht dankbar sein, du wäschst meine Hemden gut.*" (Look Muslim, you don't have to be grateful to me. You really wash my shirts well.)

Soon, the whole *Block* knew about the gift, and my companions labeled me an ass-kissing idiot. I couldn't have given a shit what they said or thought. I had a full stomach for fifty-eight days and wouldn't have to worry about the next "selection."

♦ ♦ ♦

Christmas and the New Year passed with the Allies encircling Germany. Because of the constant bombing, the delivery of raw materials by rail was increasingly sporadic. Factory output plummeted. The *Kapos* struggled to keep us busy with meaningless, but still physically draining tasks. Rumors circulated that the Soviets had launched a new offensive and that their arrival was imminent. At night we could see a reddish luminescence on the eastern horizon and hear the distant thunder of heavy guns, but the only source for reliable information had dried up. I had not seen a POW at Buna for a while. I wasn't even sure if they were still in Auschwitz. At the time of the first snowfall, all the Soviet *Häftlinge* were marched out of the camps. We heard they had been moved into Germany. A few days later, the Polish *Häftlinge* followed. Every passing day we wondered if we were going to be evacuated, liberated, or exterminated. The SS had destroyed the gas chambers in November, but we all knew they had other means to quickly rid themselves of us.

After roll call one freezing morning, we assembled into our *Kommandos* as usual. But as the band launched into its first military march, news came that we weren't going to Buna until the fog lifted. Surely it wasn't the light morning fog that was keeping us from leaving, I thought. We had gone to the plant when it was much thicker. All morning we stamped around the Appelplatz, trying to keep warm. As the hours crawled by the most fantastic speculations took shape in our overheated imaginations.

"We're going to be evacuated tonight."

"The Soviets have Auschwitz encircled, and they're going to shell this place until nothing stands."

"The *Boches* are going to wipe us all out with flame throwers."

"No, no, they signed an armistice."

Toward afternoon, we were told to return to our *Blocks*. The next morning the assembly bell failed to ring. The sudden shock of change made me nervous. Twelve months of a strict, daily routine had created an odd sense of comfort—dare I even say, a sense of control—that had now been yanked out from under me. I walked aimlessly around the camp. The guard towers were still manned, but the *Kapos* were out of sight. They knew this idle time could spark one of the milling groups of *Häftlinge* into a vengeful mob.

I looked toward the east. The Soviets were closer. The sounds of battle were now tremendous hammer blows. I figured they would be here in two or three days, but would we? Would I get the chance to go freely through those gates? And if I did, should I search for Stella? She hadn't entered my thoughts for some time. If she were alive, I thought, would she be capable of caring about me anymore? My heart had become callous, but still I held a thread of hope for us. Why couldn't she?

Prisoners ran past me. Without knowing why, I followed them across the yard to a growing mob trying to break into the clothing warehouse. With an old post as a battering ram, a gang of *Häftlinge* smashed in the door. We all rushed in.

The warehouse was dark and thick with the smell of mothballs and disinfectant. I groped my way through a corridor created by massive piles of clothing in hopes of finding something to insulate myself from the January blizzards. Running my hands along the piles, I recognized the rough material of our striped "pajamas." Near the far end of the building, my hand fell upon a handle that seemed to belong to a suitcase. I yanked and then found myself buried under an avalanche of valises. Feeling as if I had been bashed by twenty *Kapos*, I struggled out from under the luggage and "organized" a suitcase that I could carry with ease.

Machine gun fire exploded from an adjacent guard tower. Bullets pierced the walls and shattered windows. I threw myself flat on my face as most of the others rushed toward the door in a screaming panic, trampling the dead and wounded. Light seeped through dangling shutters. When the shooting stopped, I jumped to my feet and ran to a window opposite the guard tower. I looked out. There was no one around. I threw the suitcase through the glass and jumped out after it.

Bullets whistled by my ears, slamming into the warehouse wall behind me. Terrified, I bent over as far as I could and rushed for the nearest shelter, the latrine. A strong shock nearly wrenched the suitcase from my grasp. I spun around, thinking someone was trying to steal my bounty, but there was no one there. I barreled into the latrine, slammed the door, and crouched breathless behind my brown leather suitcase.

When the machine guns fell silent again, I cracked open the door. The yard was deserted except for a few bodies. I closed the door. It was time to open my treasure chest. It looked new except for the hole on one side, which I could easily stick my thumb into. There was a key tied to the handle, but the clasps weren't locked. Inside were cozy wool sweaters and cardigans. I layered them on me, making sure after each one that my "pajama" top still fit. These were the first civilian clothes I had put on since my arrival. There had been times that I wore the same "pajamas" for three months— clothes made hard and brittle from filth. The clean, soft tickle of angora against my skin was overwhelmingly seductive. Some of the sweaters had odd moth holes in them, but I couldn't care less. When I slipped on the fourth sweater, I was barely able to button my jacket.

There were three cardigans left and I planned to give them to Hubert, but I couldn't walk out with them bundled under my arm. My fellow *Häftlinge* would jump me for them and probably strip me of the ones that I was wearing. I had to hide them, and the latrine's rafters were the perfect spot. When I began to fold the cardigans, a piece of metal dropped to the floor. A machine gun bullet. That's what almost ripped the suitcase out of my hand and made the moth holes in the sweaters. Shit—how close did that bullet come to putting a moth hole in me?

I was unable to find Hubert. He wasn't in his *Block* or anywhere else I thought he might be. I repeatedly called out his name as I roamed the yard. A few fellows were rushing toward the kitchen, and being an opportunistic scavenger, I followed them. With the plant idle, there was no steam for cooking, but there could be some cold leftover soup or some cabbages. To my shock, a cook was standing in the doorway handing out leftover loaves of bread, the morning bread having already been delivered to the *Blocks*. Holding that hefty loaf of dark bread in my hands, I realized that the rumors must be true. We were going to leave Auschwitz. The SS wouldn't fill our bellies if they planned to kill us. Figuring that we would be leaving in the morning, the bread joined the sweaters on the rafter.

The assembly bell rang.

"Everybody in their *Blocks*!" The *Stubendienste* yelled through megaphones.

"Line up with your blankets," the *Blockälteste* ordered.

We were going to "Pitchi Poi" tonight! I grabbed my blanket and the blanket of a bunkmate who hadn't opened his eyes that morning. As we marched out of the barracks in single file, we received a ration of bread at the doorway.

"Line up by *Blocks*!" someone was yelling through a megaphone.

As 10,000 men flowed out of the *Blocks*, I ducked into the latrine to recover my loot. I rolled the sweaters and bread in my extra blanket, tied the bundle with the shoelaces from one of the bullet-riddled corpses, and looped it over my shoulder. Wrapping my blanket around me for the journey, I darted out of the latrine and fell into rank. I called out for Hubert again, but it was useless.

PART III

THE DEATH MARCH

CHAPTER 16

The first columns of *Häftlinge* began to move. The men of my *Block* stomped and shuffled about to keep warm as we waited our turn to be ushered out. With the receding sun behind them, the peaks of the Carpathians glowed like the wicks of smoldering candles as a thinly stretched nimbus lowered a crimson veil of snow onto them. Everyone was grumbling. January was by no means the time to be taking an evening stroll. Finally, a guard in a thick field gray coat waved us forward. This time there were no musicians playing a martial tune as we walked in rows of five through the gate. The quiet was unsettling.

The SS led us back down the road that we had all traveled after unloading from the cattle cars. The Buna plant was to our right, its barbed-wire fence bordering the road. The plant itself was a looming silhouette against the winter twilight. No lights shone inside, no smoke spewed from its multiple chimneys. The Nazis had deserted it. Buna was a dying monster. How I hated and feared that beast when its heart furiously pumped methanol through its snarled network of veins. And now that it was innocuous, I should have felt happy—overjoyed—but I wasn't. Hadn't I dreamt of seeing it like this? Yes, but the slave had become overacquainted with his task-master. I knew what it expected from me and that I could endure its many tortures. What monster was I being herded to now along this icy path? Could I survive its demands, its torments, or would it be the one to finally devour me and spit out my ashes?

Rumors circulated that we were headed to the town of Gleiwitz. No one knew exactly how far that was, but it became increasingly apparent that we would be walking all night. We slipped through the darkened town of Auschwitz, which was situated near the main camp. As I chewed over whether the SS had also emptied Auschwitz and Birkenau, I caught glimpses of town folk watching us through the cracks in their closed shutters. I imagined that the Poles were glad to see the Nazis leave, but were wracked with fear of what would come when the Soviets marched through their streets. For my fellow *Häftlinge* and I, the Red Army meant only one thing: freedom. But as a *Muselmann*'s fate would have it, we were being forced to flee from our liberators.

The snow was becoming deeper, filling my wooden shoes and turning my feet into icicles. I feared frostbite wouldn't be far off. It would have been nice if my benefactor had packed a pair of galoshes with all those warm sweaters. I had no way to judge the distance we had already traveled, but I was pretty sure we had been on the move for about four hours. Deep bomb craters now bit off large chunks of the road, slowing our advance. The whole Polish countryside looked wounded and forsaken.

The wind-ravaged skeletons of trees were the only things mark-ing the road as we started up a hill. Our ranks began to break as *Muselmänner* struggled to plow through snowdrifts. The gusts be-came more violent, causing my eyes to water and burn, and it seemed nearly impossible to get the frigid air into my heaving lungs. I wrapped my blanket tightly around me, wiping away the frozen snot under my nose.

The wind lifted the snow in eddies, covering the tracks of the men in front of me. I tripped over an unexpected obstacle—a man's body covered by a thin blanket of snow. A few moments later I came upon another body, this one with an SS bullet in his neck. Walking farther, I realized that the dead were forming a steady line along the side of the road. I kept my eyes on the footprints of the man in front of me. It was tempting to drop down next to the dead and drift into much-needed sleep, but I wasn't going to heed that siren song. By no means was I going to become a mile marker.

At the crossroads on the hill's summit, a metal sign read GLEI-WITZ, 55 KM. The rumors were true. I stared at the sign in disbelief—thirty-five more miles? Our SS guards must surely be planning to enter that town alone. Toward the east a red aureole enveloped the horizon as the wind brought the rumble of cannons. I looked down at the seemingly unending gray string of humanity weaving itself into the snow-shrouded valley. I was stunned by the sheer number of *Häftlinge* before me. I had no idea that so many *Muselmänner* had outlasted Auschwitz and Birkenau.

I was overcome with daggerlike stomach cramps, probably from the frozen cabbage I "organized" from the kitchen when I received my loaf of bread. I went to the side of the road and squatted among the dead bodies. Feasting crows screeched and scattered. I recognized familiar faces as the columns hobbled by me. Once I was finished, I tried to get up, but the cramps were still twisting my guts. A growling German Shepherd sniffed at me, his stinking breath full in my face. Yapping, he circled around me, then sat down.

"*Los weiter!*" (Keep going!)

An SS pushed me with the butt of his gun. Not about to get shot in the head for taking a shit, I darted back into line, pulling up my pants as best I could.

They marched us until daybreak, then herded us into a bombed-out tile works that had a perimeter fence that was still intact. I wanted to search for Hubert, but being past exhaustion, all I did was collapse on a pile of bricks and pull my blanket up over my head. Fearing I would freeze to death, my sleep was fitful at best. A couple of hours later, the SS called for assembly. My legs were painfully stiff and heavy when I stood. How many more miles could they handle?

Back on the road, we moved like snails. Everyone was at the end of his strength, even the SS, who took turns riding in sleighs. It was a gray day with bursts of snow flurries, but mercifully the cutting wind had ceased. Someone behind me was walking on my heels, and my right heel was already raw and bleeding and hurt like hell. I swung around ready to hit the blundering idiot. My fist dropped. It was the *Vorarbeiter* of Hubert's *Kommando*.

"*Entschuldigen sie, bitte*" (Please excuse me), he wheezed.

That was a switch. I had never heard a "prominent" *Häftlinge* say "I'm sorry" before, but now they, too, were just striped pieces of meat in this cattle drive. I asked if he had seen Hubert.

"He must be a few rows back."

I stepped to the side of the road and waited. Hubert saw me first. We fell into each other's arms. "I was searching for you in the camp," Hubert told me.

"So was I, so was I. I have a birthday present for you."

"It's not my birthday."

"It is now." I reached into my rolled blanket and tore off a piece of bread for him. The barking of a guard dog sent us back in line.

They pushed us all day without rest. The crack of rifles and pistols putting holes in the laggards had stopped turning heads. Did the SS actually think those crawling skeletons could find safe haven? Throughout the afternoon, lines of *Häftlinge* from other camps flowed in from side roads and filled the gaps left by the dead. Once in a while, we had the good fortune of waiting at a grade crossing as a train went by. Almost in unison, everyone dropped into the snow as if felled by a volley of machine gun fire. When the track was clear, only the kicks and rifle butts of the SS would raise us again.

By evening each step I took was torture. I could see my blood seeping through the rags wrapped around my wooden shoes. The glands in my groin had become agonizingly swollen, which meant my feet were infected. My head was filled with thoughts of escaping, but in my condition I would only be serving myself up for target practice. I staggered on, leaning on Hubert, who would yank me to my feet every time I was ready to give up and drag me along. I marveled at his stamina and how lucky I was. Without him I would have been a mile marker. Maybe he got the strength from the loaf we shared through the day. If that was the case, why was I such a pitiful mess?

"Any *Kommando* in Buna would be better than this," I coughed.

"*Mon ami*, hold on. I know there's a warm *Block* waiting for us in Gleiwitz."

His lies and strong back kept my bleeding feet moving forward. Somewhere out on that road I slipped into delirium. It was as if my head were being held underwater. I heard Hubert's voice, but couldn't understand his words. I thought a blurred figure standing at the side of the road was my father. Why didn't he say hello? I wanted to go back and ask him, but the white hot Mediterranean sand of Grimaldi Beach was scorching my feet. A flash of bright light jerked me back to reality. In front of me, like moths, columns of *Häftlinge* followed a searchlight's beam into the Gleiwitz camp.

Hubert and I went to find a bunk, but all the *Blocks* were full to bursting. Seeing men still streaming into the camp, a dismayed Hubert led me to the wooden steps of one of them. "This is at least better than lying in the snow."

Hubert folded his blanket for us to sit on, and we covered ourselves with mine. We huddled close to each other.

"Is there any of my birthday present left?"

I reached into the blanket wrapped over my shoulder. There was a mouthful for both of us, then I remembered the sweaters.

"This is definitely the best birthday present I've ever gotten," Hubert said as he pulled the third sweater over his head.

We awoke in each other's arms just as dawn began to break. The blanket covering us was frozen stiff. Laid out in front of us on the snow-covered ground were grotesquely contorted bodies. One frozen man was just about to take a bite of bread. There were crumbs on his tongue. These men had dragged themselves all the way from Auschwitz for nothing. Hubert and I knew we were lucky.

Without the loaf of bread and the sweaters layered over our bodies we would have been part of that icy mortuary.

For three days we mindlessly milled about Gleiwitz without anything to eat. The dead were everywhere, stacked in the snow like kindling, piled behind the *Blocks* like discarded rags or just left where they dropped. The SS made no attempt to remove any of them. For three nights Hubert and I slept on those steps, and the more our bellies cried, the colder it seemed until we could barely sleep at all. The only crumbs of hope came from the distant sounds of battle.

On the fourth day, the *Häftlinge* who were squatting in a barn-like structure in the center of the camp were driven out into the snow by the guards. The guards then emptied the *Blocks*, lining us all in front of the entrance of the "barn." The rumor circulated that we were going to leave as we filed into the building one by one. The SS were handing out bread rations at the door.

Nearly a hundred *Häftlinge* had entered by the time it was my turn. Since the "barn" had no windows, I was momentarily blind when I stepped through the doorway with my bread. I held both hands out in front of me so I wouldn't bump into anybody. Someone tore the bread out of my hands and ran. I tried to catch him, but I slammed into a wall of bodies. I yelled to Hubert, who was behind me, to guard his ration well.

How could one of my fellow *Häftling* be that dirty? Easily answered, but how could I have been that careless? Stupidity like that could cost me my life. Thankfully, Hubert was willing to share and wouldn't take no for an answer. When the SS couldn't squeeze another *Häftling* into the "barn," they marched us out. I eyed my fellow prisoners. Which one was the thief? There was no way to tell, so I put a jinx on the whole bunch.

Our guards led us to a train parked on a solitary track next to the camp. I happily climbed into one of the open freight cars. My heels hadn't recovered enough to endure another trek on foot. Hubert was right behind me. There were at least seventy men in our car. I pulled the door shut to keep any more from getting in. Four

Kapos and their *Piepels* stretched out on the floor, taking up space for twenty. Hubert and I crouched down in one corner. I was thankful that I had enough room to sit comfortably and move my stiff limbs.

The train sat idle for hours. The falling snow that settled on our caps and shoulders slowly melted, until the car seemed to be steaming. A few squadrons of German fighter planes flew over us. How close was the Red Army? I wondered. The frantic voices coming from the other cars made me think we were all asking the same question: Would this train become one of their targets?

I heard trampling outside our car. The SS were bringing up another pack of "pajamas." A *Häftling* climbed up and looked into our car. All he saw were the lounging *Kapos*. "*Na, die liegen da wie ein Gott in Frankreich!*" (They're lying there like God in France!) he exclaimed in a shrill voice.

From the accent, I could tell the bastard was Hungarian. His words flooded another forty men into our car. Now we all had to stand like asparagus in a can. The *Kapos* cursed and threw blows, but there was simply no more room. We should have lynched them as soon as they had spread out on the floor, but the whole lot of us could barely walk, let alone kick open someone's skull.

Toward evening a sharp jolt signaled that a locomotive had been attached to the train, and shortly thereafter we began to roll. The icy wind, choked with biting, black smoke, whistled in my ears, stung my eyes, and made me spit coal soot. Wrapped in our blankets, we looked like a shipment of veiled statues. We rode standing all night, but somehow I must have gone to sleep because the next thing I knew it was getting light. Some of the statues around me looked as if they had been placed on pedestals. I slowly grasped that they were standing on corpses. The *Kapos* were now sitting comfortably in a corner. Hubert whispered that they had made room by beating and strangling as many *Muselmänner* as they could get their hands on. This had put everyone on edge, and the tension was palpable. An accidental kick would start a rabid fight that would set off others like wildfire.

Somewhere, two men were swearing at each other. I recognized the strident voice of the asshole who had created this whole stew. A *Kapo* did as well. He stood up and barreled his way to the Hungarian. He grabbed him by the throat and pounded him unmercifully. The Hungarian fell back onto other men, who flung their fists at him. He cried out, pleading for his life, but no one was listening. Pulling himself up, he straddled one of the walls of the car. The speed of the train seemed to frighten him more than the blows he had received. The *Kapo* charged and knocked him off, but somehow the Hungarian hung on by his fingertips. Wild-eyed, he struggled to climb back in. Hands and fists rebuffed him. He hung there one minute, two, then the *Kapo* lost patience and took off his boot. Bringing the heel down like a hammer, he crushed the man's fingers. Screaming, the Hungarian fell. A burst from a submachine gun bid him a bon voyage.

The second day in the car, Hubert came down with a fever and began coughing terribly. I made enough space for him to sit and to enable me to shield him from the train's frigid draft. I fed him snow to quench his fevered thirst. "You have to hold on, Hubert. We'll be in a warm *Block* soon."

"We'll be going fishing again, won't we?" Hubert coughed.

On Thursdays, when the schools in France were closed, a few of us would pack a picnic lunch and pedal to the Pointe St. Hospice, a cape between Nice and Monaco. We were always able to catch enough fish for a hearty pot of *bouillebaisse*.

"Hubert, do you remember the novices?"

His eyes seemed to light up. Everyday at noon, the good sisters from the convent took the novices in their white dresses for a stroll on the path circling the cape. The trail passed over a grotto where we would sip beer and lie in wait. The elements had washed a crevasse in the pavement right over our heads. It forced the novices to take a wide step.

"I only remember the novices who weren't wearing panties," Hubert murmured.

"I only remember the one who straddled the gap as she admired the view. Boy, did I get sand in my eyes that day."

Hubert went into a coughing fit. I realized that conversation, even if it was about girls, wasn't the best medicine for him, so I fed him more snow and let him doze.

The screaming of the train's brakes and the cars' bumpers banging and shuddering jarred me from my snooze. It was a starless night. My senses were numb, but one thing was crystal clear: I was starving. Hubert was slumped over motionless. His raspy cough let me know he was still with me. I heard someone yelling from outside the train. Was it what I thought they were calling out: "Five-minute stop for lunch?"

"*Alle Leichen ausladen!*" a *boche* repeatedly screamed.

No, it was only my wishful thinking. The SS were ordering us to unload the dead bodies. After being in this car for three days, I thought, a little exercise would do me well.

With the ever-present threat of Allied bombers, only dim blue electric lights illuminated the train station. From all the cars, bodies started raining onto the snowy platform. It looked as if the *Muselmänner* were erecting a bulwark of flesh for a last stand against the Nazi crusaders. In pairs, we dragged the bodies to the last car, which the SS had cleared out. There were still mounds of dead when that car was filled, so a second morgue car was started.

On my fourth trip I came across a body I could handle alone. I took hold of the corpse by the trousers, but the cord used as his belt gave way and I fell on my ass with the pants in my hands. A couple of *Häftlinge* passing by with a corpse had a good chuckle at my Laurel and Hardy pratfall. Their laughter might have seemed somewhat perverse, but for many of us a sense of humor was the only thing that preserved what little sanity we had left. In Monowitz, I had witnessed a couple of *Häftlinge* laugh with the noose around their necks. That was true gallows humor. Laughter really pissed off the guards at Buna. Swinging their rifle butts, they would scream, "*Lachen verboten! Lachen verboten!*" as if they thought we were enjoying our holiday in hell.

The body of a tall yellow triangle, barely older than I, landed at my feet. Taking hold of his ankles, I started to drag him across the platform when he began to move. He blinked his big dark eyes and breathed deeply. The snow must have revived him. He tried to speak, but he couldn't utter a sound. He licked his lips. I knelt and put a handful of snow into his mouth. He tried a grateful smile, but it came out as a grimace. I brought him to his feet. I wasn't about to put him in that morgue car.

"This boy is still alive!" I yelled as I hoisted him into a car, a task I wouldn't have been able to accomplish if he hadn't been a *Muselmann* of the first order.

After dragging another body to the morgue car, I found the kid lying on the platform again. He had the look of someone who had wakened from an unfathomable dream. I was flushed with anger, and before I knew it I was shouting into the car.

"*Was ist los mit euch Drecksäke? Der lebt doch noch!*" (What's the matter with you dirt bags? He's still alive!)

"Go screw yourself! He's croaking!" someone barked back, a *Kapo* no doubt.

I turned around to find that my fussing and fuming had attracted the attention of a young SS officer. The kid must have seen him, too, because he rose feebly, staggered, then fell on his face.

"*Was ist denn mit dem los?*" (What's the matter with him?), the officer asked me.

"He's still alive."

"I'll show him where to go."

The SS unholstered his Luger.

"*Nein, nein,*" the kid said and started crawling away on all fours.

The Nazi smirked. He must have found the kid's futile struggle quite amusing. Play possum, you fool, and he might not waste the bullet.

The barrel of the gun was only inches from the back of his head when the *boche* pulled the trigger. The kid went limp and sank into the snow. Thin whiffs of smoke rose out of the hole in his skull.

The officer holstered his gun and walked away. He didn't say anything. He didn't look twice. He didn't even blink. Why should he? He was only exterminating vermin.

There was a noble innocence to the boy's struggle that transfixed me, reminding me of the stranded baby sparrow I had found when I was seven. It didn't cry out or look frightened; it was just determined to fly back to its nest. I figured I would adopt it until it was truly ready to be airborne, when an alley cat pounced. At least that animal had a reason behind its act of violence, I thought, as I dragged the boy's body to the second morgue car.

What was it inside that boy, inside me, inside Hubert, and inside so many others on the train that made us still want to live? Were we clinging that tightly to the fairy tales society had sold us before it went insane? Is the instinct to live that Herculean? Or were we that overwhelmed by our fear of the unexplored void of death? I didn't have the answer, but after witnessing men at their most foul, I was straining the limits of my creativity to find a good reason to keep moving forward. But as I glanced at the handful of *Muselmänner* around me dragging our dead and the ever present SS, I realized there was a good enough reason, an imperative one. With the Allies closing in, staying alive, keeping Hubert alive, was now a form of warfare on the *boches*. The more of us, the more of them who couldn't aim a rifle at a Soviet, British, or American soldier. Also, surviving would ensure that we would have our day of vengeance. I was going to be the one to permanently wipe the smirk off that SS officer's face, I dreamed, as I filled my cap with snow for Hubert.

CHAPTER 17

I found Hubert on the opposite side of the car, in the area where everyone was relieving himself. He was sitting in the filth and dampness.

"Pierre, Pierre," he cried. His trouser legs were soaked with blood from being stepped on, and his eyes were glassy and dull from his burning fever. I felt incredibly guilty. I had been gone for only a short while, but I should have anticipated this. I shouldn't have left him. Hubert held out his hand to me. It was covered with black-ish goo. "Chocolate," Hubert murmured.

The smell left no doubt what it really was. I took a ragged blanket, which wasn't much cleaner than his hands, and wiped away his illusionary confection before he could eat it. I lifted him to his feet and jammed him against the wall.

"You stole my chocolate," Hubert whimpered.

"I'm sorry."

There were tie-downs on the walls. I grabbed an ownerless blanket, pushed it through one of the rings, weaved it under Hubert's armpits, and made a knot over his chest. With his blanket wrapped around his head and shoulders, he dozed off right away. I sat down. My legs were swollen and soft, and yellowish flesh was bulging over the tops of my wooden shoes. In another day, perhaps two, I wouldn't be able to stand.

Hubert awoke delirious, calling out my name over and over again. Nothing I did or said could quiet him. As the train raced down a hill, I shared a blanket with Antoine, a red triangle Frenchman who had been in one of my *Kommandos*.

"Why don't you throw him overboard and end his suffering?"

I shook my head. "I couldn't live with myself."

Again I tried to quiet Hubert. I didn't want his whining to get on anyone's nerves, especially those *Kapos*. How had my hallucinating friend only a few days before managed to drag me to Gleiwitz? Was his effort to keep me alive the reason he was sick now? Probably. I must not allow anyone else to die so I could see tomorrow. I could not be propped up by Hubert's bones.

Somehow I fell asleep against Antoine's shoulder. He nudged me awake. It was dark and Hubert was still calling for me.

"It's okay," I told Antoine, "he'll quiet down."

"No, it's not your friend. Look over there." He pointed at a couple *Häftlinge* bent over a corpse. "We better stay awake."

I didn't know what Antoine was talking about or what I was supposed to be looking at until I saw one of the *Häftlinge* lift out the corpse's liver. The pair slinked off to an empty corner and killed their hunger. No one moved, no one reacted, no one seemed to care. So this is what we have been reduced to. They finally succeeded in turning us into subhumans.

Once more they made us unload the dead bodies. I asked Antoine to watch over Hubert, then I climbed out of the car, hoping to find something edible while knowing that at least I would return with a cap full of clean snow. The second morgue car was nearly full. It struck me that Hubert would fare better with the dead than with the living. At least we could lie down. I hobbled back to the car as fast as I could. Incoherent, Hubert couldn't understand and Antoine seemed more repulsed by my plan than by those hyenas eating the liver. I freed Hubert from his sling, placed him on the blanket, and dragged him to the end of the train. I was lucky that he was keeping quiet. We couldn't afford to draw any attention.

"Don't worry, my friend. This is going to be much more comfortable."

It took every once of strength I had to push him up into the car. Even with the corpses packed tightly, it was hard to get my footing and I fell a few times pulling Hubert to the center of the pile. I dropped breathless next to him, trying to ignore the hundreds of unblinking eyes staring at me. No one was yelling in German to get those two living corpses out of there, so I knew my scheme had worked. But my gush of pride was tempered by a new fear—if they uncoupled the two cars from the rest of the train, we would be as good as dead. Suddenly our car rocked forward and back. The train was coming alive. I patted Hubert's still hand.

"*Cela va marcher, vieille noix.*" (It will work out, old nut.) Once the train was out of the station, I gathered together as many jackets and trousers as I could and made a bed out of them. I hadn't had such comfortable sleeping quarters since I was shipped out of France.

The din of the train passing over a bridge snapped me awake. I broke out in a cold sweat, thinking we were being bombed. The burned-out carcasses of trains that I had seen lying on the side of the tracks were haunting me. The wind whistled and howled over me as I stood up and looked around. The train was rushing down-hill at full throttle. The dead men's garments flapped and waved, and their bluish flesh shone in the moonlight. All we needed, I thought, were a few spider webs and "the god with the moustache" at the throttle to make this phantom train complete.

The next day we passed through some of the finest scenery in Europe as the train lugged along the foot of the Bohemian Mountains. Unfortunately, from where I sat I couldn't savor their beauty. I was too tortured by my hunger and thirst. I thought of the two *Häftlinge* who had eaten the dead man's liver. I was sure the same scenario was playing out in every car. No, it was better to die than to come to that. I pondered why it was the cannibals, the ones with no restraint, no scruples, who seemed to survive and prosper? I had no answer and figured I never would.

The train began to slow. I looked out. The area ahead had been thoroughly bombed. Along the embankment were the smoldering remains of a freight train. Our train stopped, and the morgue came to rest below a bridge. A Czech railway worker looked down in horror. What an unimaginable sight a freight car full of corpses must have been to the uninitiated. I waved to him. From the look on his face he must have thought that I had risen from the dead. He opened his shoulder bag and tossed down a little package to me. I was about to pick it up when a shot rang out. The man sagged onto the railing, where he hung for a moment, then tumbled down into our car. Now I was the one staring in horror. Hubert awoke, calling out my name. Fearing that the SS would swarm into the car at any second, I threw myself on top of him.

"*Tais toi et ne bouges pas! Daida Lou Bodu!*" (Keep shut and stay still! The goon is coming!), I hissed in Hubert's ear as I put my hand over his mouth. *Daida Lou Bodu* is Nice slang that we used to warn classmates when the teacher was coming. I flattened myself on top of Hubert and took only short breaths. If the guards came they would be right on top of us because the dead civilian was only an arm's length away.

Finally the train started moving. I rolled off Hubert and looked at the railway worker's prostrate body. I turned him over. A stream of blood was running from where his right eye had been. Why had they killed him? Were they afraid of partisans? Had they taken the package he tossed for a bomb? Or had this civilian become an embarrassing witness, unwittingly spying the Nazi underbelly? I opened the package he had dropped—a piece of bread and a sausage. Inside his shoulder bag I found the rest of his lunch. Hubert and I devoured the food so quickly that we almost choked. Suddenly I was no longer afraid of dying from starvation before arriving at the next "Pitchi Poi."

The railway man's wedding band made me think of his wife. I pictured her anxiously standing on the stoop, waiting for him. She would never know how or why he had suddenly disappeared, or that the lunch she made her husband gave two emaciated teens another chance at survival. The man looked about the same age as my father. He probably had sons and daughters. Had it been his paternal instincts that compelled him to be a Good Samaritan? There would be tears, curses, and questions by family members for months, and I was the only one who could tell them that the "god with a moustache" and his goons had propped me and Hubert up with their loved one's bones.

Hubert fell fast asleep and awoke in the late afternoon a different person. Those few calories had done wonders.

"Do you think that some day you will run your family's business?" I asked in an attempt to gauge his mental state.

"Well, if you should ever find and marry that girl Stella, you'll have a roomful of our finest carnations," he smiled.

It amazed me that he remembered her name because I hadn't mentioned Stella for some time. I became sad. I hadn't given Stella much thought. Truthfully, close to none. If she was even alive when we left Auschwitz, I couldn't imagine her surviving the march. And if she was alive on some other train, I hoped that she had more confidence in my tenacity than I did in hers.

I awoke to find the train stopped on a sidetrack. I looked over to Hubert, who was peacefully gazing at the sky.

"How long have we been here?" I whispered.

"An hour or more."

"Why? Have they unloaded the cars?"

"I don't think so. I've only heard *boche* voices."

I carefully inched over to the edge. From the snatches of conversations I caught, it seemed that no one had been moved yet. There was a question if the nearby camp, Mauthausen, could absorb us. I truly hoped they couldn't. In Auschwitz, I had heard that Mauthausen was one large quarry, and breaking rocks for twelve-hour stretches in the winter was not appetizing, whatsoever. I crawled back to Hubert and told him what I had heard. He complained that if he had to lie still much longer, he would be frostbitten. I reminded him that he would be much colder with a bullet in his brain.

Three or four hours later, with the sun setting, I heard an SS guard say to another that there wasn't enough room to take the whole load. I guess breaking rocks wasn't killing *Muselmänner* fast enough. Shortly thereafter the train started moving again.

♦ ♦ ♦

"*Alles raus! Alles raus!*" the SS ordered. I peeked over the rim. We were stopped at the foot of a steep hill, and the guards were beginning to line what *Häftlinge* were left next to a trail leading up to barbed-wire and pine tree shrouded barracks. This I presumed was our new "Pitchi Poi." The guards had their backs turned to the morgue cars so it was easy for Hubert and me to slip out and fall in with the others. We all threw ourselves on the ground and greedily ate the snow. Glancing back at the train, I saw that every car had practically become a morgue. It looked as if we had lost about 80 percent of our fellow "pajamas."

We stumbled along the train track, which disappeared into a tunnel at the foot of the hill. The tunnel's entrance was camouflaged with a canopy of netting woven with greenery and guarded by a fortified pillbox. Next to the tunnel was a pile of gigantic cylindrical aluminum sheets that looked like cigars sliced in half. They had been meticulously camouflaged. I couldn't imagine what they could be used for, but my mind wasn't altogether clear. I could barely hold up my head.

The guards ordered us onto a trail that veered away from the tunnel's entrance, then zigzagged up to the camp. It took everything I had to keep Hubert on his feet as we went up those switchbacks.

This camp seemed newer, smaller, and better constructed than Monowitz. At least from the outside, it appeared that the *Blocks* were built for human beings, not animals. I wondered if the Germans had planned this to be a vacation resort after their victory.

We were immediately ushered to the showers. Once again, all our clothing was taken from us. Bye, bye, wool sweaters. Again, a shower that went from freezing to scalding. From the bitching of the *Häftlinge* from Majdanek and Gleiwitz, I realized that every single camp had the same design: to kill *Untermenschen* by inches.

When we came out of the showers they lined us up for a "selection." I held my breath as Hubert threw out his chest and summoned his last reserves of strength, but they shoved him among the *Muselmänner*, or rather, the super-*Muselmänner*. There were tears in my eyes as I watched him totter away. My puny chest was filled with whimpers of protest, and somewhere in my numb brain I felt the urge to go after him. But I knew that opening my mouth or running after Hubert would just get me killed, too. So, I stood silent like a good *Untermensch*.

I had helped Hubert to the limit of my endurance, when I could barely stand myself, and it hadn't been enough. The *boches* had pressed the last drop of blood and sweat from my friend, and now they were going to fertilize some cabbage field with his ashes. For the first time I grasped the hell of watching family, loved ones, trudge toward Birkenau's belching chimneys. As we were being led into this new camp, I had seen a brick chimney. I knew the SS had shut down the Auschwitz crematoriums in November. Were they still burning here? I couldn't assume they weren't. That was hope, and the longer I treaded in striped "pajamas," the more I believed hope was a cancer.

Dressed now in light summer "pajamas" and felt slippers, we were herded through the snow to a large frame building. The sign at the door read Kino, the German word for "cinema." We sat down on rows of wooden benches. To keep myself from dwelling on Hubert, I studied the faces of the men around me. Oh, we were a sorry lot. Even the green triangles who had left Auschwitz in much better shape than the rest of us were now faint shadows. We had survived, but it was a hollow victory. We were still breathing as slaves behind the barbed wire that encircled a camp called Dora, and me without my *vieille noix* ("Old Nut") to share my suffering with.

Barrels of soup were brought in. It was the first warm food we had received in two weeks. As we slurped up the soup, rumors circulated that there was an underground factory in the tunnel and that only those who were craftsmen in metalworking would be kept in the camp. The hell if I was going to go on another Nazi joy ride, so when the SS asked, I told them I was an electrician.

PART IV
DORA

CHAPTER 18

"*Links, zwei, drei, vier; Vordermann und Seitenrichtung!*" (Left, two, three, four; straighten up front and side!) the *Kapo* called off. After a week in quarantine, I tottered more than marched down the hill that I had climbed with Hubert. Near the camp's gate, a potpourri of musicians from different camps struggled to play harmoniously. The virtuosos in Monowitz had spoiled my ears. Unfortunately, most of them had arrived here as corpses. The kettledrum's beating still echoed in my ears when I reached the bottom of the hill.

We followed the *Kapo* along the train tracks to the main tunnel. About a hundred yards away was a sister tunnel that also had tracks coming out of it. A maze of "blast walls"—large blocks of concrete—were positioned in front of both entrances. They were designed to protect the factory inside the tunnel from the shrapnel and conflagration of Allied air raids. These heavy obstacles had to be removed every time a train brought in supplies.

A pleasant rush of warm air greeted us as we marched under the canopy of camouflaged netting and into the main tunnel. Boxcars with signs reading ACHTUNG SPRENGSTOFF! (Beware of Explosives!) blocked our path. "*Zieht die Bäuche ein!*" (Pull in your stomachs!) joked the *Kapo*.

Hell, he was the only one who needed to suck in his belly. I hugged the tunnel wall and squeezed by the freight. In front of me were flat cars loaded with the aluminum hulls that had so intrigued me when I arrived. These sixty-five foot hulls were fully assembled, making them look like metal dirigibles. I felt as if I had stepped into a Jules Verne novel. Did the Nazis want to send us "undesirables" into space, using our ashes to turn the moon into one big cabbage patch? On racks near the flatcars sat the guts of these vessels, intricately contorted assemblages of pipes, hoses, sphere-shaped tanks, and valves. From my physics studies I knew that these were jet propulsion engines. Whatever their purpose, I thought, these metal dirigibles must be drastically important to the Nazis for them to be built in such an elaborate underground factory.

A row of hanging lights stretched down the tunnel as far as I could see. The *Kapo* led us past a series of immense transverse tunnels set up as workshops. The bursting of explosive rivets that came from the workshop assembling the hulls sounded like Bastille Day fireworks. I was thankful the *boches* hadn't drafted me as a riveter. No amount of cotton could save one's eardrums from sixteen hours of that racket. From other workshops came the shrieking of lathes, the hissing of paint guns, and the rattling of milling machines. We passed ten tunnels before we came to the relative calm of the electricians' shop.

Unlike the *Elektriker Kommando* in Auschwitz, there was no barrage of questions from the Kapo, no impromptu test of my knowledge and skill. I was just assigned to a workbench and given a color-coded schematic. My job was to assemble and mount switches, gages, and instruments on panels of Winidur, a German PVC. It was all relatively new to me, but to my own astonishment and relief I managed well. I shouldn't have been that surprised. As a kid I took toys apart to see what made them tick, and spent hours in my room with my Erector set. In high school, physics had been my favorite subject, while at home I happily did all the electrical repairs. In Buna I watched the electricians, asked the right questions, and became familiar with the German names for their tools and their symbols for volts, amps, and ohms. In the pipe shop, I had even helped solder circuit boards subcontracted by some unknown German company. Now, thankfully, it was all paying off.

As the days went by I realized how enormous and elaborate the underground plant was. The two main tunnels, which were about a mile long, worked as assembly lines fed by a total of forty-six tunnel workshops. If the top of the Kohnstein hill were shaved off, the plant would look like a ladder. The two German *Häftlinge* who became my mentors at the workshop told me the names of the strange contraptions we were building: the V-1 and V-2 rockets. Both in their late twenties, Bruno and Siegfried had been *Luftwaffe* technicians working at Peenemünde, which was on an island in the Baltic sea, where the Nazis created and first tested the rockets. When the island became a target for Allied bombers, the Germans moved the construction of the V-1s and V-2s to Dora, which had been a gypsum mine.

While working in Peenemünde, Bruno and Siegfried carried on affairs with a couple of Danish cuties. When their wives got wise to their infidelities, they went straight to the Gestapo and the two men were stripped of their uniforms and stuffed into "pajamas."

"That was a dirty trick those bitches pulled on you," I said, wanting to sound sympathetic. "Just because they were jealous?"

Bruno raised his bushy eyebrows. "No, because we were associating with the enemy. Our wives are good Nazis."

"Basically, they did us a favor," Siegfried laughed. "We're much safer in this tunnel."

From them I learned how lethal and intricate those futuristic-looking weapons were. The V-1s carried 551 pounds of explosives, but they weren't effective because their accuracy depended solely on the direction and speed of the wind, which made the V-1 an easy target for a fast fighter plane.

The V-2s were a different matter. These long-range missiles flew at twice the speed of sound, carried over two thousand pounds of explosives, and had guidance systems. With a sarcastic smirk, Bruno informed me that "the god with the moustache" had promised that the rockets would turn the tide of the war. Even if Bruno had his doubts, I was determined to do all I could to ensure that "the god with a moustache" couldn't keep his promise.

The slightest shock would render the precision instruments I installed in the electric circuits useless, and I saw to it that they got it good. Who could accuse me of sabotage? There was no way to prove I was responsible because it couldn't be detected until the rocket was fired. They would have to write it off as a manufacturing defect. I daydreamed that some of the V-2s might errantly explode over Berlin. Finally I was able to do real damage to the Nazi war machine—at least that was what I told myself.

One day the SS discovered sabotage in one of the shops. They didn't bother with an investigation. They simply hung the whole *Kommando*, *Kapo* and all. Fifty men were tethered to a rail that was then hoisted into the air by a crane used to lift the V-2s. They were left hanging near the tunnel entrance as a reminder to us to be good little slaves. Passing before those dangling bodies—that row of purple faces with protruding eyes and tongues—didn't deter me from my sabotage. It just gave me more fuel to be relentless in my mission.

After a sixteen-hour shift, climbing the hill back up to the camp strained the limits of my endurance. I would stumble along that frozen trail with heavy legs, and many times my heart would palpitate, then seemingly stop beating. I'd put my hand to my chest and wouldn't feel a thing. I would become dizzy. Everything in front of me would begin to fade. And just when I would think I was dying, my heart sparked and I would have enough energy to drag myself to my bunk, where I wondered in astonishment how I had held out for another day. Luckily there were times we stayed in the tunnel for a couple days straight, taking catnaps at our benches or wherever it was comfortable. That was okay with me. I was safe from the Allied bombs, and I didn't have to drag my ass up and down that damn trail.

Our *Blockälteste*, Ludwig, a green triangle from Hanover, was a vile dog. He had been dismissed from his teaching job for clobbering his pupils and had been locked up for printing phony money.

Having been wounded on the Western front during the First World War, Ludwig was a fanatic Francophobe and picked only those who spoke French for his daily trouncings. In his sadistic rages he even beat a few *Muselmänner* to death. After I found myself under his lash, I joined a group determined to kill him.

"This must look like a natural death or the SS are going to hang the whole *Block*," I told them. "I'm not going to die because of that prick. The end of this war is too close."

From the tunnel I smuggled a small container of glass cleaning fluid, a mixture of ether and detergent. The following night, two Belgians, a Fleming and a Walloon, whose ethnic feuding was centuries old, started a noisy, diversionary fight at the piss pails. Once the night watchman and the *Stubendienst* were distracted, five of our most able-bodied cohorts charged into Ludwig's private quarters while I stood lookout. They pinned him down and covered his face with a rag soaked with my lethal contraband. After his body went limp, they opened the window, and I rushed over to separate the Belgians. In the morning, Ludwig looked very peaceful.

♦ ♦ ♦

For lunch the Nazis delivered an infusion of roasted acorns that they had the gall to call coffee. In my workshop I was assigned the lucky task of returning the empty container. There was nothing in the bottom except a few drops and the grounds, which had no nutritional value but appeased my stomach for a while. One day after delivering the container I went to the toilet and found a *Häftling* struggling on the plumbing of one of the bowls. He was lying on his stomach, swearing in French and banging his tools. I coughed and the fellow rolled onto his back. I stared at him astounded. It was Marius, the Corsican plumber who befriended me in Drancy. He looked me over in disbelief, then jumped up and hugged me, blowing his trademark garlic breath in my face.

"Boy, you look like shit!"

He didn't have to rub it in. I knew that without the assistance of a mirror. "Well, you're the expert on shit. You look pretty good in 'pajamas.'" He had hardly changed. "How long have you been here?"

"About a year. Before that I was in Compiègne."

Compiègne was a camp in northern France, by the Marne River. "I heard that camp was only housing the so-called 'enemy aliens.'"

"Well, there are two camps," Marius said. "Remember that couple from Honduras with the twins? They put them in that camp and dumped me in the political one. I repaired the plumbing in both. The bastards liked my work so much they sent me here."

"In what tunnel is your shop?" I asked.

"I'm all over this place, wherever I'm needed. I even have those bastards and some of the civilian workers from Nordhausen bringing me their faucets and the like to repair. They slip me extra food."

That's how he got the garlic.

"Ciao, I have to get back. Look me up when you have a chance. I'm in the electric shop."

"You're an electrician? Good for you, boy. My trade has saved my ass."

It was encouraging to see someone from the train to Drancy alive and weathering the ordeal well. It made me think that someone else might have been lucky, too.

◆ ◆ ◆

"See if you can repair this," snapped my *Kapo*, Kristian Berg, a sea captain who was rumored to have killed four prostitutes in a Hamburg brothel.

I stopped tapping threads into Winidur, and he handed me a pressure gauge. My ingenuity had gotten me christened the "Doctor Fix-it" of our shop. This one was a cinch. The pressure gauge wasn't working because its tiny right-angle gearbox was jammed. Once I warmed up the grease inside, the bevel gears engaged smoothly.

Holding that gearbox in my hand I thought, if I had this in Auschwitz I could have been co-owner of a successful *Häftling* dental practice. When I was in the pipe shop in Buna, a dentist from Salonika, Greece, mentioned that if he had even the most primitive tools he could treat *Häftlinge* with toothaches during our lunch breaks. His words stuck with me, and after the first bombing raid I salvaged a bicycle and the speedometer cable from a burned-out car. In the pipe shop's supply room, I soldered a small drill bit to the speedometer cable, then attached the other end of the cable to the bike's dynamo. When someone pedaled, the drill bit whirled at a good speed. The dentist was pleased with my contraption and we went into business.

With me on the bike, the Greek drilled out cavities, then filled them with plaster we had "organized" from one of the construction sites. Our rate was one bowl of soup, which we split. Because the dentist could drill only on a bias, the drill bit would always slip off the tooth. This caused unendurable pain for the patient and the screams scared off business. With one of those pressure-gauge gearboxes the dentist would have been able to drill straight into the tooth. However, even with the gearbox it still would have been a short-lived venture because two weeks later my contraption was blasted to bits along with the shop in the second air raid.

◆ ◆ ◆

At dawn, after a sleepless night thanks to the bed bugs and the cramps in my stringy calves, I would walk around the camp looking in the moss for acorns that the squirrels had missed. A pocketful could last me the whole day. Many mornings the SS had no bread for us to eat because of the Allied bombings of their trains. They substituted boiled rotten potatoes, but those earth apples lasted only a few days. So there were many days I went to work with my stomach running on empty. One March morning I was hunting for acorns along the barbed-wire fence. The snow had melted and a

light breeze shook the branches of the oak and pine trees. Somewhere above me a nightingale was singing. In the valley, the morning light reflecting on the roofs and medieval towers of the town of
Nordhausen created a storybook illustration. Stopping at the barred
front gate, I couldn't help but think of the commencement speech
that the principal of my high school had given two long years ago.
"Graduates, you are the elite of our youth and now all doors are
open to you."

Damn dirty liar.

The reveille bell sounded and the nightingale shot out of the
pines. I hurried back to my *Block*, where I found a table piled high
with loaves of bread. To my disbelief, each of us got a whole loaf,
which normally would have been rationed for six. Later I learned
that the shipment was intended for a camp that had already been
liberated by the Americans. I went to work with a lighter heart,
wolfishly devouring half of my bread on the way down the trail.
With a full belly I could see myself witnessing American tanks
smashing through those gates and making my principal's words
come true.

When I reached my workbench, I put the other half of the loaf
in a drawer. An hour later I couldn't resist temptation. I cut the
bread into thin slices with a coping saw and made my dream of
eating toast come true by putting the slices on my electric soldering
iron. When they brought the coffee, it was already cold. Why not
heat it the same way, I thought? I took the iron and dipped it into
the liquid. The sudden cooling cracked the filament. A sickening
feeling sank into my gut. Since I was the one responsible for my
tools, the *boche* could accuse me of sabotage. What was I going to
do? I took the iron apart in hope of repairing it. My *Kapo*, Kristian,
came up and watched over my shoulder.

*"Wenn det heute Abend nicht geht, kriegste fünf und zwanzig, auf'n
Arsch."* (If that isn't in working order by this evening, you'll get
twenty-five on your ass.)

He knew as well as I that it would be impossible to repair the
iron. I couldn't let a day that had begun so well turn completely

sour. I came up with a scheme. The tool room clerk inspected our tools when we returned them, and he would immediately know that mine was broken, but he wouldn't be able to if I returned it hot.

I went to the tool room with a metal chit that had my workbench number stamped on it, and got an identical *Löteisen* (soldering iron). Back at my workbench I used the good iron to heat up the broken one. A short while later, holding my breath, I turned in the broken soldering iron. Burning himself on it, the clerk swore and threw the chit at my head. I ducked and with a smile picked it off the floor.

◆ ◆ ◆

Whenever I could I collected the discarded cigarette butts of the civilian plant workers for my own smoking pleasure. To ensure I didn't burn my fingers trying to puff out the last slivers of tobacco, I made a sharp-looking cigarette holder from scrap electronic parts. A German technician took a fancy to it and bought it for a pack of cigarettes that I in turn swapped for a few bowls of soup. Soon I had a thriving business, and I even gained weight from the extra soup.

One day I decided to make myself a good luck charm, a heart made out of Winidur. As I was working on it, a hand grabbed the heart and another my right ear. A Luftwaffe major, whom I had neglected to notice, led me toward the loft where Kristian had his desk. I didn't dare stumble as the officer climbed the stairs two at a time or my ear would have been upstairs without me. Seeing the officer, Kristian jumped to attention with his cap at the seam of his trousers.

The major threw the heart on his desk. Kristian stared at my primitive jewelry while I bowed my head in feigned contrition. His powerful punch sent me flying across the deck, and I thought my head was going to snap off my neck. I played possum, bracing myself for a barrage of kicks, but both Germans were satisfied with the results of the right cross. The major left to continue his inspection and Kristian returned to his desk. "Back to work, you asshole!" he yelled.

Rubbing my jaw and split lip, I slowly picked myself up and slinked down the stairs. Later, Kristian came to my bench and looked over my shoulder. "How's your jaw? Nothing broken?"

"You have a hell of a fist," I said.

"That was for your stupidity. You're lucky I held back. If it had been SS, I would've bruised my knuckles and sent you to your ancestors toothless."

"Well, thanks." I painfully smiled

"No more cigarette holders, you idiot."

"You knew?"

"I got smokes and you got some. No civilian would dare talk to you without asking me first. By the way, whose initials are on the heart?"

"My mother's."

"Here, go hide your bad luck charm."

Kristian returned to his desk. I squeezed the heart between my hands. Even the slightest act of kindness seemed like a hallucination. For a green triangle, Kristian was more decent than I could have hoped for, and I had my high school German teacher to thank for it. Mr. Claudel, who hailed from Alsace, demanded that we write our assignments using an old German alphabet. Everyone in the class despised him for it. Not only were the letters of this alphabet extremely hard to replicate, but it was fast becoming obsolete. Thankfully I had been an obedient student. Kristian, besides being very impressed, appreciated that a non-German made the effort to fill out reports using this elaborate alphabet. In any other circumstance it would have been comical how one could take advantage of a German's nationalistic vanity.

◆ ◆ ◆

One morning, my *Kommando* arrived at the plant to find a crate, almost seven feet high and sitting on a dolly, blocking the entrance to our shop.

"What the hell is this?" Kristian swore.

He tried to push it aside, but it wouldn't budge. It took five *Häftlinge* to finally move it out of the way. Kristian fetched an engineer, who looked over the invoice glued to the crate. The night shift had screwed up and it would be our job to deliver the crate to the right location. Kristian rounded up six French *Häftlinge*, then turned to me.

"Since you speak both French and German, you're in charge."

Three *Häftlinge* manned the rope that was attached to the four-wheel dolly and the rest of us got on either side of the crate to keep it steady.

"Don't leave yet," Kristian ordered. "You need an overseer, or whatever his title is, to accompany you."

Our watchdog turned out to be a fifteen-year-old Hitler Youth, who was decked out in a brown shirt, swastika armband, and short pants, and who had an Italian carbine slung over his shoulder. Showering us with insults as we struggled with our load, he led us down the tunnel farther than I had ever gone before. We came to a locked gate guarded by a *Landswehr*, an elderly reservist. Germany was sure scraping the bottom of the barrel to keep its war machine sputtering along. The Hitler Youth swaggered up and ordered the old man to open the gate. The guard didn't appreciate the kid's cocky tone, but did as he was told.

We entered a ballbearing factory that none of us *Häftlinge* knew existed. One of the dolly's wheels jammed into the railroad track. With the kid swearing and kicking at us, we struggled to dislodge it. We attempted to lift the dolly, but it wouldn't budge, and this sent the Hitler Youth into a rage. His tantrum attracted two young secretaries dressed in flowery print dresses. The pair stared aghast at the seven of us. Obviously they didn't know such creatures existed on the other side of the gate. The Hitler Youth decided to show off for them, pounding us with the stock of his gun.

"*Genug! So behandelt man nicht Hunde!*" (Enough! You don't treat dogs that way!) one of the girls screamed.

The shithead turned his attention to the girls, which gave us a momentary reprieve from his adolescent brutality. "Shut up, you whore! They're the enemy!"

The girls fled with tears in their eyes. Reluctantly, the Hitler Youth allowed me to go search for something that would help free the dolly. When I returned with a length of pipe and a brick, the kid and a middle-aged civilian in a suit were screaming at each other. The secretaries watched from a distance.

"I'm in charge here, you snotty brat!" The civilian barked as he pointed to the swastika button on his lapel. "I was a Party member before you were born."

The kid flipped the bayonet out from under the barrel of his gun and pointed it at the man, who continued spewing insults. Neither one of them was willing to lose face. The other *Häftlinge* were cowering behind the crate. If this kept escalating, I was certain the brat would pull the trigger and mow us all down. I took a breath and stepped up to the screaming jackals.

"Could you two move a little so we can free this?" I asked in German.

Surprisingly they stepped to the side but didn't stop arguing. If it hadn't been for the gun, the whole thing would have been farcical. I slid the pipe under the dolly and used the brick as a fulcrum.

"*Dèmarez tout le monde pousse quand je souslève, pour qu' on puisse s'enaller*" (Everybody push when I lift, so we can get out of here), I ordered my crew.

But freeing the dolly had no affect on the German hotheads. I came up with an idea. I took off my cap and stood at attention. Using my best Berlin slang, I respectfully addressed the brainwashed little creep. "*Herr Wachtmeister, wo sollen wir die Kiste abladen?*" (Sir watchmaster, where should we unload the box?)

They stopped arguing and looked at me surprised. My Berlin dialect had hit them like a bucket of ice water. I'm sure they were asking themselves how this cockroach could be speaking their language. The civilian pointed to a corner. The kid lowered his gun and without a word followed us as we unloaded the crate.

The civilian called me over and pulled a half a pack of cigarettes out of his shirt pocket. "Thank you. Distribute those to your men."

I slipped one to each of my crew and kept the rest for myself. After all, I was the big shot who had saved the day.

The Hitler Youth kept quiet as he led us back to the shop. He and I reported to Kristian.

"No problems?" Kristian asked.

"Everything went smoothly," I said.

The brat nodded in agreement.

Back at my bench, I thought about the stunned looks those two secretaries gave us. I wondered, as I did when I stared at the bullet hole in the railroad worker's forehead, how much the civilian population really knew about the concentration camps. How were they going to feel when they found out the whole truth? They all knew that Jews had been rounded up, but what would they say when they learned how many cement bags their ashes had filled?

♦ ♦ ♦

With the Allies rolling farther into Germany, not a day passed without an air raid. Nordhausen was constantly encircled in a red halo. The fire brigades were no match for the firestorms caused by the bombings. The civilian workers would come into the tunnel coated with black soot and dust, and you could see the demoralization in their eyes. I could also see it in the eyes of the SS and, as in Auschwitz when the Red Army was edging closer, our fate became my overriding fear. Soon there would be no place the Nazis could keep us. Were they planning to kill us all, eradicate the witnesses to what had to be the crime of the century, or would we wake up one morning to find that they had stole away in the night?

CHAPTER 19

One fine April morning we started out for work as usual, but we were halted half way down the hill. From the edge of the trail I could see a waiting train and the guards beginning to cram *Häftlinge* into the boxcars. I knew there was no way the Germans had any provisions or water for us on that train. Those boxcars were our coffins.

I heard the roar of an airplane and turned to see a fighter with a white star on the side strafing the entrance of the tunnel. I could clearly see the American pilot as the plane zipped by. Our guards hit the ground. The American looped back, and in a steep dive dropped the bomb strapped to the belly of his plane. It exploded on the tracks between the entrance and the train. The Nazis stayed prone with their hands clasped over their head and their weapons lying next to them as the American plane circled above us like a hawk. I looked at the cowards and thought how easy it would be to overwhelm them if a few of us would just grab their guns.

Two *Häftlinge* ran toward the camp, disappearing over a hill of bulldozed earth. I ran after them. This is the only chance I have to be left behind, I thought, zigzagging up the slope so I wouldn't be an easy target if there was a guard who wasn't cowering.

Back in the camp, I hid in an empty *Block*. The fighter could be scouting for an advancing column of American tanks. Was freedom only a few hours away? My wait lasted until the next morning, when I was awakened not by the sound of tanks crashing the camp gate but by dogs barking. The Nazis rousted us strays and marched us down the trail. Now at least I was prepared for the trip. Hidden in my blanket were three containers filled with water that I had scrounged during the night. Having slept alone in that *Block*, I was surprised to see that there were about a thousand of us filing into twenty cattle cars. Some of the men probably had come straight from their shift in the tunnel. With only forty of us in the car, at least I would be comfortable for the journey to the next "Pitchi Poi."

Once the train started rolling it didn't stop until the next morning, coming to a halt in the middle of pine trees and heath. Surprisingly, they let us out of the cars to walk about. There was smoldering brush on either side of us. I could see down the track the skeletal remains of a bridge. We had missed being on the primary target by a couple of hours. I picked up from the guards' conversations that they were waiting for orders as to where to deliver us. Squatting to relieve myself, I spotted some wild onions. They went down like fire into my empty belly. Luckily I found some young, tender dandelions to soothe the burning. The SS brewed coffee and ate by a campfire while we watched with dripping tongues. We'd had nothing to eat for the last forty-eight hours.

The SS got their orders and we started off on foot. We soon reached a village of prosperous-looking dwellings. Everywhere we heard cattle, chickens, and pigs. A rooster crowed from its perch on the fence of a white farmhouse with a red tile roof as we went by. I couldn't believe it. Even German farm animals were Nazis, teasing and torturing our ravenous stomachs. It had to be a Sunday, for people were coming out of the church. They were all big and fat, clean and well dressed. They turned their backs when we passed by or spat with disgust. Others let loose their dogs or chased us with pitchforks when we tried to drink from their pumps. I guess "Love thy neighbor" must have been ripped out of their Bibles. They couldn't give a damn how many cement bags the ashes of *Häftlinge* had filled.

As night fell we followed a road that ascended the Harz Mountains. Multicolored explosions lit the western horizon, and little silvery birds passed in front of the moon. Again we were fleeing before our liberators and marking our trail with corpses. I had to escape now if I was going to witness the Nazis' demise. We reached a forested plateau, but with the dogs at our heels there was no chance to make a break. Then the road zigzagged downward and at each bend there was a culvert. From the road, all the culverts seemed to have plenty of mud that I could burrow myself into. I checked behind me. The SS and their dogs were at the end of our column.

At the next bend I jumped into the culvert, but instead of landing in mud I kept falling. My shithouse luck had picked a pipe that was on an extremely steep incline. Pressing my knees and elbows against the slimy walls, I struggled to break my fall. It was hopeless. I couldn't get a grip anywhere. I shot out the other end and landed flat on my back in a muddy ditch. I stood up scraped and dripping wet, only to find the head of the column coming around the bend. There was nothing to do but fall back in line.

When we reached the valley below, they marched us across desolate grazing land to a waiting train sitting on a rusty track overgrown by weeds. I could tell that the march over the mountain had thinned our ranks considerably because we had even more room in the cars. They left the door to our car open, and sometimes there would be a guard sitting there and sometimes there wouldn't. The SS at Auschwitz would never have such an inconsistent routine. Things were so desperate and chaotic for the Germans that they were probably wishing we would all jump out of the train and die.

The effects of the Allied bombing raids were evident everywhere. Charred remains of buildings and military equipment dotted the landscape like so many funeral pyres. A perfect postcard to send to the Allied generals. Problem was, I didn't have a camera or a stamp and I was riding on a high-priority target for their bombers. There were bomb craters on both sides of the track. The train would roll for miles, then stop for hours as workmen fixed the mangled tracks ahead. When the rails were repaired they were still far from being sound.

While the train sat idle one afternoon, I stepped over to our guard who was sitting in the doorway with a copy of *Der Stürmer* and read over his shoulder. The bold headline gave me a shock: "Roosevelt Tot."

Roosevelt was dead. I slumped down in a corner, crying. I feared his death would alter the outcome of the war, or at least prolong it. At this point every minute counted for a *Muselmann*.

The train began to move slowly. Wheels squealing, our car wavered on the poorly repaired track. We were approaching the outskirts of a town when air raid sirens started to wail. The train lurched forward at full throttle in the engineer's attempt to escape harm's way. He was taking a hell of a chance on those unstable rails. Everyone in the car either plastered themselves against the walls or dropped to the floor as the train rocked and bounced through a burned-out train station. The guard's newspaper scattered, then was sucked out the open door. I slid across the floor, expecting us to derail at any moment, but by some miracle the track got smoother and we hurtled onward to "Pitchi Poi."

That night a young Romanian who was talking to himself woke me.

"Let me sleep," I grumbled.

He looked at me with dull eyes and continued to mutter. Poor bastard, he's out of his mind. Someone jostled him and he leapt to his feet howling like a rabid beast. The other man fell over backwards and the Romanian grabbed him by the throat. Foolishly I tried to separate them, and the Romanian came after me with a homemade knife. I grabbed his arm, but he twisted away. I felt a sharp sting at the nape of my neck. I knocked the Romanian over. Seeing the knife still in his hand, I jumped on top of him and kneeled on his arm. He tried to bite me, so I jammed my other knee into his neck. I could feel blood streaming down my back as he scratched and hit me with his free arm. I sank my knee into his throat. Gasping for air, the Romanian finally let go of the knife. With my hand over the gash in my neck I rolled off him, exhausted. One of the *Häftlinge* circling us picked up the knife and threw it out of the car. A few others flung the Romanian out after it.

PART V

RAVENSBRÜCK

CHAPTER 20

The loss of blood from the knife wound had debilitated me. A malnutritioned man needs to spill only a few drops to render him a useless shell. I was catatonic for the rest of our train ride. We could have traveled days, weeks, or maybe only hours, before I was overwhelmed by sunlight. I found myself staggering behind a procession of *Muselmänner* on a dirt road leading to a camp called Ravensbrück. Once we were all inside, the guards locked the gate and stayed on the other side of the wire. I stumbled into a *Block* and passed out.

When I awoke I was shocked to find myself not in the lowest tier of a bunk but in a normal bed. The whole *Block* was filled with single beds. Still weak and woozy, I slowly sat up. Other than the dandelions and wild onions, I'd had nothing to eat for five days. I asked the *Muselmann* in the bed next to me if the *boches* had passed out any rations. He didn't acknowledge me. He was on his way out, and it looked like the rest of the men in the *Block* were heading in the same direction. I dragged myself outside. There was barely a soul in the yard, and the *Häftlinge* who were milling about seemed to have the same goal I did: finding something to eat. Young dandelions were sprouting around the *Blocks* and I filled my belly with them.

Back on my bed, I put my hand on my neck. My scabbed-over wound was swollen and hot to the touch. I scrounged around the *Block* for something to use as disinfectant. To my surprise I found dirty, ragged dresses, skirts, and blouses. Obviously. Ravensbrück had been a women's camp. I ventured into another *Block*. Most of the *Häftlinge* were lying motionless, and the few healthy ones were clowning with the women's clothing that they had discovered. I came across the remnants of a make-up kit that must have belonged to the *Blokowa*. There was some toilet paper and a few drops of the famous German 4711 cologne in a lipstick-smeared bottle.

Dizzy from the slight exertion, I crawled back into my bed with a scarf of cologne-soaked toilet paper around my neck and blacked out. I spent close to the next four days prone in that bed. The Nazis didn't bother us, which was fine except that they also didn't feed us. They also didn't pick up the corpses, which made the camp a petri dish for an epidemic.

A rumor shot through my *Block* that Red Cross packages had arrived for us. This made me sit up. "*C'est une blague!*" (It's a joke!)

I laid back down and shut my eyes. A Parisian who was wearing a Greek mariner's cap awakened me. Where he scrounged up that damn cap I will never know. "Get up. I need a partner to get a package. We have to split them up."

I rolled onto my side and said, "Another joke? Leave me alone. I'm not getting up unless it's absolutely necessary."

He kept on insisting, but it wasn't until other *Häftlinge* came in holding boxes with red crosses on them that I followed my "partner" outside. What a pair we made as we crossed the yard, him with his fishing cap and me with my flowing scarf of toilet paper. I followed him into a *Block* and was dumbfounded by the stacks of Red Cross boxes towering in front of us. With a contingent of German soldiers observing, members of the International Red Cross had us sign a ledger, then handed us each one of the cardboard boxes. A GIFT FROM THE AMERICAN PEOPLE was stenciled across the top. In German, *Gift* is "poison." It took a lot of convincing to get some of the *Häftlinge* in my *Block* to believe that the boxes weren't filled with Zyklon B, the poison used in the Auschwitz gas chambers.

Examining our treasure at my bedside, my partner insisted we open all the tins at once and divide the contents. I told him he was an idiot. We had no means of keeping the food from spoiling. Either we would have to stuff ourselves or watch it rot.

"Let's split a tin."

"No."

"Okay, you have the Spam, and I'll eat those sardines."

The fool wouldn't hear of it, but after opening a couple of cans he yielded to my logic. I unwrapped a chocolate bar designed for U.S. paratroopers in the field. The label warned in English to consume only a small section a day because it was spiked with special drugs and vitamins. I dropped into a deep sleep after I ate some of the Spam and a small chunk of the chocolate bar.

I awoke to a familiar scene. All around me were dead and dying. Our long starvation had caused many of my comrades to go at their food so voraciously that they had eaten themselves to death. Since most couldn't read English, the chocolate bar became the *coup de grace*. Everywhere in the camp *Häftlinge* were losing their guts, some literally. There were some who were actually struggling to push their protruding intestines back inside. I opened one of the packs of Lucky Strike included with our tins of food, and blew the smoke of the American cigarette through my nose to mask the stench. Diarrhea would be a lethal scourge for days. Many men's last thought had to be that their Red Cross package was a German *Gift*.

All the *Häftlinge* in Ravensbrück came from camps that had fallen to the Allies. Some of these men didn't have triangles, others had only numbers, and most didn't have a tattoo on their left arm. Outside the wire stood the guards from these different camps, a mix of SS and their mercenaries. These mercenaries were real bastards. With truncheon, rifle butt, jackboot, or fist, they were much more sadistic dealing out punishment than the *boches*. They had to prove themselves to earn their pay and the favor of their masters, but they also seemed to get an orgasm from it.. With Ravensbrück north of Berlin, it would be Soviet troops who would burst through the gate, and there was no doubt what they would do to those mercenaries, since the majority of them came from Ukraine, Hungary, and the Baltic states. I and many of my fellow *Häftlinge* believed we were entitled to front-row seats for that bloodletting.

Having no idea when we would be liberated, and with the Nazis not feeding us, that Red Cross food became treasures worth killing for. With safety in numbers, I talked my moron partner into banding with four fellow Frenchmen from Dora. I forged a true friendship with two in the group, Jean and Michel. They were in their twenties and single—construction workers from a small town in northern France—and they had been sent to Germany in a contingent of forced laborers. In an agreement between the Nazis and the Vichy government, they were classified as volunteers. For minor infractions like tardiness, absence without a medical excuse, or drunkenness, these "volunteers" would find themselves incarcerated in camps as black triangles. Because they were new arrivals in Dora, Jean and Michel were in better shape than the rest of us, and they would have been able to fight off any thief, but thankfully it never came to that. I valued Jean and Michel for their common sense and street smarts, and they were dependent on me because their German was limited to a couple basic phrases.

There were moments, sometimes, while we heated our food at one of the campfires in the yard or when, perched like swallows over the shit trench, the six of us found the strength to be optimistic and plan for the future. But planning brought on apprehensions about what we would find or not find when we arrived home. Since I had given the Nazis a false name, I wasn't concerned about the Gestapo harassing or arresting my mother or father. It was the errant bomb or bullet that troubled me. I knew through the POWs in Auschwitz that Allied troops had invaded southern France shortly after D-Day. But, as strange as it might sound, I was more concerned about how angry my parents would be with me for being dumb enough to get arrested and giving them over a year of grief.

The knife wound in my neck had gotten infected, and the egg-sized boil was affecting my hearing. It was unfortunate that the knife had been thrown out of the train along with the Romanian because I could have used it to lance the abscess. The camp's infirmary was locked up. The doctor had left with the women *Häftlinge*. I had to find Martin, a French Canadian POW who had come with us from Dora. He was a stocky blonde from Vancouver who had driven an ambulance before becoming a paratrooper medic. The Germans had transferred him to Dora after his third escape attempt from a Stalag. Martin was also a homosexual with an insatiable sexual appetite. At Dora, he had a connection with a cook who provided him with boiled potatoes, and his many partners stuffed themselves with those morsels while he stuffed them.

"It will take four guys to hold me down," I informed him when he propositioned me.

"That would ruin our romantic privacy," he laughed.

He had already tried to seduce half of Ravensbrück, so I had no trouble finding him.

"That boil looks mean," he told me. "It needs immediate attention."

Since the guards posed no obstacle, Martin and I walked over to the HKB, pried open a window, and slithered inside. Lucky for me, the infirmary wasn't completely cleaned out. Martin found a scalpel and some rubbing alcohol, and with one deft stroke he opened the boil, sending green pus shooting everywhere.

"Boy, that thing would've killed you if it had gone to your brain," he said as he pressed and squeezed the poison out. He rolled strips of toilet paper around my neck.

"What's your fee, doctor?" I joked.

"That's all right, I won't take it out in trade. You look like a young priest with that collar around your neck. Not my taste."

Ironic that it was religion, or the appearance of religion, that saved my ass this time.

◆ ◆ ◆

When the old men of the *Landsturm* replaced our SS guards, rumors flew.

"They're fighting in Berlin."

"Berlin has fallen."

"Hitler is dead."

"The Russians will be here by morning."

The red-starred fighter planes strafing barges on a nearby canal and the continuous flood of German refugees streaming by the camp gave some credence to the hearsay. The sounds of fierce battle delivered by the eastern winds made me ask if the heavy cannons I heard could be the same as those I heard four months ago in Monowitz. Over the last tin of Spam I told Michel and Jean how I feared that, even with defeat imminent, the *boches* would herd us once again on a death march. With a wink, Jean assured me not to fret.

One day the Nazis ordered all the Jews to report to the *Block* where we had received our food packages. Word was that the Red Cross was going to transfer them to the neutral country of Sweden. I was shocked to see *Häftlinge* rush over. How could they be that gullible after all the Nazis' deceit? Had these fellows gotten the wrong head circumcised? Hadn't they learned anything? In my deadened heart, I felt this could be only a final, desperate attempt to exterminate what was left of "the Jewish problem." But there was something inside me that hoped they would soon be sleeping on Red Cross cots. Maybe somewhere Stella was getting the same offer of safe haven.

◆ ◆ ◆

"Come on, Jean," I said, leaning out of the attic.

Standing on a rickety chair, Jean reached for my outstretched hand.

"A little more. Come on, I got you. Yes, there you are."

Jean crawled past me as I pulled up the chair by the rope tied to its back. I handed it to Michel, then closed the hatch. I could still hear German commands and the shuffling of fellow *Häftlinge*. The *boches* were evacuating once again, and Jean and Michel had made sure that the six of us weren't going to be part of that flock of sheep. They had planned our escape well, finding a hiding place the day before where the dogs wouldn't be able to sniff us out and "organizing" enough water and food to last us at least two days.

Two hours later, we heard voices and the sound of footsteps in the yard. The Red Army so soon? I cautiously lifted the trap door and peered out. Our fellow "pajamas" were back. Curious and confused, the six of us came down from the musty attic and mingled with the others. The guards had turned them back because the road was choked with German refugees.

When the bell for assembly rang the next morning, the six of us moved quickly for our hiding place, but sitting on the *Block's* stoop were two *Landsturm* guards. We had no alternative but to follow the others out the gate. Where were these old men taking us? There couldn't be any camps in the sliver of land that the Nazis still held. Michel and Jean told me not to be concerned; with all the pandemonium there would be plenty of opportunities for escape.

The two-lane country road was so clogged with Germans and their horse-drawn carts that we stood more than walked. Going one way were young soldiers—cannon fodder pulled straight out of high school classrooms. It struck me that they appeared as cocky and brainwashed as that brown-shirted brat in Dora. Stupid boys playing with guns. We followed the refugees. There was no cockiness in their eyes. Many of them had stolen Slav land after the blitzkriegs, and now they were running scared from a vengeful enemy. Even back at Buna I heard German civilians fret about the retributions the Red Army might exact.

Residents of Ravensbrück village stood on the side of the road, watching the parade. These farmers were resigned to their fate. They couldn't afford to abandon their only valuable possession. A group of women with their children around them looked at us with genuine surprise. One said, *"Da sind ja Männer; wo sind den die Frauen?"* (These are men; where are the women?)

A four-year-old girl with blond braids tied off with blue ribbons waved at us. No one waved back, but one *Häftling* did lean toward her and smile. The girl held out her hand. "*Onkel, Bonbon?*" she begged.

He softy broke off a piece of paratrooper chocolate and the child grabbed it before her mother could pull her back.

A *Häftling* standing near him hissed, "You Nazi lover."

Others began punching and kicking him. Most of them I'm sure had lost their precious daughters, nieces, or sisters to the ovens. If it weren't for the intervention of the guards, the fool's benevolence would have cost him his life. There was no tolerance in our hearts for even the most innocent of Germans.

To move us faster, the guards led us onto a path that cut through a dense forest of firs and oaks with heavy underbrush. They marched us in small groups, each guarded by a *Landsturm* and a dog, and those mutts did the job of ten guards. The trail narrowed as it followed the bank of a small brook, and we were forced to walk single file. I was between Michel and Jean. We agreed that the time was ripe to make our move. When the trail took a sharp turn, the three of us jumped across the stream and threw ourselves flat among the tall ferns on the other side.

Our *Landsturm*, an old goat who was more concerned with keeping his porcelain pipe lit than doing his guard duties, came down the trail with his rifle catching on tree branches. He was oblivious to our disappearance. However, his guard dog sniffed the air, then sniffed our footprints on the bank. Michel, Jean, and I lay like corpses. It felt as if the dog were looking right at us. The guard whistled and the big beast pricked up his ears, dipped his tongue a few times in the clear water, and went off barking. More groups passed, and none of those dogs picked up our scent. We were safe among the ferns, but we knew it would be hours before we could make our next move.

It began to rain. Hail beat down on the leaves, but I had ears for nothing except the distant Soviet batteries. Ragged bunches of civilians came down the trail. Many stopped at the brook's bank to fill a pail or bottle. Even though they were terrified and on the run, we stayed flat: anyone fleeing from the Red Army was our enemy. As night fell, the traffic on the trail tapered off. I stood up and was greeted by the rain. I felt strange. I never had so much energy coursing through me. I was free. I was finally free, and I told myself that no man was ever going to take that away from me again.

Heading in the direction of the advancing Soviets, it took us the whole night to make our way through the forest. Toward morning we were at the woods' edge, staring out at broad fields of asparagus. Past the fields, on a road bordered with poplars, were retreating Nazi convoys. A brick barn with a tile roof stood about one hundred yards in front of us. We would never be able to cross that much open space without being spotted.

"If we have to spend the day here dripping wet, we will die of it for sure," said Michel. Luckily, we didn't have to wait long. The rain started coming down harder, reducing visibility. We dashed across the asparagus field and arrived safely at the side of the barn. There was a pile of potatoes, and I stuffed as many as I could into my pockets. We moved toward the barn's gate, but stopped when we heard women's voices and the crying of a child.

Horses were pawing the ground and noisily shaking their harnesses. We were ready to beat a retreat into the forest, when the sound of squeaking hinges made me look up. The hayloft door was flapping in the wind. There is no such thing as a hayloft without a ladder, I thought, and before I could say a word, Jean found one half-buried in the mud.

PART VI
WUSTROW

CHAPTER 21

The sweet smell of hay greeted us. A thick blanket of the loose fodder covered the loft's floor. We moved about carefully and whispered so as not to attract the attention of the people in the barn below. Through a skylight we could see the woods we had trekked through. A window gave us a partial view of a nearby lake and the small town that sat on its far bank. Michel discovered a padlocked trunk in a corner that we were convinced was full of warm, dry clothes, but unfortunately we couldn't break the lock.

We stretched out our exhausted, wet bodies in the hay and attended to an extremely important matter—sleep. When I woke up it was dark. My companions were still snoring. The echo of a commanding voice from below made me stiffen. Alarmed, I pressed my ear against the floorboards. *"Diese Scheune wird von der Armee besetzt. Alle Civilisten müssen raus."* (The army has taken over this barn. All civilians must leave.)

"But we are refugees from the east," an old woman pleaded.

"Alles raus, und schnell!" (Everyone out, and fast!)

Someone lit a lantern. Rays of light came through the gaps in the floor. I could see men and women reluctantly picking up their multicolored bundles and shuffling out. An elderly man led a team of draft horses out of the barn while cows mooed. Once they were gone, heavy, blue cigar smoke rose into the loft. Wehrmacht officers were squatting around a map. Couriers began to arrive with reports. The shattered German forces in the area were regrouping. I woke my friends.

"What do you want?" Michel demanded, his eyes still closed.

"Damn, my ribs hurt. What the hell have I been sleeping on?" Jean began to swear.

"Shh! Do you want to be caught by the *boches* down there? We're sitting above their command post."

Jean's eyes widened. Michel peered through the cracks. "Shit," he whispered. "I was hoping you were having a nightmare."

"What should we do?" I asked.

From beneath the hay Jean pulled out a bottle a wine. "Look what I've been lying on. Someone must've forgotten this during the harvest."

"Might as well get drunk. We're not going anywhere," Michel said.

Jean handed me the bottle. I forced the cork down the neck and took a swallow. My mouth puckered and beads of sweat broke on my forehead. The wine had turned to vinegar. Jean and Michel choked back laughter.

I was drawn to something one of the officers said and leaned my head against the floorboards. I couldn't believe my ears. Jean and Michel drew close. "This is no joke. This barn is in between the lines. We're right in the middle of this battle royal."

"What are the odds of picking such a shitty place to dry out?" Jean asked.

As the Nazis prepared for their last stand, we resigned ourselves to fate and washed down bites of raw potatoes with the spoiled wine. As tractors and cargo carriers pulled heavy cannons into position, and foxholes and trenches were being dug in the asparagus fields, I fell asleep with a familiar worry: would I survive through tomorrow?

The first Russian shells whistled over the barn around noon the following day. The officers below us screamed orders as their cannons came to life. The barn walls trembled, and large chunks of plaster broke from the bricks. I crawled over to the loft window. Spooked horses reared and stamped in a courtyard filled with Nazi vehicles, and a terrified ox and cow raced for the woods. The asparagus field was dotted with the white puffs of exploding mortar shells. Clutching their machine guns and Panzerfausts (antitank weapons), the *boches* waited for the Soviet troops gathered behind a hill. Red Army tanks would emerge over the crest, lob a blind salvo, then vanish. An immense column of black smoke rose from the town while the ripples from errant shells shivered the fire's reflection on the lake.

I slid back over to my friends, and we sat in a silent circle, our eyes darting toward each explosion. A blast disintegrated the far corner of the roof, and suddenly there was shiny silverware hanging from the rafters like icicles. My hip felt as if it were on fire, and I looked down to find that a fork had pierced the skin of my bony hip. Unscathed, Jean and Michel stared dumbfounded at the trousseau decorating the roof. I yanked the fork out of my hip. Blood was dripping from the prongs. I dropped my pants and poured the wine on the puncture holes. Michel pointed to the source of the projectiles: the padlocked trunk. The shell had split it open like a melon.

Another shell came screaming through the air. Instinctively I ducked. A thunderous roar erupted and I found myself tossed into the air. Gathering my wits, I realized that I was now bathed in sunlight. There was a gaping hole in the roof above me, and another in the loft floor in front of me. Stunned, Michel stared at the hole while Jean was on his knees rubbing his ass. The armor-piercing tank shell had spared us and exploded below on the stable's cobblestone floor.

More explosions ripped through the air. Overcome with panic, I could think of only one thing: I have got to get the hell out of here! I slid down a grain chute, hoping the shell had killed the Germans below. Lucky for me I was surrounded only by eviscerated cows. Nitrate fumes choked my throat. There was a little door that led out to the asparagus fields. I opened it a crack and saw a German soldier running toward me. I slammed the door and looked for a way to bolt it. A horseshoe was hanging on the wall. By the time I grabbed it, the Nazi was pushing the door open. I planted my weight against it, but it wasn't enough to allow me to drop the horseshoe through the eyebolts. The door blew open and I found myself sandwiched between the door and the stable wall. Oh, how I wished I hadn't come down from that loft.

The panting soldier flung the door closed and fell against it, inches away from me. His eyes would adjust to the stable's darkness in mere seconds. He took off his helmet and wiped the sweat from his brow. I slammed the horseshoe against his temple. To my relief, he dropped like a stone. I picked up his submachine gun. The weapon transformed me like a magic wand. I went from trembling fugitive slave to eager warrior.

I cracked the door open. The field was littered with Nazis corpses. Ten breathing *boches* still manned foxholes. I poked the gun's barrel out the door and pulled the trigger. As it barked, I realized what a foolish thing I was doing. I ducked into one of the pens, fully expecting the door to be shot to splinters, but there was no return fire. Puzzled, I peeked out a window and saw the remaining soldiers running toward the burning town. I was quite certain that it wasn't my hotheaded cowboy shooting, but the rumbling of the approaching Soviet tanks that had sent them scrambling. Still, I felt pretty proud. I had participated, I had made a contribution to the Allies. Yes, it was miniscule at best, but I, a *Häftling*, had made it.

With the shelling over, I slipped into the courtyard. Looking around, I realized this was no ordinary farm, but a country estate. The only things left of the Nazis were a few discarded guns, a couple of crates, and a two-wheel wagon with a horse dead in the harness. On the wagon was an enormous wheel of Swiss cheese. A dead German soldier was lying at the entrance of the courtyard. His boots looked like they might fit me, but the spray of bullets coming from four Soviet tanks kept me from retrieving them. There was no sense getting mistaken for the enemy, so I ducked back through the open stable doors.

Jean and Michel were crouched beside the German soldier.

Michel looked up at me. "We thought you ran away. Say, you have a machine gun."

"Did you shoot this one?" Jean asked. "I don't see any blood."

There was no time for explanations. One of the four tanks had pulled up in front of the stable doors. The turret hatch opened and the tank's commander peeked out. Thankfully I had picked up some Russian while in Auschwitz.

"*Nitchevo, tovaritch!*" (Don't do anything, comrade!) I cried.

The commander ordered us to come out. When he saw what sorry specimens we were, he sat himself on top of the turret. He was young, unshaven, and had sweated through his tunic. "*Germanski?*"

"*Tree Franzusie. Germanski.*" I pointed in the direction that the Nazis had fled.

"*Da,*" he frowned and jumped down from his tank. He took large gulps of water from the pump, then without a word climbed back into the turret. The tank pivoted, its metal treads sparking on the cobblestone, then rumbled off, choking the courtyard with diesel smoke.

Better get those boots, I told myself. As I started toward the courtyard entrance, the remaining tanks sped by. The first ran over the body, popping open the skull. The second tank's treads crushed the legs and chewed up my boots. Shit! All that I could salvage was a bayonet and a pouch that contained a shaving kit and a few cigars.

Soon after, the Soviet infantry arrived like a horde of locusts. On foot, on horseback, and on anything with wheels—Russians, Cossacks, Tartars, Ukrainians, Mongols, Georgians, men and women, swept by. Because of the warm weather, many of the soldiers had shed their coats and shirts. Even women stripped to the waist, their breasts bobbing with every step.

With tears in our eyes and cigars in our mouths, Jean, Michel, and I cheered on our liberators, far into the night. When we finally climbed back into the loft, we realized our asses were peppered with wood splinters from the tank shell. Ecstatic that the war was over for us, we disregarded our pain and the fact that the Red Army had confiscated our wheel of cheese, which left us only raw horsemeat to eat, and we dropped into peaceful slumber.

The following morning I butchered the horse with my German bayonet. Growing up, I had cut up chickens and rabbits, but never an animal that large. Luckily I had done well in my zoology class. Stepping over a few Nazi corpses, I then gathered fresh asparagus. From the snickering of passing Soviet soldiers, I guess I was a real pathetic sight crouching there in the dirt. Since the kitchen in the manor house was still well equipped, I was able to boil the asparagus with a pot of potatoes. On the side of the house I built a makeshift spit and barbecued two beautiful horse tenderloins. The rest of the mare went to fill the ravenous bellies of the Red Army.

After eating our first civilized meal, complete with white linen, crystal glasses, antique porcelain, and silverware from the trunk, I found Michel and Jean trying on fine tailored clothes in front of the master bedroom mirror. An armoire stood empty; the clothes that had been hanging inside were now strewn across the floor. Every pair of pants had its pockets pulled out. On a dresser stood a framed photo of an SS officer greeting the Führer. Whoever lived here was definitely a big shot in the Nazi Party. In those custom-made clothes, and after a few more hearty meals, Michel and Jean could certainly pass themselves off as the heirs to the estate.

"For the time being we better keep our 'pajamas' on," I said. "The last thing we want the Soviets to mistake us for is three *boches*. At least I have a tattoo."

Michel and Jean sadly agreed.

"Forty-eight hours ago I would have been shot on sight walking around here in these putrid rags," Michel murmured. "And now they're going to keep me alive in this god-forsaken place."

The next day we continued scavenging around the farm in between extended visits to the outhouse. There was a price a *Muselmann* had to pay for enjoying such a rich dinner.

We kept our distance from the bands of Soviet soldiers who would come and sleep for a couple hours in the house or barn, then leave with whatever they could carry. I never saw an organized regiment, battalion, or platoon that one would expect from a victorious army. The soldiers seemed to be no more than marauders, and many were surprisingly ignorant. They were expert marksmen who could shoot sparrows on the wing, but they behaved like children on Christmas morning when they had their hands on a bicycle or a discarded toy. They were mystified by the simplest household items. With one Georgian, I swapped a dented old alarm clock for a superb gold chronograph. They would discard their uniforms whenever they found something better to wear, even if it was an article from a German uniform. A Red Army truck driver discovered a tuxedo in the armoire that tickled his fancy, even though the coat wouldn't button over his potbelly. With his helmet on his head, the strap buckled under his chin, and the tails tucked into his pants, he left ready for the ball.

These soldiers were also not particular about what they drank. As soon as they saw that a liquid might contain alcohol, it went happily down the hatch. I had discovered a suitcase full of perfumes and eau de colognes in one of the bedrooms. At gunpoint, a female soldier liberated them from me and enjoyed a few sips. She offered me a drink from a heart-shaped bottle, but I respectfully declined. Shortly thereafter, a burly sergeant joined her. Once they had polished off the larger bottles, they drained the small-necked ones into a goblet. I guess that was their dessert cocktail. Later I found the couple asleep in the stable, nestled naked on a bale of hay.

On the heels of the Red Army came Russian peasants, traveling in canvas-topped wagons drawn by horses or oxen. These *muzhiks*, whose ancestors had been the serfs of Russian aristocrats, had received parcels of farmland after the Russian Revolution, but Stalin took their lands and bunched them into large communes. When the Nazis invaded Russia, the retreating Red Army scorched the earth, forcing the *muzhiks* to roam like nomads for four years. Now they hoped to settle down again, no matter how or where. With their tools and kitchen utensils hanging from their wagons, they looked like the American pioneers I had seen in movies grabbing up Indian land. Their manner and their way of life, though, spoke more of medieval times. They took possession of German farms; and if the properties weren't abandoned, they would run off the owners or kill them.

On the third day of our liberation, Germany still hadn't conceded defeat. From the kitchen I heard explosions. German teens were making craters in my asparagus field with a discarded Panzerfaust. It made me uneasy, and I wished I hadn't left the submachine gun buried under the straw in the barn's loft. A little later, as I was smoking my last cigar, a Russian tank rumbled into the courtyard. Four young women with open shirts popped out and cooled themselves at the pump. I greeted them in broken Russian, which brought surprised smiles to their faces. Watching them climb back into their tank, I thought, if Russian women make a habit of prancing around in open blouses, then Moscow is the perfect summer vacation spot for me.

As the tank proceeded toward the village, one of the German teens emerged from a manhole and fired the bazooka at the rear of the tank. The base of the turret exploded and the tank shuddered and died. I couldn't believe that the punk had disabled the tank, and neither could he, standing like a statue next to the manhole with the Panzerfaust still saddled on his shoulder. The turret hatch opened, but only one soldier jumped out, and she slid into a growing pond of fuel spewing out from underneath the tank. As she tried to pick herself up for the second time, there came a sound like a thousand gas stoves being turned on and fire sprang from the fuel. She yelled only once as the flames swept over her. The radiating heat told me there was nothing I could do. The teen disappeared back into the manhole as heavy, black smoke began obscuring the tank.

A half-track came racing to the scene, but there was nothing they could do to save their comrades. I whistled at the driver and pointed at the manhole. He nodded, raised the manhole cover, and dropped in a hand grenade. He ducked as the cover flew up in the air, then glanced into the shaft and dropped another one. The hamburger must not have been ground fine enough for him.

Even after everything that I had gone through, I couldn't help feeling that I had witnessed a pure waste of young lives on both sides. It was disheartening, and I questioned whether, as a society, we had the fortitude to ever overcome the bestiality so deeply embedded in our fabric. I went back into the kitchen and started cooking dinner. I had no stomach to ponder philosophical questions or watch those soldiers scrape the women out of that tank.

That night I was awakened by the cackle of chickens. First, I thought that a fox or porcupine had entered the hen house, which was located on the side of the barn adjacent to the manor house. The noise abated, then I heard someone shoveling. I woke Michel and Jean, and the three of us climbed down to investigate. A lantern was lighting up the hen house. Inside, a Russian tank driver stood watch with a tommy gun strapped to his chest as a German civilian dug up a box. The German ordered us to leave and to forget what we saw. The Russian threw us cold stares, but never uttered a word. We climbed back into the loft and watched the pair walk off with a bulging gunnysack and a couple dead chickens.

Naturally we went back to the hen house. The ground was littered with empty velvet jewelry boxes of all shapes and sizes. By the number of boxes I could tell those two had dug up a fortune. The store names on the cases left no doubt that they were all confiscated from Jewish jewelry stores during the Nazis' occupation of Holland. In their haste, the two had dropped a few spoons made of bent gold coins and twisted gold wire.

"Tomorrow we move," I told my friends.

"Why?" Michel asked.

"When there's no logic I get worried."

"No logic to what?"

"I heard the civilian speak only German to the Russian."

"So?" Michel said. "The Russian speaks German."

"Why would that German lead a Russian tank driver armed with a gun to such loot in such an isolated location?"

My buddies were silent.

"And why would the Russian split the jewels with a *boche* when he could easily keep it all for himself by pulling the trigger?"

"Because we surprised them," Jean guessed.

"Doesn't it seem strange that the German did all the talking? That it was he who told us to forget what we saw."

"What are you getting at?" Jean demanded.

"I think the Russian was a Nazi in disguise. He looked a lot like the SS officer in that photo on the dresser upstairs."

"You're crazy," Jean laughed.

"Fine, but tomorrow we might not fare as well if they return for the silverware," I said, nodding toward the splayed trunk, "or some other buried loot."

Jean and Michel agreed with me on that point.

With my Nazi submachine gun in my lap I kept watch until morning, then we loaded a wheelbarrow with all the goodies we had "organized" from the house and headed for the lake. Michel and Jean had discovered a vacant cottage there during an attempt at fishing. It had been ransacked, but there were still mattresses on the three beds. We couldn't ask for more and made it our home.

While cleaning the cottage we found a couple of shotguns and a box of shells under one of the beds, and Jean and Michel made plans for a hunting trip in the nearby woods. I told them it was foolish to be trekking around with guns when there was a lake stocked with bass, perch, smelt, eels, crawfish, and northern pike. They complained that they didn't have much to show for the hours that they had spent "dipping a line."

"That's because you guys don't have any experience. You have to think like a fish to catch a fish."

"Well, you do smell like one," Jean shot back.

I did know a thing or two about angling. Every day since kindergarten I had fished the Mediterranean before going off to school, and I "dipped a line" every summer morning during my family's annual vacation in the Alps. When I fished in Lake Geneva, the hotel where we stayed would put fish on its menu because the cooks knew that I would bring them a gunnysack full. I gave Jean and Michel a crash course, and they returned that evening with enough bass and pike to feed us for a week.

CHAPTER 22

We were in the town of Wustrow, which was more a village than a town. You needed a powerful magnifying glass to find Wustrow on any map. There were three hundred inhabitants, and a fair number of them were relatives who had escaped Berlin and other German cities the Allied bombers had targeted. Most of the homes were collected along the main road, which ran from Ravensbrück to the city of Reinsberg. There were ten cottages on the lake; two or three seemed like permanent residences, and the rest were summer homes for well-to-do Berliners. Most of Wustrow's residents made their living from the land, but because of the war most of the fields were untilled that spring. Only two men seemed to be making their livelihood from the lake. Not knowing who had been card-carrying Nazis, I kept my distance from most of the residents, and they made no effort to associate with a *Häftling*. I would see other "pajamas" pass through Wustrow, but I think Jean, Michel, and I were the only ones bedding down there.

Our cottage gave us a solitude and safety that the estate could never have provided. It was encircled by pine and oaks, which kept us out of view from the Soviets and assorted riffraff traveling the main road. The serenity of our new home was a stark contrast to what I had become accustomed to since Drancy, and I realized that I would have to consciously teach myself how to relax. How to go about that was beyond me. What I did know, especially when my sciatic nerve made me limp, was that before I could truly relax I had to take care of some unfinished business that was eating at me.

The day we were evacuated from Ravensbrück we marched by a farmhouse that had a huge pile of potatoes near the cellar chute. A few of us dashed to "organize" some of the earth apples. A bulldog-faced farmer jumped off his porch and kicked me with his heavy boots. It felt as if he had cracked my tailbone. I fell and dropped my stash. Limping back into line, I heard an awful scream. The *boche* had plunged his pitchfork into the thigh of one of the other *Häftlinge*. So, as Michel and Jean plied their newfound fishing skills, I headed back toward Ravensbräck to kill that farmer. Stuffed under my coat was a German hand grenade that I had found in the asparagus field.

At a bend in the main road, I was met by a familiar stench, but being on a crusade I had no time to investigate. I passed a mill with a spectacular water wheel turning in a canal choked with plump smelts. I made a mental note to come back with a net. Passing the spot where we had taken the trail into the woods, I began to nervously fondle the bulge under my coat. My hand fell limp when I arrived at my destination. The farm was now a heap of ashes and blackened walls.

"A direct hit?" I asked a neighbor.

"No, the Red Army torched it. You see, Kurt lost his mind when some Russian soldiers backed up a truck and took his damn potatoes. The idiot charged them with his pitchfork. I couldn't believe my eyes. The soldiers shot him, threw him into the house, then burned it down." Heading back, I tossed my weapon into the woods. I had to admit I was relieved that the Soviets had done the dirty work.

When I arrived again at the bend in the road, I followed my nose and discovered an arm sticking out of the ground with a swollen, blackened hand crawling with maggots. The markings on the green sleeve were that of an Italian uniform. It was peculiar that there would be Italian soldiers this deep into Germany. My attention was drawn to something under a nearby bush reflecting the setting sun. It was the chrome buckle of a knapsack stuffed with Austrian cigarettes. German money was worthless, but cigarettes were gold, and that knapsack would make the trip back home much easier. What a splendid day it turned out to be.

We received news of "the god with the moustache's" death and the end of the war days later, possibly even two weeks later. In Auschwitz, I had dreamt that the day he died would be a joyously drunken day, but it turned out to be anticlimatic. Possibly I had anticipated it too much. Maybe it was anticlimatic because there was no dancing in the streets. But what kind of celebrations could I expect in the country of the defeated enemy? Maybe it was because I knew I still had a hell of a long way to go before I would be home. More than likely, it was because his death didn't erase what I had endured and seen in the last eighteen months. The one thing that I did rejoice, and I quietly celebrated it every day, was the fact that my German submachine gun would prevent any *boche* from ever ordering me around again.

The Soviets put up notices stating that no one—German or "displaced persons"—could travel without a permit. These traveling papers could be acquired only at the Soviet provost marshal's office in Reinsberg, which was about seven miles south of Wustrow. We woke up early and trudged down the empty main road. We came upon two Mongol soldiers with their heads shoved under the hood of their truck. Luckily they knew squat about engines, and Michel had spent time in a garage. Not that the problem, a slipped distributor cable, needed a mechanic. Grinning from ear to ear, the Mongols were more than happy to let us hitch a ride.

Ten minutes later we were floundering in a motley throng of refugees and displaced people in Reinsberg's marketplace. Reinsberg wasn't much bigger than Wustrow, but they did have a bank and that was where the Soviets had set up their provost's office. Seeing that it would take days to receive our traveling papers if we waited our turn in line, I elbowed my way to the entrance where a Red Army guard was sleeping in a red velvet armchair.

"*Drasvicshem, tovaritch*" (Good day, comrade), I blurted in my broken Russian.

The soldier, who had been snoring loudly, opened one eye.

"*Trois Franzus, tovaritch*," I said, pointing to Michel and Jean.

"*Franzus, tovaritch?*" he repeated, unimpressed as he twisted the ends of his long handlebar mustache.

I slipped a few of my Austrian cigarettes into his hand. His smile revealed a row of blackened teeth.

"*Da, Franzus, tovaritch, da, da!*"

Deaf to their complaints, the guard pushed away those at the head of the line and planted us. Back on his throne, he pulled out an old edition of *Der Stürmer* from his jacket pocket. He tore off a square of the newspaper and rolled a cigarette with the tobacco from the ones I had given him. All the soldiers from the Russian countryside seemed to prefer the taste of newspaper to cigarette paper, since that's what they rolled their *makhorka* in back home. Blissfully the guard breathed in the first puff, and slowly the corner of a swastika became smoke.

An hour later a broad-shouldered female private ushered us inside. The bank was no more than a small office with a few chairs and a well-worn desk. Sitting behind it was a Russian noncommissioned officer who looked to be in his thirties. He asked in halting German where we intended to go. From our "pajamas" he knew where we had been. While the officer began to fill out our traveling permits, Michel stared out the window.

"If I'm not back in five minutes, wait for me at the edge of town," he whispered, then ducked out.

Seeing that the officer was sympathetic to *Häftlinge*, I told him I had discovered that a "Nazi farmer" in Wustrow was hiding two draft horses and those beasts could make our return to France easier. The Russian smiled and wrote out a requisition on bank stationery.

As he said he would be, Michel was waiting for us at the edge of town. He had a Russian helmet pulled down over his ears and a bicycle hidden in a bush.

Jean pointed to the helmet. "How did you get that?"

"Simple. I saw a Russian park his bicycle in the courtyard behind the bank. He hung his helmet on the handlebars and went into a shithouse. When I got back there I could tell from the sighs he was heaving that he was going to be there for a while. Nobody blinked when I came riding out on his bicycle with this pot on my head."

With that Red Army helmet bobbing on his head, Michel furiously pedaled back to Wustrow with me perched on the handlebars and Jean sitting on the small luggage rack over the rear wheel. We sure got some stares from the people on the road. Hey you German fools, get a good look at the three-clown *Häftlinge* circus riding by!

The next day we all went to the Wustrow garrison, which was a small house on the southern edge of town. I showed a soldier the requisition. He acted like it was meaningless to him. I wasn't sure if he was illiterate or couldn't be bothered. I asked in broken Russian who was in charge. A sly smile flashed on his face, and he led me behind the house to a girl's bicycle, which was lying on a gravel path that cut through a meadow. He pointed to a knoll and waved me on.

I walked through thigh-high grass and almost stepped on the officer in charge. He was soaking the biscuit with a stunningly beautiful Slav girl in her early twenties, who had her skirt hiked up and blouse open. I turned my back to them and profusely apologized in German. I braced myself for a Russian tongue-lashing, but all the chagrined young officer did was turn his back to me, yank up his pants, and brush the grass off his uniform.

Still on the ground half-naked, the girl laughed at our reactions, making me feel silly and immature. Holding out the requisition, I explained in German why I had come to the garrison. The girl jumped up, snatched the paper from me, and read it aloud. Her smooth pink cheeks mesmerized me. She had the most beautiful skin I had ever seen. It had been way too long since I had laid eyes on such a fine creature. I asked myself how that lucky son-of-a-bitch had gotten his skin against hers. His officer stripes, of course.

She gave me a smile.

"Oh, don't worry, he was all through. Your horses should come first, anyway."

Either something had gotten lost in the translation or the officer in Reinsberg had expedited things the best way he knew how. The requisition read that the Wustrow garrison was to assist us in recovering "our stolen horses." The girl ordered the reluctant lieutenant to confiscate the horses immediately. He nodded, and I wondered if he had accidentally put on her uniform. I thanked her profusely and again expressed my apologies.

"I'll catch up later. Anyway, he needed a breather," she winked.

The officer quickly rounded up a couple soldiers and Jean, Michel, and I led our military escort to the barn where the draft horses were being kept. The farmer's protests fell on deaf ears. The officer had only one thing on his mind and it wasn't his duties. I couldn't blame him.

Jean and Michel led a pair of well-kept Percherons to the country estate. We calmed the animals with a couple buckets of oats and a bale of hay. Since they were too fat to saddle, we needed to "organize" harnesses and a wagon. That wouldn't be an easy task. The Soviets had confiscated nearly every vehicle in Wustrow. We had gotten the horses and our permits quicker than expected, so we were confident that we would jump this new hurdle and be on our way home in a couple days.

"*Ou nous pouvons revivre, aimer, aimer*" (Where we can live again and love), Michel laughed as he led the horses into the stalls. I was holding Stella the last time I heard that refrain. I walked into the courtyard with tears welling in my eyes. I had lost almost all faith of ever holding her again.

One of us was always in the barn keeping guard over our new prized possessions. There were no secrets in such a small town, and once the farmer learned of the horses' new home he made daily visits. He would brush their coats, hug their necks, and kiss them on the nose, all the while blubbering like a four-year-old. He tried to make us feel sorry for him. Without those draft horses he couldn't work his fields, but we had no pity. One time he even offered me a smoked ham for their return. I shook my head, no. "Go break your back tilling your fields just as we broke our backs digging ditches for your glorious Führer."

It would be a long and arduous trip to the French border. At least four main Germany rivers—the Hafel, the Elbe, the Weser, and the Rhine—must be crossed. No one knew if there were any bridges still standing. The rubble-filled towns might not present opportunities for "organizing" provisions en route. So, in between scouring the countryside for anything with wheels, we canned a sheep and fruit preserves. We lived off a stray goat that I shot while leaning out the cottage's back window. That was the last time I fired at anything in Germany, because the Soviets posted notices forbidding the carrying of weapons. Nevertheless, Jean and Michel went off with the shotguns for a morning rabbit hunt. When I pointed out that their activities might prove dangerous, Jean replied, "Those signs don't apply to us. We're on the Allied side."

All morning I heard them sniping away in the woods. Around noon, a truck filled with soldiers rumbled up the road. Hearing the shotguns, the truck stopped. The soldiers seemed unsure of what to do. Coming out of the house, I could hear them talking. The truck turned down a trail and disappeared into the woods. When my two friends didn't return that evening I was certain that they'd had a run-in with the soldiers.

At daybreak I followed Michel's and Jean's tracks to the bank of a stream, where their footprints mingled with a multitude of heavy bootprints. I walked over to the garrison, hoping that they could tell me something. The guard standing near the front door didn't question me when I walked inside the house. Wearing "pajamas" was almost as good as having an authorized pass. To my surprise, the Soviet lieutenant's stunning lovebird was sitting behind a desk in the front room. She had a white piece of cardboard pinned to her blouse with her name, SONIA and DOLMETSCHER, German for "interpreter," written across it. Her gorgeous smile turned to a frown when I told her why I had come.

Without hesitating she said, "I have a driver making a round trip to the provost in Reinsberg. You can catch a ride. They might have some information."

"Can't you call?" I was in no hurry to leave. Gazing at Sonia was too enjoyable.

She shook her head. "The telephone lines are still down."

Sonia went to an open window, barked in Russian, then handed me some paperwork for the driver. She touched my arm. "I'm sure your friends are fine."

The driver was a gray-haired reservist in his fifties who had worked the oil fields in the Caucasus. His deeply creased face complemented the battle-scarred Nazi amphibious car he was steering. He drove slowly because he feared the cracked windshield might shatter in our faces. Avoiding the numerous holes left by tank and mortar shells seemed to be wearing him thin. I handed him one of my Austrian cigarettes.

"*Danke Schön.*"

He parked the clunker to the side of the road so he could light his smoke. "I, too, was a prisoner in Germany," he said in halting German, "but in the First World War."

Exhaling smoke, he released the clutch. The gears groaned and the car jerked forward. He waved his cigarette at the surrounding meadows. "This is nice country when you're on the right side."

At the Red Army headquarters in Reinsberg, a plump major, his chest covered with hardware, deigned me a few moments of his precious time. Through his interpreter, who looked like a farm servant and stuttered incomprehensible German, I deciphered that the major hadn't received a report of two Frenchmen hunting in the woods. I wanted to ask more questions, but the major turned his back to me. My time was up.

I hoped that Jean and Michel were in some Russian prison, but it was more than likely their swollen bodies were floating down the river. Either way, I was now alone, and my urgency to leave dissipated. I wanted my parents to know that I was alive, that I had survived, but the road home had excessive perils—too many unknowns to go it alone. If I was patient, the right traveling companions would eventually come along. So I took the whining farmer up on his offer and gave him back his horses for the smoked ham hanging in his chimney.

CHAPTER 2 3

I had become friendly with a plain-spoken former truck driver whose property I crossed every time I went into town. Arthur Novak was a stocky man in his fifties. The Nazis had thrown him into Oranienburg Penitentiary, a massive prison on the outskirts of Berlin, in 1935 because of his membership in the Communist Party. Our conversations were short but never frivolous, always touching on politics and the events of the last twelve years. When he learned of Jean and Michel's disappearance, he invited me to stay with him. Since I knew his political leanings, and that we had a mutual hatred for "the god with a moustache," I accepted without hesitation.

Arthur owned a small lakefront cottage that he shared with his wife and seventeen-year-old niece, Trautchen, whose parents had been killed during one of the bombing raids on Berlin. I slept in the guesthouse, a converted greenhouse situated between the house and the main road. Under the bed I stored my only possessions: two knapsacks, one with my cigarettes and the other stuffed with the silverware from the loft. Although Arthur didn't ask anything of me, I kept his table stocked with fish and asparagus.

A couple days after I moved in, the Soviets appointed Arthur the mayor of Wustrow because he was the only obvious anti-fascist in the area. Proud as a peacock, Arthur strolled through the village wearing a red armband that Mrs. Novak made. SAROSTA, the Russian word for "mayor," was stitched across it. He was the liaison between the residents and the garrison, but his title didn't impress the drunken gangs of Red Army looters who tore through Wustrow night and day. Not being able to speak their language, he would show them his armband when they stumbled and banged through his house.

"*Sarosta! Sarosta!*" he would scream.

The thieves would answer with dismissive laughs.

When helping Arthur and Mrs. Novak clean up after such a visit, I asked him, "When you paraded through the streets of Berlin with your fist in the air, didn't you yell 'All for one and one for all'? Wasn't that your motto?"

"Yes, but pretty soon I won't have anything left."

"You're only a bourgeois trying to protect your property. When you have only one ragged shirt on your back, when you have nothing more to lose, then you'll be a good communist again," I teased.

"You snotty brat. You sure think you know a lot about politics."

"That's right, and most of it I learned the hard way." To steer the conversation away from me, I asked Arthur why he became a communist. "You owned property and you were self-employed."

"Anyone who had their eyes open could see the Nazis were thugs and Bavarian beer-swilling hoodlums. The communists were the only ones willing to take the brown shirts head on, fist to fist, gun barrel to gun barrel. But when the army backed Hitler, we were done for. Who knows how many of us they locked up or killed." He paused. "I don't think a real peace will ever be possible on this planet. There's just an overabundance of hate and greed."

"You know, the one thing I realized in the last eighteen months is that we should take handfuls of healthy kids from every country, raise them with one language, no religion, and sterilize the rest of the world."

Arthur eyed me incredulously. "Are you saying you want to create a master race?"

"No master race, no race at all—just mongrels. Beautiful mongrels with plenty of *Lebensraum*" (space to live).

Arthur sucked air through pursed lips. "You've been quite mute about your time in that camp, Pierre."

I shrugged. "I don't want to sound like a cry baby."

I was hesitant to utter a word about Auschwitz or Dora. I had no desire to revisit the brutality and death I had barely survived. The moments I did want to relive I fought to keep the furthest from my memory because I knew I would never get another chance to press my lips against Stella's red hair. And although he had been locked up in Oranienburg, Arthur had no idea of the extent of the mass murder in Auschwitz and the other extermination camps. Because a few wealthy Jews had been released from Oranienburg after obtaining visas, he thought that all German Jews had safely left the country. I was flabbergasted when he asked if I had seen any Jews in Auschwitz.

"Yes, mostly going up in smoke." The unsettled look in his eyes when I explained myself made me wish I had kept my mouth shut.

I should have wished harder, because at dinner the next night my conversation with Mrs. Novak got my tongue wagging on the maladies *Häftlinge* had to endure. "We had all kinds of abscesses, cysts, and tumors in the camp and we were always operating on one another. We only went to the infirmary for grave emergencies and then reluctantly because of the 'selections.'"

"What's a 'selection'?" she asked.

I cringed. I had unwittingly dropped Pandora's box onto the dinner table. I kept silent. Mrs. Novak repeated her question. I looked over to Arthur, who nodded his consent.

"A 'selection' is when they picked a whole bunch of us to be executed."

"Why?"

"Because they were judged too weak and worthless to do any more good for the Reich."

"*Diese Biester sind mit Menschenhaut überzogen!*" (Those beasts coated with human skin!) Mrs. Novak spit. Yet it was the look in her eyes that made me feel like an interloper who had proved that her God was dead.

While I was getting ready to go to sleep, Mrs. Novak came out to the greenhouse with a glass of Danziger Goldwasser liqueur. Sitting on my bed, I reluctantly accepted it, bracing myself for more questions about Auschwitz. She would get no answers. No more stories, no more recollections. I had learned my lesson. Perplexed, she just stood over me, silent. I took a sip, then watched the gold flakes swirl about the clear liqueur. She laid her hand on my head.

"You brave boy," she whispered.

I looked up at her. Mrs. Novak had tears in her eyes. She bowed her head and quickly left. Don't pity me, I thought, I'm still alive.

As the liqueur brought on its desired effects, I couldn't help but question what bothered her more—the realization that it was our bodies, *Häftlinge* bodies, that fueled the Nazi war machine, or the embarrassment that it was her countrymen who ground our bones into that fuel. When I woke up the next morning I still didn't have the answer. What did it matter, though? Wasn't Mrs. Novak a victim of the Nazis, too?

Since the only boat dock was on Arthur's property, the underfed Soviet soldiers were constantly using his boat for fishing expeditions. They would row to the middle of the lake, toss hand grenades, then calmly wait until the stunned fish floated to the surface. They netted all the fish they could, from the largest carp to the smallest minnows. Arthur was in despair. The lake would soon be empty, and fish was the staple food of Wustrow since the Soviets had taken all the cattle. When a drunk Kalmuck soldier blew himself and Arthur's boat into guts and splinters, the Red Army declared a ceasefire on the fish.

Arthur was greatly relieved when the Soviets finally set up a mayor's office for him. Since his appointment, a multitude of women had been knocking at his door at all hours. Not only were they looting, the Soviet soldiers were raping any female they could get their hands on. The Soviet officers shrugged their shoulders at Arthur's reports, saying that the Nazis did it to their women first;

but it was former female *Häftlinge* and non-German refugees who were also being sexually molested. So Arthur kept a record of all the victims in a leather-bound ledger.

Many German women were in hiding, in the woods, attics, haylofts, and cellars. Since the Soviets' arrival, Arthur's niece had barely left the attic. I would see Trautchen once in a while in the kitchen, but our conversations never got past hello. One stormy night, the soldiers discovered the attic door, forcing Trautchen to climb out a window and hide in the woods. She returned the next morning wet, pale, and coughing badly.

"The girl can't stay up there any longer," Mrs. Novak declared.

Arthur decided that she would stay with me.

Nestled in an overstuffed armchair, Trautchen fell off to sleep at once, worn out from her adventure the previous night. I looked at her for a long time in the thin moonlight filtering through the dusty glass roof. It had been a long, long time since I had been alone with a woman in a bedroom. Trautchen would breathe heavily for a while, then stop suddenly to move or mutter a few incoherent words, her golden hair shimmering against the red velvet of the chair.

On the third night I was awakened by the grinding of truck brakes and drunken singing. With one leap, Trautchen jumped into my bed and hid underneath the quilt. She was just in time. A Russian began kicking at the greenhouse door, which wasn't even bolted. The door flew open and the soldier fell flat on his face, his gun crashing down next to him. Petrified, I sat up in the bed as Trautchen flattened herself against the mattress. I brought my knees to my chest to tent the quilt. If the rest were as inebriated as the one lying motionless on the floor, then I was going to be spared witnessing Trautchen's rape. The soldiers that filed in burst into roars of laughter when they saw their comrade. Every one of them must have bathed in a trough of vodka. The beam of a flashlight played on the wall, then struck me full in the face.

"*Nix Panienka*" (No girl), one of them slurred.

Thankfully I wasn't a good enough substitute, and leaning

against each other, they slithered off. When the drunken shouts stopped and the truck's diesel motor clattered to life, I assured Trautchen that the danger was over. She was trembling, so I doubt she noticed that I was, too. I lay back down and she brought her head out from under the covers. She pressed herself against my body and kissed me on the mouth. A soft warmth overtook me.

We remained locked in an embrace for a few moments, then she ran her hand over my body. I held my breath. In the darkness I was sure she was turning expectant eyes toward me. My time in the camps had rendered me impotent, but I was hoping that her caresses would cure me. I began to panic. Nothing was happening down there. It would be unbearably embarrassing to tell her the truth. She wouldn't understand, since everyone in Wustrow seemed so ignorant about the camps. Where the hell is Arthur? Why hasn't he checked to see if everything is all right? Was he that sure I could keep his niece safe or was he playing the sly matchmaker?

"*Dass kann ich deinem Onkel nicht antun*" (I can't do that to your uncle), I lied.

She untangled herself from me and dropped into the chair, sobbing convulsively. I couldn't stand it. Embarrassed and feeling guilty, I slinked out of the greenhouse and spent the rest of the night on the dock. When Trautchen announced the next morning that she would feel safer hiding at a neighbor's house, Arthur gave me a strange look but never asked any questions.

◆ ◆ ◆

The Soviets had requisitioned the front room of a small house by the marketplace for the mayor's office. The room was empty except for a wobbly table and two mismatched chairs.

"Will you help me as long as you're here?" Arthur asked.

"As your secretary?"

"No. You'll be the *putz*. The two of us might be able to put some order to this mess."

Putz was German slang for "cop." Me a *flic*, in Germany?

"Why not," I said.

"If the Führer could only see us now," Arthur laughed as he dragged one of the chairs behind the table and completed his first mayoral duty, making himself comfortable.

Mrs. Novak made me an armband with Polizei stitched on it. My main function was to take reports from the rape victims. In Arthur's ledger I would write the woman's name, put little crosses for each occurrence, and then lie that I would notify the Soviet commandant. The ledger was filled in no time, and I wondered how many bastard Russian children were now on their way. The biggest problem, though, was that venereal diseases of all kinds were spreading like wildfire through the countryside, and there was no medicine to treat them.

My knowledge of languages was Arthur's greatest asset. Displaced people trying to make their way home came to the office every day, and it was my job to decipher their needs. When a group of Greek Jews came looking for help, we conversed in Spanish, a language that had been handed down to them when their ancestors fled the Spanish Inquisition. English was the only way I could communicate with a Serbian professor. With Jews who had been rounded up during Rommel's campaign in Libya and Tunisia, I spoke French. Unfortunately, on matters of repatriation, the most I could do was point them in the direction of the Soviet garrison, but few dared to seek them out. Rumors were rampant that the Red Army was rounding up able-bodied refugees to rebuild the devastated USSR.

Arthur and I were able to provide short-term shelter to some of these errant souls, leading them to the still-vacant country manor. I would ask any female I even suspected of spending time in a camp if she had crossed paths with a young French girl with red hair who had been in Auschwitz. The answer was always the same.

During dinner one night I made the mistake of talking about all the crosses in the ledger. Mrs. Novak was devastated. Feeling guilty, I tried to lighten the mood. "It's ironic. There's no happy medium. Here are all these women, many of them now widows, who during the war dreamed of tender, romantic companionship. The Russians are only helping them catch up on lost time."

I thought it was funny, but Mrs. Novak was incensed and stormed out of the dining room. Arthur shrugged. "You shouldn't have joked about that. My wife has no sense of humor about those types of things. She was raised by a stern Lutheran mother who believed sex was dirty."

Oh, you poor man, I thought.

Mrs. Novak gave me the cold shoulder for days, which made staying under their roof unbearable. On reflection, I realized I had messed up, but I didn't think my off-color humor was crude enough for an apology. To my surprise, the following Sunday Mrs. Novak invited me to go to church with her.

"No disrespect, but four horses couldn't drag me there. The clergy of all religions make a good living selling you a hereafter that they have no proof exists."

"Well, I read the Bible every night," she shot back.

"The people who wrote the Bible all those years ago would be writing romance novels now."

"Your soul will burn in hell."

Mrs. Novak was spitting mad. I thought she might even slap me, but I couldn't keep my mouth shut. "Mrs. Novak, the Bible says God created man in his own image, right? Well, I have seen men at their worst, and if there is a God he had better get off his ass and find a new blueprint."

She never asked me to church again.

◆ ◆ ◆

One morning a Cossack colonel, wearing a Persian lamb hat and black uniform weighted down with medals, rode into Wustrow on a white stallion. I watched from the window as he tied his horse to a lamppost next to "city hall." With a cartridge belt slung across his torso, saber, and polished black boots, it was as if he had charged straight off the pages of *War and Peace*. As a child I attended a performance of the Don Cossacks with my parents, but none of those men cut such an impressive figure. Arthur and I froze when the colonel stepped inside our office. It seemed extraordinary that a man dressed for a ball at the Summer Palace would want to speak with us.

"My name is Boris," he announced in Old German. "For the time being I'm the senior officer of the garrison."

He explained that he and his soldiers were passing through with a massive herd of cattle that they had driven all the way from Bavaria, and he was now waiting for transportation either by sea or rail. Otherwise he would have to drive the cattle through Poland, which meant he wouldn't reach Russia till the onset of winter. The herd and his men were now camped at the lakeshore.

Hesitantly, I asked the colonel if he had learned German in school. He fixed his gaze on me and furrowed his brow. "I was adopted by a Volga German family whose ancestors had settled in Russia centuries ago. When the Germans approached Stalingrad, they were all deported to Siberia."

When he learned that I was from France, he demanded that I be the one to shave his head every morning. I didn't dare refuse. Was he under the impression that every Frenchman was a barber? Or was he leery of the Russians and Ukrainians in his platoon, fearing they might try to slit their colonel's throat in mid-shave? I had grown up believing that everyone in the Soviet Union was Russian, but the Red Army troops flowing through Wustrow had quickly dispelled me of that fallacy. The only thing that was keeping the ancient ethnic rivalries from flaring up among the diverse republics was Stalin's blood-stained iron fist.

Around noon the next day, Boris arrived on his stallion and handed me his razor. All evening I had practiced with Arthur's straight razor on my own cheeks. It wasn't that I feared the colonel would beat me if I nicked his scalp; I wanted to do my best for him. Shaving him well could grease the wheels for any future favors I might need. I sat Boris down in the middle of the office, softened his stubble with towels soaked in a pot of hot water, then lathered his skull. As I began to shave him, a group of Russian soldiers came running down the street. Cossacks on horseback were herding and whipping the breathless men who looked more like *Muselmänner* than soldiers.

"What's going on?" I asked.

"We liberated those cowards from a German Stalag, and they're being shipped home today. Stalin is going to have a hell of a reception for them," Boris said matter-of-factly.

The colonel's Red Army cowboys were a wild bunch. Every night from the dock Arthur and I watched them have an orgy in the light of their campfire. Afterwards, their female companions would splash at the edge of the water to cool off their overheated organs. We agreed that vodka was one hell of an aphrodisiac.

"If we could break their bottles, I bet all the rapes would stop," I ventured.

◆ ◆ ◆

My life in Wustrow was good. I had no complaints whatsoever. But even though Arthur and Mrs. Novak treated me like a son, they weren't my parents and Wustrow wasn't Nice. Having heard BBC reports on Arthur's shortwave radio about the ghastly finds the Allied armies had made in the camps, I realized how cruel it was to continue to keep my parents in the dark about my well-being. They had to be expecting the worst. And truth be told, I ached to go home, figuring that the farther away from Germany I was, the easier it would be to put behind what the Nazis had forced on me.

One afternoon, a pale, anemic man in his thirties with a nasty cough and a blue-eyed blonde who had been badly beaten came into the office. She grimaced as she slowly eased herself onto the chair across from the desk. The man stood behind her like hired help.

In German I asked the woman her name.

"Ilse."

"You were raped?"

She nodded.

"When?"

"Last night." She pointed to her companion. "Carlos promised to protect me. He said he was '*Policia en Madrid, Policia en Madrid,*' but they lifted him up like a sack and hung him on the coat stand."

I turned to Carlos and asked him in German how many Russians had been involved? He shook his head.

"*No hablo aleman.*"

I asked him in Spanish.

"What could I do against five Russian goons? It was awful. I saw the whole thing. Five times," Carlos said shamefaced.

I turned to Ilse and asked in German if it was true that they had hung Carlos on a coat rack?

She glared at Carlos and hissed, "He looked pathetic hanging there, like a worthless scarecrow."

Carlos may not have known German, but he got the general idea from Ilse's tone. He waved five fingers.

"There were five of them," he protested in Spanish. "Five! I couldn't fight them all. You know, she left me dangling there all night."

I tried to mask my amusement. I asked Ilse if she left him up there.

"I couldn't move. It was a miracle I was even breathing. That Spaniard is lucky that I even bothered to fetch a neighbor this morning."

I wrote down Ilse's information, then turned to her ineffective bodyguard. "Carlos, what's your full name and where's your home? I need it for my records."

"My name is Carlos Puerta. I was a Republican policeman in Spain, but my wife and two kids now live in France."

After the Spanish Civil War, the French government had located all the anti-Franco refugees in a camp in the southern French town of Gurs. Carlos informed me that the Vichy government emptied the camp, handing the Spanish men over to the Gestapo. Carlos landed up in Ravensbrück where he contracted tuberculosis.

That explained why he coughed up blood twice while I took their report. When I told him I was from Nice, he clapped his hands.

"My family is in Menton. They're right in your neighborhood," he said in French.

Malheure! What a harsh accent, but he was right. Menton was twenty miles from Nice.

As they headed for the door I asked Carlos if they planned to stay in the house Ilse was renting.

"We will be leaving soon. Ilse has a place in Berlin. It'll be safer there," he said as they walked out. I jumped out of my chair and ran after them. I had found my traveling companions.

CHAPTER 24

A huge lazy pike had made his home under Arthur's dock, and for a week I tried to catch it with an array of baits, but this was one fish that knew how to get dinner without getting hooked. I told Arthur that we needed to nab it before some Russian blew up his dock trying to make a meal of it. After delivering slices of ham and preserves to Ilse and Carlos, I baited my line with a lively nightcrawler and went down to the lake. I dropped my hook, but the damn pike wouldn't budge. As I bobbed the line, I debated how to break the news of my imminent departure to the Novaks.

Ilse and Carlos were recuperating nicely. The bruises and swelling in Ilse's face had receded, revealing a pleasant-looking thirty-two-year-old. Unfortunately she was still bleeding, and it would be a few days before she could walk without any pain. She was eager to get to Berlin for medical attention because she feared those five brutes had infected her. Carlos wasn't coughing as much and had put on some weight, but he wanted to get to a hospital as soon as possible, too.

Carlos and Ilse's relationship was intriguingly odd. They were completely incompatible. The only reason they were together was that the group Carlos was traveling with left him at her doorstep.

Being a war widow, Ilse was thankful for any companionship, and in many ways Carlos acted like a thankful stray puppy dog in her presence. They definitely weren't romantically involved. How could Ilse be attracted to a man she could so easily swat away? If Carlos had been a cop in Spain he must have held a desk job.

For me they made the perfect traveling companions. With no common language there wasn't much chance of a protracted argument grinding the journey to halt, and I would see to it that all translations were watered down. I trusted both of them, certain that I wouldn't wake on the road to Berlin abandoned and my knapsacks gone. Ilse knew that two men at her side would keep her out of harm's way, and since Carlos couldn't speak German he needed me more than I needed him.

A half-hour had passed and the pike still hadn't gone for my bait. I was thinking about finding a frog to use as bait when Mrs. Novak yelled from the house.

"Hurry, the soldiers are pilfering your room!"

A soldier went running from the greenhouse toward a truckful of his comrades parked on the road. In his hand was one of my knapsacks. Screaming in French, I chased after him. He jumped onto the rear of the bed and the truck started rolling. I kept running and cursing. To my astonishment, the truck stopped. Twenty rifle barrels suddenly pointed at me, but I didn't care. I grabbed one of the knapsack's straps. Inside were some clothes, a Hitler Youth dagger that I had confiscated from a German teen the day before, and the silverware. For the trip home those forks, knives, and spoons were my currency. Holding onto the other strap, the soldier looked inside. With a triumphant grin spread across his unshaven face, he held up the dagger, then let go of my knapsack. The guns dropped as the other soldiers burst into drunken laughter. Either they were happy for the thief or they found a *Häftling* chasing after a Nazi knife positively amusing.

I was shaking when I returned to the greenhouse. How did I pull that off? I could easily have gotten myself killed or booted to Stalingrad as more slave labor. Was it my striped "pajamas" and

POLIZEI armband that saved me? That night I had nightmares about my little stunt. I was too close to the end of my journey to be taking such foolish risks.

The next morning I went straight to Ilse's and told them that no matter what, we were leaving in three days. Neither of them argued. I broke the news to Arthur and Mrs. Novak while eating our usual dinner of ham and asparagus. Arthur was grateful that I had stayed as long as I had, and Mrs. Novak made it clear that I was welcome to stay on, but they both knew I needed to get home. As usual, after dinner we listened to music on the shortwave radio. Arthur excused himself early. The next day he handed me a letter, hoping that a commendation from the mayor of Wustrow would help with any problems I might encounter on my trip.

The Novaks must have told everyone in Wustrow, because people stopped me on the street or came in the mayor's office and shoved marks into my pockets.

"Do take it. Money is worthless here. We live on a barter system, but it might come in handy for you." I ended up with several hundred marks. Well, if I don't spend it, it might become a collector's item or at least a souvenir, I thought.

The Novaks' neighbor, Irma, arrived at the house with tears rolling down her cheeks. Irma had trusted me to lance a seriously infected boil on her neck, which was healing nicely. She gave me a piece of smoked ham and a green striped tie that had belonged to her husband, who was "missing in action."

Still feeling guilty about my insensitive remarks in front of Mrs. Novak, and my reluctance to notify the authorities about the rape victims, I took the ledger to the garrison. It also gave me a good excuse to have one last visit with Sonia. She was berating two soldiers like an older sister who had caught her brothers snooping in her underwear drawer. She seemed genuinely happy to see me, which made me ask myself why I hadn't come around more often.

"Where are you from?" I asked her.

She named a town in Poland. I never heard of it, but to impress her I nodded as if I knew.

"I came here as a so-called volunteer three years ago. Otherwise the Nazis would've cut my parents' food rations," she told me.

"I suppose this was a quaint, peaceful little town."

"Not for us. We were treated like dirt and worked like cattle in their fields and as their domestics."

She asked me what I had in my hand.

"It's a list of all the rapes that have been reported."

Sonia shrugged her shoulders. "I was raped, too."

"Lately?"

"Oh, no. I'm safe now. The word got around that I'm private property. It was a couple of years ago. My complaint went right into the waste-paper basket. He was a Nazi official."

"Are you going home soon?"

"No. I'm waiting for that bastard to return so I can get even."

"I wish you success," I said and dropped the ledger on her desk. "I promised the women I would deliver this. What you do with it I could care less."

As I returned to the mayor's office a group of women milling about in the marketplace caught my eye. They were wearing camp garb, striped uniforms, or civilian clothes with red X's painted on the back. A few clutched bundles under their arms, most likely clothes and valuables left by fleeing Germans. None of them was older than forty. Seeing a survivor over that age would have been a rare sight, indeed. Approaching the women I heard two of them chatting in French. From their tattoos I knew they had been in Auschwitz.

"*Ou allez vous?*" (Where are you going?) I asked.

"We're going to Berlin to be repatriated."

I asked her my usual question.

"A young girl with red hair named Stella? It's quite possible."

The other French woman, who had a distended stomach, grabbed my arm. "Yes, yes, Stella. We left her and some others on the other side of the lake, twelve miles or more from here. We had to make a big detour because there wasn't any road. You can't miss the house. It stands all by itself on the top of a hill."

"Are you sure her name is Stella?"

"I'm certain."

I asked her three more times. The woman was positive that it was my Stella. I could barely contain myself.

"You better hurry. They've been there for three days, and they were all very ill, the poor things."

As I sprinted to the mayor's office, she called after me.

"Be careful, I think it's typhus!"

Typhus! If Stella has typhus and has gone three days without medical attention I would have to fear the worst. But the woman did say "she thought." It might be influenza.

Arthur had a hard time understanding my German when I excitedly asked what was on the other side of the lake.

"A woman told me there's a house up on a hill."

Arthur thought for a moment. "There's a hunting lodge. I was there once, a long time ago. I don't think there's anything else over there. Why?"

"I'll be back as soon as I can," I told him and bolted out the door.

It was late in the afternoon, and I decided that the quickest route would be to cross the lake. I knew that the owner of one bungalow had a canoe stashed in the reeds. Having watched the man from Arthur's dock, I also knew he hid the paddle in a nearby bush.

The canoe's hull grated against gravel as I pushed off. Startled ducks flew off quacking. Looking out in front of me, the lake never seemed so vast. I paddled frantically, struggling to keep a straight course. I was skilled at canoeing, but I had never been so desperate to get to a destination. Muscle fatigue quickly set in, calming my stroke.

For a stretch, the lake was placid and I glided briskly over the glassy surface. Green patches of water whipped up by the wind began to blossom, bucking and bobbing the canoe and threatening to pull the paddle out of my hands. A huge gust came close to stopping me dead in the water. These blasts became frequent, steadily increasing in fury. When my efforts couldn't keep the canoe moving forward, I threw down the paddle and let myself drift.

I was in the middle of the lake. Black clouds rimmed with gold were gathering above me and had already covered the setting sun. A screen of opaque grayish rain was over the town. I began to look for a place to beach the canoe. Off to my right was a small island surrounded by rushes and home to a few willow trees. In my haste I had forgotten to take any provisions, but I decided to spend the night on the tiny island without food, then return and make the whole journey again in the morning.

Dead tired, I pushed my way through the reeds and drew the canoe onto solid ground. Great drops of rain began to fall. I gathered up a few willow branches, piled them together for a bed, and put the canoe over me. As the rain beat down I thought of Stella. It had been raining when we were separated. Those showers had mocked our tears, and this storm seemed to conspire against our reunion.

Toward midnight the rain and wind relented and the sky cleared. The moon glowed over the hills. In the distance a few lights shone in Wustrow. Even though I was spent, I couldn't sleep. Stella was too close. My mind was spinning with anticipation and possibilities. I slipped the canoe back into the water.

With a slight breeze against my back I was able to cut a quiet path. I slipped by floating white orbs—gulls sleeping with their heads tucked under their wings. To my right a black band bordered the lake; it was the woods Jean, Michel, and I passed through on our escape. Off to my left were the meadows that the Cossacks' cattle grazed on. One of Boris's men was rekindling a campfire. From a tent came the melancholic notes of an accordion. I considered stopping to beg a little food, but the drunken soldiers probably would have taken me for a Werwolf* and filled my hide full of holes.

---

* *Werwolf* was a Nazi guerilla/terrorist movement formed by Heinrich Himmler in 1944 to harass Allied troops in occupied parts of Germany.

Silhouetted hills rose up in front of me. The house the woman spoke of must be on top of one of them. Only a couple more hours, I thought.

A rosy hue was tinting the sky when I finally arrived at the foot of the hills. The shoreline was deserted—no bungalows, no docks, no footpaths. It appeared that no one lived on this side of the lake. I made my way through the brush as best I could, and a little later was trampling through the thick damp grass covering the slope. When I reached the summit, a new sun had risen. If only the lake were as small as it looked from where I stood. On an adjacent hill a short distance away I saw the hunting lodge, a solitary building with its wet tile roof glistening in the sun.

The next thing I knew, I was standing in the lodge's courtyard, wet, muddy, and out of breath.

"Stella, Stella," I called, my hobnailed boots echoing on the paving stones. "*Ist da jemand?*" I yelled in German. "*Quelqu'un?*" I asked in French.

No one answered. My heart skipped a beat. Was I too late?

The courtyard was littered with rags, old paper, and broken boxes. The doors of the lodge were open and all its windows shattered. There was no smoke coming from the chimney. I bounded up the front steps and into a big room. The reek of mold and rot was heavy. Puddles of water sat under the windows. The furniture was no better than kindling. On the walls I could see where pictures and hunting trophies had once hung. Even with all the wreckage it was apparent that this had been a clubhouse for affluent sportsmen.

My boots crunched on shards of glass as I went from room to room. The beds were stripped of their mattresses, and tufts of eiderdown floated before me like lazy butterflies. In the kitchen I slipped on rotten vegetable peelings and bumped into pots and pans filled with moldy food. Dirty and shattered dishes were scattered everywhere. I could tell by the coat of dust that it had been months since anyone had used the two large stoves.

There wasn't a hint of a living creature anywhere in the lodge, so I went back into the courtyard. Where could Stella be? Was it possible that she and the others had recovered and moved on? Hell, there was a damn good chance that Stella wasn't even among the group of women. I looked around not knowing what to do next. It was then that I caught a glimpse of a red tile roof beneath the branches of an apple orchard. Moving closer, I discovered a walkway that led to a long, wooden structure that seemed to be a hen house.

"Stella? Stella?"

Pigeons cooed from the rooftop. A rabbit that had been gorging on cabbage scrambled off. Against one wall, a tub of manure steamed in the sun. Swollen from the rain, the hen house door wouldn't budge. Something awoke inside and it now sounded like I was going to enter a beehive. That meant only one thing. I said to myself that fate wouldn't shit on me like this. The French women could have confused another for my Stella. It's not such an uncommon name.

The hinges groaned as I kicked the door open. The pigeons took flight. A noxious odor that I was overly familiar with struck me in the face. A few tentative steps forward and I was inside.

I squinted. In the faint light I could see five female bodies lying in a row on a low wooden platform meant for nesting. A cloud of horse flies swirled above them as parasitical clusters feasted. Swatting them away, I bent over the bodies with my hand over my mouth and nose. Turning over those that had rolled onto their side, I looked at each one's pale bluish face. None of them looked like the Stella I remembered, but that was eighteen miserable months ago. The body farthest from the door was the only one that was her size.

To get a better look and to escape the stench, I placed the rigid emaciated body on a wobbly bench outside the door. Her eyes were closed. Her lips stretched over teeth that were clenched on the tip of her purple tongue. Strands of red hair peeped from beneath a brown scarf tied around her head. She wore an off-green print blouse and a soiled black skirt. Her ankles were swollen and her legs were tattooed with fresh rat bites. She must have outlived the others because she had the fewest bites.

Could this be my Stella? Staring at her face gave no answers. Would I even recognize my Stella if she were breathing and standing in front of me? I had been avoiding mirrors, but I knew my mother would have to look three or four times before she could be sure I was her Pierre.

I slid my hand under the palm of her swollen left hand. The rats had done too much damage for me to tell if there was the pyramid scar that I had run my fingers across as we sat on that staircase. I let the hand drop. It slapped onto the bench like a fish tossed onto a cutting board.

It hit me. Stella's eyes. No matter how much weight she had lost, no matter how hard she had slaved, no matter how broken her spirit, her eyes, her light brown eyes, would not have changed. I lifted her right eyelid. I couldn't see the color of the pupil. The whole eye was coated with what looked like coarse white talcum powder—fly larvae.

Sickened and caught so off-guard, I stumbled backwards. My stomach clenched as I fought the urge to get sick. With all those flies I should have known what was going to greet me. I hugged myself to stop from shaking. There was no way I was going to be able to say without hesitation if that corpse was or wasn't Stella.

I hadn't prepared myself for this. Paddling across the lake I envisioned either finding Stella alive or finding her dead, or else finding a body that I knew wasn't Stella. Not once had I considered not being able to tell one way or the other. I grew angry—angry with myself for wanting something to happen that could happen only in storybooks. I was not a child. I was not a teenager. After everything I had gone through, I was a man. Maybe not a wise or good one, but I was a man now and I wasn't going to let anyone say differently. But here I was, wanting a happy ending straight out of a schoolgirl's fairy tale. Was I too weak, too dependent on the dreams I created in Monowitz to admit that this was Stella? Or was

I too afraid to hold onto hope for a reunion with my Stella? Hadn't I lost enough?

I sat down next to the body. I pulled down the right eyelid. The harder I willed myself to believe the corpse wasn't Stella, the further from assurance I seemed to lead myself. And the more I stared at her dead face, the less confident I felt that I had found my Stella. The chances that she survived Auschwitz were laughable. Then, again, maybe shithouse luck had been on her side, too.

I had an urge to run away and forget what I found—forget that I ever sat down in that canoe. What would remembering accomplish? Nothing but anguish. Even with the nagging doubt, I couldn't let the body rot with the rest of them. If this body isn't Stella's, I thought, then maybe some day we would find each other. If it is Stella, then at least I got to say goodbye and see that she had a proper burial.

I went back to the house to find a crate or trunk that might serve as a coffin, but there wasn't any large enough. While I was in the courtyard mulling over if I should bury her without one, I bumped against a tree trunk that had been hollowed out for a drinking trough. I dragged it into the orchard, then carried the body over. With my eyes shut, I laid her inside. I closed the coffin with boards that I had broken over my knee and a few rusty nails.

I dug the grave in the shade of the apple trees. I hadn't held a shovel since Auschwitz. As I ripped open the rain-soaked earth, something inside me kept telling me that it was Stella who I was burying. Where inside me this new conviction came I had no idea, but I accepted it. I was too drained to squabble with myself any longer.

Now I sobbed as I carved out a hole in the earth. I didn't want to believe that this was all that remained of the girl I had loved in Drancy and had dreamt about in Auschwitz, Dora, and Ravensbrück. That she died alone, far from home, unable to ask her mother to hold her tight or have her father sing her a lullaby. I felt wrong hoping that she had thought about me, but I couldn't help myself.

Why had she come this far, paid so dearly for a freedom she would never enjoy? Why did she have to endure the death rattles of those four other women and feel the rats scurry over her to get to their meals? Why couldn't she have died in Auschwitz? Why couldn't she have hid in a neighbor's cellar? Why couldn't these be tears of joy?

I don't know how long I cried, but at some point I realized that I couldn't stand in that hole with a bowed head any longer. If I was going to return to Arthur's before nightfall, I had to act now. By the sun I could tell it was mid-afternoon. I finished digging and slid the coffin into the hole.

In Monowitz I had fantasized what my life in Nice would be like with Stella. I would have proudly showed off my prized jewel to family and friends. With the bells chiming midnight, Stella and I would have strolled out of the cinema hand in hand, like movie stars. After dinner at my parents we would have gathered in the parlor and enjoyed my mother's singing and Stella's violin. Oh, I saw us with a flock of healthy, red-headed brats and living a joyous life.

Standing next to the open grave, I realized that if my Stella had lived (or was alive), more than likely the memories of our experiences and hardships would have torn us apart, never allowing us to find the innocent hearts that we had in Drancy. I doubt either one of us would have wanted to bring offspring into such a vile, rotten world.

CHAPTER 25

Arthur and Mrs. Novak were listening to classical music on their shortwave when I returned that night.

"How did it go?" Arthur asked.

I shrugged. "I'm tired. I'm going to make myself something to eat and go to sleep."

"I made you dinner," Mrs. Novak chimed.

"Thank you."

I braced myself for a barrage of questions, but Arthur must have seen in my face that I wasn't much for conversation. I went into the kitchen with a familiar ache in my stomach, something I had longed never to feel again. I ate without tasting, then went out to the greenhouse where my exhausted body dragged me to slumber.

If I had nightmares I couldn't recall them in the morning. I awoke early, but stayed in bed staring out the glass roof at the cloud-filled sky. By the time I forced myself out of bed, Arthur was already attending to his mayoral duties. I visited my traveling companions to make sure our departure was still on schedule. Indeed, it was. Carlos and Ilse had been concerned that I hadn't stopped for a visit the day before. I told them about Stella.

"What a shame," Carlos said, then he went on and on about

the rumors that one bridge on our route might not be standing. Ilse gave her condolences and went back to making lunch. It seemed that they were relieved that nothing or nobody was going to interfere with my will to leave Wustrow. I was stung, but I couldn't fault them. Like so many in Europe, death was now all too common for Carlos and Ilse. Carlos had witnessed the Spanish Civil War and lived through the camps. Ilse had survived the bombings of Berlin. To be affected by the death of a person they had never met was pointless, a waste of precious energy. There were more pressing issues to deal with. Those women lying next to Stella didn't move me emotionally. I didn't bury them. I didn't know them. Carlos and Ilse didn't know Stella. She was just another faceless corpse.

After lunch I loaded some jars of preserves into our wagon, a discarded stroller with one missing wheel, that Carlos had "organized." To make it a fairly sturdy, I moved the remaining front wheel to the center of the thin axle. Carlos attached a rope to the buggy so we could pull it.

As Carlos helped Ilse pack her belongings in the buggy, I said, "Athos, Porthos, and Aramis."

"How about D'Artagnan?" Carlos asked.

"He wasn't one of the Musketeers," I informed him. "*Tenemos que salir mañana en la mañana.*" (We have to leave tomorrow morning.)

Ilse looked at me bewildered.

"*Morgen früh ziehen wir ab.*" (Tomorrow morning we pull out.)

My next stop was the mayor's office. Over a game of chess I told Arthur about my dreadful reunion with Stella.

"Of all the things I wanted to be for her, why did I have to be her gravedigger?"

Arthur sat silent for a moment. "I thought you said you weren't sure it was her."

"Well, yes. Not absolutely sure, but . . ."

"But sure enough to bury her."

I nodded.

"Then I hope you remember her as she was when you fell in love with her."

I didn't think that was possible, but I kept that to myself.

Arthur changed the subject. "Do you think Ilse is up to the long trip?"

"I hope so. You know I should apologize to your wife about those remarks about the rapes," I admitted.

"Don't worry, she doesn't carry a grudge for long. Besides, some of these Nazi bitches deserved it. Don't tell my wife that."

"Were there many women in the Party?" I asked.

Arthur nodded.

"Without their vote he never would've been chancellor. I'll never understand what excited them about that Austrian nobody."

Neither of us could remember whose turn it was and we abandoned the game.

I knew Arthur had told his wife about Stella because at dinner she was overly attentive. She kept looking at me while clearing the table. Suddenly she took my hand and expressed her condolences. I thanked her and blurted out, "If she wasn't meant to survive, why couldn't she have been gassed on our arrival?"

"It's hard to understand God's will."

I bit my tongue—hard.

I could barely sleep that night. Stella, the anticipation of finally going home, and what I would do with my life from here on had me fidgeting under the blanket. Was my father still fighting off cancer or had he surrendered? I was pretty certain that Claude, *mon ami* who hid in my family's outhouse so long ago, had been able to stay one step ahead of the Milice and the Gestapo. I couldn't imagine Meffre not surviving. He would have a few well-deserved medals on his lapel for his service in the Maquis. I feared that my radio-loving classmate Bernard was dead. I wasn't able to picture such a sickly boy surviving any Nazi-scripted ordeal.

Would I finish my college prep classes? In France, after you graduated from high school you took a year of either math or philosophy, depending on what you wanted to specialize in at a university. I'd had six months of philosophy classes when I got arrested.

Could I fit back in? Would I be able to tolerate the carefree snickering and giggling of the other students? I couldn't imagine sitting at a desk and having the patience to listen to philosophical lectures. As far as I was concerned now, philosophy was a study for sissies with their heads in the clouds or up their asses. Learning a trade might be the best way to go. Damn, I had become an old man in a junior's body.

The next morning, after a hearty breakfast of catfish and potatoes, I hugged and kissed Mrs. Novak and Arthur goodbye with tears in my eyes, grabbed my knapsacks, and headed into town. Ilse and Carlos were anxiously waiting in front of her house. I put one of my knapsacks over my shoulder and the other into the stroller. None of us was concerned that our provisions were bending the rear axle. Carlos and I grabbed the rope and Ilse got behind the stroller and raised her arm like a coachman cracking his whip.

"*Vorderman und Seitenrichtung,*" (Line up, front and side) Carlos mumbled in his coarse Spanish accent.

It was the only German he knew. It was what the *Kapos* bellowed every morning when we marched out the gates. I turned to Ilse.

"Okay *Kapo*, let's get rolling."

This was the first time that I heard them laugh.

Outside Wustrow we turned off the highway to Reinsberg and followed a road that would take us to a train station, the first leg of our journey to Berlin. Except for the carcasses of a few German tanks, the road was deserted. In an outlying field, a Soviet soldier was tilling the ground with a plow pulled by ten German women. Ilse whispered to us to move faster.

We went around a bend and I looked back. The hill where I left Stella was gone. What unforgettable memories she gave me. Memories that my imagination embellished while I laid in those infested bunks, dug those ditches, froze during those roll calls, and withered with hunger. Stella had given me strength when I was at the end of my rope, and in those months that rope nearly slipped from my grasp every day. I had a good grip on the rope now, and it was going to get me home.

EPILOGUE

It took us three days of walking and hitching rides to reach Berlin. Although the sector had been carpet-bombed, by some miracle Ilse's apartment building was still in good shape. Carlos and I visited the newly opened French Information Office. The officer in charge wouldn't issue Carlos a visa, advising him to return to Franco's Spain and apply there. Okay. The only way to the Spanish border would be to either sprout wings or cross through all of France, and the only thing Carlos could have applied for in Franco's Spain was his death certificate. It was reassuring to see that stupid bureaucrats survived the war unscathed.

Two days later Carlos and I said goodbye to a tearful Ilse, and ten days after that we managed to reach the American zone. We hopped on an Army truck with some GIs from Texas to get to a Red Cross train. On the way to the station Carlos was in his glory, chatting up the Spanish-speaking soldiers. I thought of butting in with the story of how Carlos became a Red Army coat hanger, but he just had too big a smile on his face. Maybe I had finally mastered biting my tongue.

♦ ♦ ♦

The Red Cross train, stuffed with soldiers, displaced persons, and Red Cross nurses, snaked through Holland and Belgium. Eight days later I was in a Paris military hospital, where I finally wrote my parents that I was alive and would be home soon. Four weeks after the letter, a friend of the family arrived to see why I was still in Paris. My parents were quite upset when the friend phoned and said the reason was a young waitress, which was not quite the truth. I was in no hurry to get home because I was afraid of what I would find, or more exactly what I wouldn't find, in my hometown.

The train to Nice was crowded with Allied servicemen heading for a well-deserved furlough on the French Riviera. I rode in first class, courtesy of the French government, and was the only civilian in the dilapidated compartment. I sat next to a husky, barrel-chested U.S. Navy officer and remarked on all his medals and battle ribbons. The officer replied, "If Hirohito doesn't throw in the towel pretty soon, I may still see some action and then I'll run out of space on my chest."

I stood alone on the Nice train platform that had been the starting point of my odyssey. There was no welcoming party for me. Wanting to put off the inevitable tears, hugs, kisses, smiles, and questions as long as I could, I made sure no one knew I was arriving home that day. On the way to the streetcar stop I passed the Hotel Excelsior. What room had Stella and her parents been locked up in before the Nazis marched them to the train? I wondered. The hotel windows were broken and bullet holes pockmarked the walls.

"The Resistance killed some of those bastards when they stormed the building during the liberation," an elderly gentleman with a red rosette of the Legion of Honor in his lapel volunteered. He noticed the tattoo on my arm, shook my hand, and saluted.

Walking up my street, I found my apprehension compounded by the sight of our front yard overgrown with weeds. The front door was ajar and the doorknob was missing. I entered the vestibule and then the living room, both rooms bare of furniture. What had happened? A noise came from the dining room. My father was eating at a ramshackle table. We stared at each other in silence for a very long time. He raised himself painfully from his chair. Tears were running down his cheeks.

"You just missed Claude." He said in a trembling voice.

My mother came in from the kitchen. She stood open-mouthed in the doorway and dropped the pan she was holding.

I was home.

◆ ◆ ◆

At that time I had no desire to put my ordeal down on paper, no need to purge myself of Nazi-induced nightmares. Frankly, I'd re-acclimated rather nicely to my former life in Nice. I attended a branch of the University of *Aix-Marseille* so I could finish my philosophy degree (even though I still believed it was all crap), and took a night course in jewelry making (something practical). My parents had weathered the war relatively unscathed except for having our house looted and occupied by Gestapo goons.

Claude had avoided the Gestapo and the *milice* and had become somewhat of a hero in the Maquis. Carlos was now working in a thermometer factory in nearby Menton. Bernard was gone. Like so many in France and throughout Europe, he was unaccounted for, and the likelihood of ever learning his fate was nil. His mother was hysterical. Bernard was her only child. Every time I went to see her, she'd ask if I was positive I hadn't seen her son in Auschwitz. Finally I just couldn't take it anymore and stopped coming by.

In August 1945 a picture of the A-bomb dropped on Hiroshima was framed and hung in the office window of the Nice newspaper *Eclaireur*. A few months later, the doctor who'd been treating my father's cancer with radiation and loads of arsenic advised him to go to America, where they were fighting leukemia with the radioactive fallout from A-bomb tests. When our visas finally arrived in 1947, I was working part-time for the French army as an interpreter for German POWs and had been offered the position as head inter-preter in Normandy. I would have gotten officers' pay, but I couldn't abandon my parents at this critical juncture. So we flew to New York City, then made our way to Santa Monica, California.

For me, America was a happy-go-lucky place where there was no bitterness and animosity toward neighbors who'd collaborated with the enemy, no postwar food rationing, and no embarrassment from being occupied by "the god with a moustache." I was riding the buses and streetcars and walking the sidewalks of the country that had liberated *mon pays* (my country). I was in the land of giants. Naturally, the scars of war weren't as apparent as they were in Europe, but now and then I'd see a man with an empty suit jacket sleeve or a young man with crutches instead of legs.

Work was tough to get then. There was a depression on. Most jobs created by the war had vanished with the victory. Many GI's stepped back into their old jobs while many more pounded the pavement alongside me. There were times, as I stood at bus stops, that I kicked myself for leaving such a plum job back in France. Finally, I got hired at the BB Pen Company in Hollywood as a maintenance man, which meant I did a little of everything.

Every so often someone would notice the tattoo on my left arm and ask what it meant. A few would ask me more questions, but most didn't care. It was painfully obvious that a majority of Americans knew very little about the 11 million men, women, and children who passed through the concentration camps. They were more concerned about the boys who died on Okinawa and other Pacific Islands that no one had ever heard of before and their country's devastating new weapon.

On the swing shift one night at BB, this riveter—a tall blonde who was in her forties—asked me if it was rough in the Nazi camps.

"You have no idea," I told her.

"Did you get enough to eat?" she asked.

When I told her I was half my body weight at the end of the war, she paused for a moment then said, "Yes, it was rough here, too. All we had to eat was chicken."

I nodded, thinking that if in Monowitz somebody had given me the choice between a night with Miss America or a chicken leg, I'd . . . Well, by now you know the answer to that one.

Riding the bus back to Santa Monica that night I decided to put to paper what I'd gone through, a belated diary if you may, so I wouldn't forget. That was the fall of 1947. I'd write whenever I got the chance—on the bus to and from work, on my lunch breaks, and on a bench overlooking the Pacific Ocean. I wrote it in French. I could speak English pretty well, but the written language gave me fits. I wrote on notepads that my mother would then type. I titled it *An Odyssey of a Pajama*.

In 1952, I paid a UCLA French-language student, a friend of a friend of my mother, two hundred dollars, and five months later my *Odyssey* was translated, but I was disheartened that somewhere, somehow, my manuscript had lost its meaning. So along with working two jobs and the seeming disinterest in the Nazis' atrocities, I put the manuscript in a drawer. Living life just seemed more important than retracing the past.

In 1954, I allowed a girlfriend, a librarian, to read my manuscript, and she convinced me to submit it to the *Saturday Evening Post* and *Harper's*. Their rejection letters sent my *Odyssey* back in the drawer. And there it sat through the 1950s and the birth of the cold war, and the start of my career as a cine-technician, repairing and rebuilding film projectors, cameras, and developers. There it sat through the 1960s and the civil rights marches, the Vietnam War, and Suharto, the 1970s and Pol Pot and Pinochet, and the 1980s and Central American death squads, and countless massacres of innocent life in Africa.

The Holocaust was now a household word, and many brave survivors had already done much to ensure that the world would never forget. I still wanted to weigh in, but to be blunt, I didn't think anyone cared to hear the story of an atheist red triangle. I loathed the skinheads and neo-Nazis I saw on TV who proclaimed that the Holocaust never happened. Those morons couldn't tell you what continent Germany is on, and they exalt a coward who committed suicide after ordering brainwashed youths to their slaughter on the barricaded streets of Berlin. More than anyone else, those bigots made me want to get my manuscript out of the drawer and into the hands of someone who would help me shape it so it could sit on a library shelf.

By the fall of 2001 I was retired but working part-time as an usher at the Cannon Theatre in Beverly Hills. I discovered that the brooding young man behind the concession stand was a writer. I hadn't spoken to Brian—he just didn't seem the type to bother with idle chitchat—but when I told him I'd written about my time in the camps, he stopped setting up the cookies and candies. He said he'd really like to read it, and the next night I brought him my only copy.

The next time I saw Brian he told me he'd read my manuscript in one night and wanted to help me develop and expand the manuscript so it could grab a publisher's attention. He convinced me that this wouldn't be an insurmountable task, but it was a tough road for both of us. The manuscript needed more description and explanation. I struggled with memories and feelings that I had long buried as Brian, a perfectionist, agonized over the choice of words and sentences. Having done his research, Brian asked the right questions and I filled in the gaps. Three years later my *Odyssey* became *Scheisshaus Luck*.

◆ ◆ ◆

We have never learned from history, so I hate to admit that I'm not optimistic that the genocide and enslavement on the scope orchestrated by the Nazis will never be repeated. "The god with a moustache" didn't invent concentration camps and genocide. I have read that he used the U.S. government's handling of Native Americans as one of his blueprints. The Jewish people will never let it happen to them again. Yet we all know that the extermination of innocent human beings designated as "the other"—whether because of their skin, their religion or lack thereof, their politics, their ancestral tribe, or just because they're the most convenient scapegoat—

continues unabated and unchecked. That doesn't mean the voices of reason and the victims of atrocities should ever stuff their thoughts and recollections in a drawer. We'll never find utopia, but that doesn't mean we should stop seeking it. Just maybe, some day, the human race will conquer its learning disability.

AFTERWORD

Joseph Robert White,
*University of Maryland University College,
Adelphi, Maryland*

Although there are many French gentile accounts of Dora, the same cannot be said of Auschwitz-Monowitz. Two Jewish testimonies, by Georges Wellers and Paul Steinberg, have been published, but only Steinberg's is available in English. For this camp, reliable gentile accounts of any nationality are rare. Most were contributed by Poles, in a few instances by prisoners allegedly complicit in the elimination of Jews. Pierre Berg's account, therefore, makes a welcome addition to the Monowitz testimonies.[1]

Mr. Berg attributes his arrest and survival to "*Scheisshaus* luck." If not eloquently expressed, it undoubtedly captures the feelings of many surviving victims. Too often, the general public and even historians insult survivors with the impossible question, "Why did you survive?" Mr. Berg's emphasis upon the terrible misfortune leading to his arrest and to the rare moments of good fortune give a sense of the contingencies that always lurked beyond a prisoner's control under the Nazi regime. As his account shows, confusion over a prisoner's number or the mix-up over a brand-new shirt made the difference between life and death.[2]

Mr. Berg's privileges derived mainly from his facility with languages. Unlike Primo Levi, who passed a life-or-death interview in academic German at the I.G. Auschwitz Buna Polymerization Detachment, Mr. Berg spoke the language fluently, after frequent childhood vacations in Germany. His multilingual experience underscored Levi's memorable description of the I.G. Carbide Tower as a modern-day "Tower of Babel." Besides French and German, Mr. Berg spoke Italian, English, and Spanish on the I.G. building site. His technical skills and problem-solving abilities likewise were fortuitous, although he endured months of backbreaking work in labor crews.[3]

The Monowitz Hospital Book records Mr. Berg's admission to the *Häftlingskrankenbau*, or prisoners' infirmary. The volume submitted into evidence at Nuremberg records 15,706 patient admissions between 15 July 1943 and 27 June 1944. Among them, it listed 766 patients as dying in hospital, as indicated by a cross stamped in the margin; and 2,599 selected for murder at the Auschwitz Main Camp or Birkenau, as indicated by the marginal annotations, "To Auschwitz" or "To Birkenau." Patient entries recorded as returning to the general population were stamped "*Entlassen.*" Mr. Berg's entry read: "Entry 21725, [Prisoner Number], Berg, Peter Isr[ael], 31.3.-13.4.44, Released." Erroneously, it listed him as Jewish, so he was in greater danger than even he realized at the time, because after the fall of 1943 the SS confined hospital selections almost exclusively to Jewish prisoners. It is not clear whether the Anglicization of his name was his idea or inspired in some way by the neighboring British POW camp, which had opened in September 1943. His hospitalization coincided with Primo Levi's, although Mr. Berg states that the two never knew each other. By January 1944, the Monowitz infirmary comprised seven blocks, so it is not surprising that the two did not meet. Levi was admitted one day earlier than Mr. Berg, 30 March, after injuring his foot while hauling an iron fitting at the job site. He was released seven days later than Mr. Berg, on 20 April.[4]

A minor detail furnishes a telling example of Mr. Berg's memory. He is the first survivor to describe the raising and lowering of a "red and orange basket" before air attacks at the I.G. plant. Only days after the massive 20 August 1944 raid by the U.S. Fifteenth Air Force, Plant Leader Walther Dürrfeld issued a directive intended to augment the existing air-raid sirens with a visual warning system. Installed at one building in each quadrant, these baskets were intended to reinforce the alarm system. This small detail does not overshadow the import of Mr. Berg's testimony—namely, that prisoners scattered helter-skelter around the plant because they were denied access to air-raid shelters. Their concern was more than theoretical, because U.S. and Soviet forces bombed I.G. Auschwitz six times between August 1944 and January 1945.[5]

Like Levi and Paul Steinberg, the real-life "Henri" of Levi's *Survival in Auschwitz*, Mr. Berg met British POWs at I.G. Auschwitz. The POWs were held at a subcamp E715 of Stalag VIII B (Lamsdorf/Teschen). E715's population rose to approximately 1,200 by December 1943, but declined to 600 in Spring of 1944, when about half were transferred elsewhere. Mr. Berg's description of the POWs as healthy "strutting roosters" dovetails with accounts by Levi and Steinberg. The British were proud of their strong military bearing, in contrast to the shabby Wehrmacht guards who controlled them. As Mr. Berg recalled, the POWs quickly caught the attention of female civilian workers, most notably Poles and Ukrainians. Although Mr. Berg characterized the POWs as "Commonwealth," they were mostly English with a small number of Canadians, Australians, and South Africans included. Realizing their special status among the plant's forced laborers, particularly their protection under the Geneva Convention, and gathering significant details about the Nazis' murderous activities, the British did what they could to aid the far more numerous "stripees" in their midst.[6]

With respect to Dora, Mr. Berg's account complements Yves Béon's *Planet Dora*. As Michael Neufeld observes, French memoirs have dominated the testimonies of this camp, despite the fact that the French were listed as the third most numerous nationality, behind the Soviets and Poles, in a 1 November 1944 SS report. What sets Mr. Berg's testimony apart is the timing of his arrival, during the winter of 1945, almost one year after the completion of the barracks and more than six months after the underground factory achieved full operational capacity. The barracks relieved the early prisoners, like Béon, of sleeping inside the tunnel. While many French prisoners were transferred to Dora after brief confinement in Buchenwald, Mr. Berg's Monowitz experience sets "Planet Dora" in a different perspective, as he arrived after the production passed its peak but before the evacuations began. Unlike many French prisoners, Mr. Berg had already experienced the shock of entering a concentration camp, after surviving one year at Auschwitz and a terrifying evacuation.[7]

As a recent immigrant to the United States, Pierre Berg wrote down his memories of wartime captivity in his native French. He started this memoir in 1947 with no immediate thoughts of eventual publication and remained somewhat reluctant, after its rejection in 1954 by the *Saturday Evening Post*, to publish it fifty years later. In the early 1950s, a University of California, Los Angeles, graduate student translated the French original into English under the title, "The Odyssey of a Pajama," but Mr. Berg did not believe that the translator did justice to the nuances of his testimony. In preparing this testimony for publication, Mr. Brock combined "Odyssey" with extensive interviews conducted over three years. I have compared both versions and can attest that this memoir is faithful in most respects to the original, except that this version helpfully elicits detail that was glossed over in the original. Regrettably, Mr. Berg misplaced the French original manuscript, but the *Saturday Evening Post's* rejection letter of 16 April 1954 helps to date Mr. Berg's original English account.[8]

Although as literature or history his memoir cannot be compared with Primo Levi's and Elie Wiesel's canonical Holocaust texts, *Survival in Auschwitz* and *Night*, Mr. Berg's Auschwitz experience reinforces these famous testimonies. Like Wiesel and Levi, Mr. Berg toiled at I.G. Auschwitz under unspeakable conditions in 1944. Like Wiesel, he was a teenager, but three years older and already well traveled. Like Levi, he drafted his original account shortly after the war, when his memory of events was most vivid. An atheist like Levi, he therefore did not situate his traumatic experience in terms of theodicy, as did Wiesel. Like Levi's *The Reawakening*, Mr. Berg recounts his odyssey back to civilization and his not-altogether-pleasant encounters with Soviet troops. One striking feature of this account absent in Levi's and Wiesel's writings is Mr. Berg's unmistakable cynicism.[9]

In the interest of full disclosure, I must confess one reservation about this account. Mr. Berg insists that he saw *Reichsführer* SS Heinrich Himmler at I.G. Auschwitz in the summer of 1944. No known primary source verifies this claim. Himmler's recorded visits took place on 1 March 1941 and 17 July 1942. Himmler's first visit concerned the expansion of Auschwitz, in order to meet the labor needs of the I.G. Farben plant, which had yet to break ground. The second combined an inspection of the I.G. construction site with a tour of the Birkenau killing center, then not yet the center of industrial mass murder it was to become in 1943 and 1944. It is likely that in 1944 Mr. Berg saw one of Himmler's many *doppelgängers*.[10]

The following comments are intended to set Mr. Berg's memoirs in the context of the Nazi concentration camp system and the I.G. Farben project at Auschwitz.

◆ ◆ ◆

When Pierre Berg entered Auschwitz-Monowitz in January 1944, the Nazi concentration camps had been operational for almost eleven years. The history of the concentration camps can be divided into six phases, each tied to the Nazi regime's changing political or military fortunes. Mr. Berg entered the camps during their fifth phase (1942–1944). In the first (1933–1934), the concentration and "protective custody" (*Schutzhaft*) camps contributed to the Nazi Seizure of Power, and to the subsequent "synchronization" (*Gleichschaltung*) of German society. The Nazi *Schutzstaffel* (SS or Protective Corps) established one of the first concentration camps at Dachau in March 1933 and the Storm Troopers (*Sturmabteilungen*, or SA) created ad hoc camps in many localities. After 1933 the total camp population declined drastically because of amnesties. It consisted mainly of political prisoners, especially communists and socialists. Career criminals newly released from prison also appeared in the early camps. During the first phase, Dachau became the model camp when its second commandant, Theodor Eicke, established severe regulations for the permanent SS camps. In July 1934, Eicke became the first Inspector of Concentration Camps (IKL), after playing a key role in the purge of leading SA members during the "Night of the Long Knives." The IKL's establishment ushered in the camps' second phase, 1934 to 1936, when most remaining early camps were closed and Eicke practiced what historian Michael Thad Allen terms "the primacy of policing": camp labor was supposed to be torture that served no rational end.[11]

The third phase of Nazi concentration camps took place from 1936 to 1939. This period saw first the limited and then mass expansion of the camps, with the establishment of Sachsenhausen (1936), near the site of the former early camp of Oranienburg, Buchenwald (1937), Mauthausen (1938), Flossenbürg (1938), and finally Ravensbrück women's camp (1939). The last early camps, including Esterwegen and Sachsenburg, closed at this time. "Asocials," who allegedly avoided work, engaged in prostitution, or whose behavior otherwise fell short of the ideal "national comrade," were targeted for mass arrest in 1937. Also in 1937, the camp authorities established a standardized triangle system for the entire camp system, which indicated the reason for arrest on the prisoner's striped uniform. As described by Buchenwalder and sociologist Eugen Kogon, this system fueled bitter prisoner rivalries and thus served the SS objective of *divide et impera*. A red triangle symbolized political detainees; green, career criminals; purple, Jehovah's Witnesses; black, "asocials"; blue, Jewish emigrants; and pink, homosexuals. Jewish detainees were identified by combining a yellow triangle with an above-listed arrest category in the form of a Star of David. The first mass influx of Jews into the camps occurred in the second phase, with the temporary arrests of tens of thousands of

Jewish men following the November 1938 pogrom, misleadingly known as "The Night of Broken Glass" (*Kristallnacht*).[12]

During the fourth phase, 1939 to 1941, the SS extended the camp system and the accompanying terror to the conquered territories. The new camps included Auschwitz (1940), Neuengamme (1940), Gross Rosen (inside Germany, 1941), and Natzweiler (1941). With Eicke's appointment to command the SS Death's Head Division (*Totenkopfsdivision*) in wartime, SS-Brigadeführer Richard Glücks became the new Inspector. An ineffectual, colorless individual, Glücks did little to stamp an imprint upon IKL. With war's outbreak, the Gestapo immediately dispatched political opponents to the camps, like Sachsenhausen, for execution, without a judicial sentence. At this time, tensions began to surface between administrators who saw the camps as intended exclusively for breaking the regime's enemies and those who desired to exploit captive labor for the economy. In this period, Eicke's protégés held the upper hand: SS overseers employed what was euphemistically termed "sport" for the purpose of killing or demoralizing prisoners, including purposeless labor conducted at breakneck pace as a form of torture. In the mid-1930s, at a time of high unemployment, Reichsführer-SS Himmler led German industrialists on a tour of Dachau, with the aim of both justifying the necessity of unlimited detention and eliciting interest in his captive labor supply. Only the civilian worker shortages produced by Nazi rearmament (1936–1939) altered the situation, however, when the SS created an enterprise to prepare building stone for Adolf Hitler's numerous monumental projects and then developed other businesses connected to the its far-flung missions. As Allen convincingly shows, the SS were disastrous managers, which when combined with "sport" meant that these new enterprises foundered.[13]

Among the fourth-phase camps, Auschwitz was originally intended to hold Polish political enemies. Founded in June 1940, over a thousand Poles were detained there less than six months later. The first Auschwitz commandant, Rudolf Höss, transferred a small number of hardened German criminals from his previous assignment at Sachsenhausen to serve as camp trusties. An "Eicke School" commandant, Höss oversaw Auschwitz's transformation from political prison to industrial complex and, most infamously, killing center.[14]

The camp's fifth phase took place when the war that Hitler unleashed turned decisively against him, with Allied counteroffensives in the Soviet Union, North Africa, Italy, and, ultimately, northwestern France. The German war economy thereupon entered the so-called total war phase, with the rationalization of war production under Armaments Minister Albert Speer, the mass mobilization of foreign workers under Fritz Sauckel, and the deployment of camp labor in private German industry under the SS Business Administration Main Office (SS-*Wirtschafts Verwaltungshauptamt*, or WVHA). In connection with the latter, I.G. Farben's erection of the Monowitz camp, discussed in detail below, furnished a model for other subcamps, with the location adjacent to, or inside, factory grounds. By late 1944, camp labor was the principal untapped workforce remaining to the German war economy, with hundreds of thousands of prisoners dispatched to work in construction, bomb disposal, and manufacturing. In the name of economic efficiency, the SS-WVHA attempted to militate against the effects of SS "sport" as practiced by Eicke commandants. The results were mixed and the WVHA did nothing about the annihilation of physically exhausted prisoners or the mass murder of able-bodied Jews during Operation Reinhard. In order to exploit their labor more extensively, private industry modestly improved detainee treatment. The camps' last phase, 1944 to 1945, witnessed the disastrous evacuations or "death marches" of malnourished and weakened prisoners from territories adjacent to front-line areas. As Mr. Berg's account demonstrates, these marches often assumed an inertia of their own, as the SS marched their exhausted victims with little sense of direction, except to get away from the Allies. Lest the proximity of Allied planes and troops raise morale, the SS warned more than once that their last bullets were reserved for the prisoners.[15]

◆ ◆ ◆

The *Interessengemeinschaft Farbenindustrie Aktiengesellschaft* (Community of Interests, Dye Industry, Public Corporation, or I.G. Farben) inaugurated its Auschwitz project during the camp system's fourth phase. Preparations for the chemical plant began during the critical nine months between Germany's frustration in the Battle of Britain in September 1940 and Operation Barbarossa, the German invasion of the Soviet Union, which started on 22 June 1941. It is easy to lose sight of these two strategic facts, which are significant for understanding how rapidly the conditions for planning this complicated project changed in wartime Germany. With the Luftwaffe's defeat in the Battle of Britain, the Reich demanded that I.G. Farben expand synthetic rubber (Buna) and oil production in the expectation of a prolonged war, despite the firm's well-known concern about the construction of excessive production capacity. Royal Air Force Bomber Command's raid on the second I.G. Buna plant at Hüls in the fall of 1940 reinforced government fears of an aerial threat against Germany's small but strategically vital synthetic rubber supply, which led to more insistent calls for the construction of an eastern Buna plant, at relatively safe remove from Allied bombers.[16]

Careful surveys by Buna expert and I.G. *Vorstand* (managing board) member Dr. Otto Ambros in December 1940 revealed a huge stretch of land in the village of Dwóry, at the nexus of the Vistula, Sola, and Przemsza Rivers as the optimal site. Its location five kilometers from the new Auschwitz concentration camp nursed unproven allegations, at Nuremberg and later, that the firm selected the site exclusively or partly because of its proximity to "slave" labor. The executives did not discuss the labor issue, however, until convinced of the site's long-term viability, which included access to essential raw materials, electrical power, excellent rail communications, and space for future growth. An oil firm's previous bid for the same property led Farben to graft oil production onto the synthetic rubber project. For the German chemical industry, this decision amounted to an unprecedented amalgamation of low-temperature polymerization with high-temperature/high-pressure hydrogenation. The Nazi Four-Year Plan (VJP) chief, Reichsmarschall Hermann Göring, ordered the firm to utilize Auschwitz prisoners in the construction of the war plant. Göring's assistant, Dr. Carl Krauch, VJP's authority on chemical questions and titular head of the I.G. Farben Supervisory Board (*Aufsichtsrat*), later boasted that *he* had secured camp labor on the firm's behalf. As historian Peter Hayes points out, evidence has not emerged to date to demonstrate that the initiative for requesting slave labor rested with I.G. Farben.[17]

However, once committed to working with the Nazi SS, I.G. quickly adjusted to the exploitation of Auschwitz labor. The project broke ground in April 1941, when the first prisoners trudged five kilometers to the building site under armed guard. The managers and German workers increasingly viewed the prisoners in SS terms, well before the first Jewish detainees arrived at the I.G. building site in July 1942. A comment by construction chief Max Faust about Polish civilian workers, in December 1941, indicated the pernicious effect of the SS on I.G.'s thinking:

> Also outrageous is the lack of work discipline on the part of Polish workers. Numerous laborers work at the most 3–4 days in the week. All forms of pressure, even admission into the KL [concentration camp], remain fruitless. Unfortunately, always doing this leaves the construction leadership with no disciplinary powers at its disposal. *According to our previous experience only brute force bears fruit with these men.* [Emphasis added.][18]

Much as I.G. Auschwitz was problematic without Germany's reversals of fortune in the summer of 1940, it would never have been undertaken if agreements had not been made before the launching of Operation Barbarossa. Contrary to certain postwar claims, I.G. executives did not know about the Führer's decisions for aggressive war. Operation Barbarossa disrupted their timetables because the German army's monopoly on the railways in the summer of 1941 cost almost four months of irreplaceable construction time when the start date for oil and rubber production was scheduled for the spring of 1943. With every passing month, the target slipped further away. Unrealistic timetables and frustration over the Krauch Office's lack of empathy for local conditions contributed to I.G.'s willingness to resort to barbaric SS methods. The failure of Barbarossa in December 1941 led the Nazi regime to reassess its construction priorities, with the closure of projects in the early stages unlikely to contribute to "Final Victory." Although the Auschwitz project had not progressed very far, it received strong endorsement from Göring, Himmler, and Albert Speer.[19]

For purely utilitarian reasons, I.G. managers alleviated some of the worst working conditions. In order to curtail the ten-kilometer daily march, a short railway line was built between the camp and the building site. To place some distance between sadistic SS guards and the prisoners, the building site was enclosed with a fence while the guards remained along the periphery outside the plant. The latter project took much longer to complete than anticipated because the Auschwitz-based SS Company, German Equipment Works (*Deutsche Ausrüstungswerke*), was unable to deliver the fence in timely fashion. Shortly after the fence was erected, and only weeks after the first Jewish prisoners started to work on the job site, typhus *and* typhoid epidemics broke out in Auschwitz concentration camp. In late July 1942, Höss responded by quarantining the camps and murdering the infected. The epidemics were directly attributable to the SS and I.G. because prisoners were forced to endure inhuman conditions with vicious treatment, starvation diet, exhaustive labor, and unrelieved stress. In coping with the temporary loss of unskilled camp labor, I.G. allocated a fourth work camp, intended originally for civilian workers, to serve as a new Auschwitz satellite, Monowitz.[20]

Erected on the building site's periphery in what had been the demolished Polish village of Monowice, the new camp opened in late October 1942. From beginning to end, Monowitz's population was overwhelmingly Jewish. The camp prominents included German criminals and a small number of German Jewish political prisoners removed from camps in the Old Reich. The latter prisoners were transferred on Himmler's order to make "*Judenfrei*" (free of Jews) the older concentration camps like Dachau and Buchenwald. Consisting mostly of Communist Party members, these Jewish prisoners formed the nucleus of the resistance and their actions made Monowitz far less deadly for the prisoners than it otherwise would have been.[21]

Nevertheless conditions were lethal at Monowitz. Between November 1942 and January 1945, the death toll reached between 23,000 and 25,000 prisoners. This estimate excludes the losses of early Auschwitz prisoners in 1941 and 1942—that is, before Monowitz's establishment. At Monowitz, the SS undertook periodic "selections" of weakened prisoners, known as *Muselmänner*, during camp marches. I.G. managers attended some of these selections. The SS dispatched the selected to Birkenau for gassing or to Auschwitz for killing by lethal injection. On a smaller scale the selections continued in the infirmary, where SS doctors ordered the transfer for killing of those prisoners whose recovery would occupy bedding space for an indefinite period. Because Monowitz was built partly in response to Auschwitz epidemics, the firm took steps to ensure that new detainees had not been exposed to typhus. These measures were not always benign. After selection at Birkenau, new prisoners were taken to Monowitz and held in a quarantine camp for several weeks. While there they worked as a segregated labor detail at the construction site. The manifestation of typhus symptoms among any new arrivals led to the murder of the entire detachment.[22]

By the time Mr. Berg arrived at Monowitz, the I.G. building site had assumed recognizable shape as a chemical plant, in spite of war-economy frictions and SS incompetence. In the fall of 1943, the plant began producing synthetic methanol, an alcohol derived from coal under immense pressure. Methanol was useful in the production of rocket fuel and explosives and constituted

I.G. Auschwitz's principal contribution to the German war economy. The plant also produced the explosives component, diglycol, and in the summer of 1944 was contracted to produce phosgene, a chemical weapon used in combat during World War I, but not World War II.[23]

With increasing need for skilled laborers to outfit the partially finished buildings, many unskilled prisoners were redeployed from the autumn of 1943 in the construction of makeshift and permanent air-raid shelters. Previously, the firm had given air-raid protection low priority, but abruptly changed course with the Allied advances in Sicily and Italy in the summer of 1943. (The capture of southern Italy brought Poland within the theoretical bombing range of the U.S. Army Air Force.) The air campaign in the summer and fall of 1944 magnified the horrors of the prisoners' daily existence, even as these attacks underscored that the Nazi regime's days were numbered. At least 158 Monowitz prisoners were killed in the course of four U.S. daylight bombing raids between August and December 1944. The Soviets also attacked the plant at least twice in December 1944 and January 1945. The number of detainees killed in the December and January attacks is unknown, but all the air attacks disrupted water, food, and electrical power, even as they also raised morale.[24]

By December 1944, the I.G. Auschwitz labor force included almost every European nationality. Its "paper" strength was 31,000, with 29,000 effectives at work. These workers included Italian civilians and Italian military internees, British POWs, Belgian and French contract workers, numerous Poles and Ukrainians (both forced and "free"), and other non-Jewish Eastern Europeans. The status of workers, free or forced, depended upon the regime's dictates and I.G. Farben's assessment of their labor productivity. Theoretically, Monowitz comprised one-third of the total I.G. Auschwitz workforce (just over 10,000 prisoners), but the number of forced laborers at the plant was smaller. In November 1944 the WVHA listed Monowitz as a new main camp, with responsibility for the almost forty Auschwitz satellites. The establishment of the

Monowitz and Mittelbau (Dora) main camps was part of the last reorganization of the SS camp system.[25]

For Monowitz's prisoners, horrible days lay ahead. In January 1945, the Soviets began the Vistula-Oder Offensive and the timing caught the German army by surprise. The Red Army consequently captured the still unfinished plant with little damage. The SS evacuated Monowitz on 18 January, as part of the larger evacuation of the Auschwitz satellite camps. The "death march" that Mr. Berg describes so vividly had begun.[26]

After four years of construction, I.G. Auschwitz remained unfinished. Under the Germans at least, it never produced synthetic oil or rubber, but wasted tens of thousands of human lives. The plant was a monument to a totalitarian dictatorship that enlisted private industry in the service of refashioning humanity along "racial" lines.

NOTES

1. André Sellier, *A History of the Dora Camp: The Story of the Nazi Slave Labor Camp That Secretly Manufactured V-2 Rockets*, foreword by Michael J. Neufeld, afterword by Jens-Christian Wagner, trans. Stephen Wright and Susan Taponier (Chicago: Ivan R. Dee, published in associated with the United States Holocaust Memorial Museum, 2003); Yves Béon, *Planet Dora: A Memoir of the Holocaust and the Birth of the Space Age*, introduction by Michael J. Neufeld, trans. Yves Béon and Richard L. Fague (Boulder, CO: Westview Press, 1997); Georges Wellers, *De Drancy à Auschwitz* (Paris: Éditions du Centre, 1946); reissued under the title of *L'étoile jaune à l'heure de Vichy: De Drancy à Auschwitz* (Paris: Librairie Arthème Fayard, 1973); Paul Steinberg, *Speak You Also: A Survivor's Reckoning*, trans. Linda Coverdale with Bill Ford (New York: Metropolitan Books, Henry Holt and Company, 2000), originally published as *Chronique d'ailleurs* (Paris: Editions Ramsay, 1996); Antoni Makowski, "Organization, Growth and Activity of the Prisoners' Hospital

at Monowitz (KL Auschwitz III)," in *From the History of KL Auschwitz*, vol. II, ed. Kasimierz Smolen, trans. Kryztyna Michalik (Kraków: Panstwowe Muzeum w Oswiecimiu, 1976), pp. 121–195.

2. Lawrence L. Langer, *Holocaust Testimonies: The Ruins of Memory* (New Haven and London: Yale University Press, 1991).

3. Primo Levi, *Survival in Auschwitz: The Nazi Assault on Humanity*, trans. Stuart Woolf (New York and London: Collier's, 1961), p. 66 (quotation).

4. National Archives and Records Administration (NARA), RG-238 (War Crimes), microfilm publication T-301, Records of the United States Chief of Counsel for War Crimes, Nuremberg, Relating to Nuremberg Industrialists (NI), roll 84, NI-10186, frames 382–383, 565–566, Monowitz Hospital Book, 15 July 1943–27 June 1944, hereafter T-301/84/NI-10186/382–383, 565–566. Pierre Berg telephone interview, 13 June 2004; Levi, *Survival in Auschwitz*, pp. 39–50; on hospital blocks, Makowski, "Organization, Growth and Activity of the Prisoners' Hospital at Monowitz (KL Auschwitz III)," p. 129. Two more blocks were added before Monowitz's abandonment in January 1945.

5. United States Holocaust Memorial Museum Archives, Moscow Central State *Osobyi* (special) Archives, Record Group (RG-) 11.001 M.03, Zentralbauleitung der Waffen SS und Polizei Auschwitz, *fond* (record group) 502, *opis* (inventory) 5, *delo* (file) 2, roll 70, Rundschreiben Nr. 8013/44, IG Auschwitz Werksluftschutzleitung, Dürrfeld, Betr.: "Sichtbares Warnsignal," 25 Aug. 1944, p. 43; on the documented air attacks, see Joseph Robert White, "Target Auschwitz: Historical and Hypothetical Allied Responses to Allied Attack," *Holocaust and Genocide Studies* (*HGS*) 16:1 (Spring 2002): 58–59.

6. Steinberg, *Speak You Also*; White, "'Even in Auschwitz . . . Humanity Could Prevail': British POWs and Jewish Concentration-Camp Inmates at IG Auschwitz, 1943–1945," *HGS* 15:2 (Fall 2001): 266–295.

7. For the nationality figures, see Michael Neufeld, "Introduction: Mittelbau-Dora—Secret Weapons and Slave Labor," in Béon,

Planet Dora, p. xx; idem, "Foreword," in Sellier, *A History of the Dora Camp*, p. x; for the history of Dora, see also Joachim Neander, *Das Konzentrationslager Mittelbau in der Endphase der NS-Diktatur: Zur Geschichte des letzten im "Dritten Reich" gegründeten selbständigen Konzentrationslagers unter besonderer Berücksichtigung seiner Auflösungsphase* (Clausthal-Zellerfeld: Papierflieger, 1997); and most importantly Jens-Christian Wagner, *Produktion des Todes: Das KZ Mittelbau-Dora*, ed. Stiftung von der Gedenkstätten Buchenwald und Mittelbau-Dora (Göttingen: Wallstein Verlag, 2001).

8. Pierre Berg, "Odyssey of a Pajama" (unpub. MSS, 1953); Berg, telephone interview, 13 June 2004.

9. Elie Wiesel, *Night*, trans. Stella Rodway, foreword by François Mauriac, preface by Robert McAfee Brown (New York: Bantam, 1986 [1960]); Levi, *The Reawakening* (New York: Summit Books, 1986 [1963]). On the Soviet occupation, see Norman M. Naimark, *The Russians in Germany: A History of the Soviet Zone of Occupation, 1945–1949* (Cambridge, MA, and London: The Belknap Press of Harvard University Press, 1995); and Antony Beevor, *The Fall of Berlin 1945* (New York and London: Viking Penguin, 2002).

10. For the recorded Himmler visits, see Danuta Czech (comp.), *Auschwitz Chronicle, 1939–1945* (New York: Henry Holt and Co., 1990), pp. 50–51, 198–199.

11. For the six-phase schema, see Karin Orth, *Das System der nationalsozialistischen Konzentrationslager: Eine politische* Organisationsgeschichte (Hamburg: Hamburger Edition, 1999); an older, three-phase scheme is outlined in Falk Pingel, *Häftlinge unter SS-Herrschaft: Widerstand, Selbstbehauptung, und Vernichtung im Konzentrationslager* (Hamburg: Hoffmann und Campe, 1978), p. 14; and idem, "Resistance and Resignation in Nazi Concentration Camps," in *The Policies of Genocide: Jews and Soviet Prisoners of War in Nazi Germany*, ed. Gerhard Hirschfeld (London: Allen & Unwin, 1986), pp. 30–72. Klaus Drobisch and Günther Wieland, *System der NS-Konzentrationslager, 1933–1939* (Berlin: Akademie Verlag, 1993),

11–75; see also Wolfgang Benz and Barbara Distel (eds.), *Instrumentarium der Macht: Frühe Konzentrationslager, 1933–1937* (Berlin: Metropol, 2003); Charles W. Sydnor, Jr., *Soldiers of Destruction: The SS Death's Head Division, 1933–1945* (Princeton: Princeton University Press, 1977), pp. 15–17; quotation in Michael Thad Allen, *The Business of Genocide: The SS, Slave Labor, and the Concentration Camps* (Chapel Hill and London: University of North Carolina Press, 2002), p. 36.

12. Falk Pingel, "Concentration Camps," s.v., *Encyclopedia of the Holocaust*, ed. Israel Gutman (New York: Macmillan Publishing Co.; London: Collier MacMillan, 1990); Eugon Kogon, *The Theory and Practice of Hell*, trans. Heinz Norden (New York: Berkley Books, 1980 [1950]), pp. 29–39; on the triangle system's origins, see Annette Eberle, "Häftlingskategorien und Kennzeichnungen," in Wolfgang Benz and Barbara Distel (ed.), *Der Ort des Terrors: Geschichte der nationalsozialistischen Konzentrationslager*, vol. I: *Die Organisation des Terrors* (Munich: C.H. Beck, 2005), pp. 91–109.

13. Allen, *The Business of Genocide*, chaps. 1–2; Reinhard Vogelsang, *Der Freundeskreis Himmler* (Göttingen, Zürich, and Frankfurt: Musterschmidt, 1972), pp. 88–89.

14. Rudolf Höss, *Commandant of Auschwitz: The Autobiography of Rudolf Hoess*, introduction by Lord Russell of Liverpool, trans. Constantine FitzGibbon (Cleveland and New York: The World Publishing Co., 1959), *passim*.

15. On the direction of the German war economy, compare Alan S. Milward, *The German Economy at War* (London: University of London Athlone Press, 1965); with R. J. Overy, *War and Economy in the Third Reich* (Oxford: Oxford University Press, 1994). On the SS-WVHA, Allen, *The Business of Genocide*, *passim*. Christopher Browning, *Nazi Policy, Jewish Workers, German Killers* (Cambridge and New York: Cambridge University Press, 2000), p. 86.

16. "Safe remove" is a relative term, because Edward Westermann demonstrates that in 1941 the Royal Air Force's Wellington bombers had the hypothetical range to attack Auschwitz. See his

"The Royal Air Force and the Bombing of Auschwitz: First Deliberations, January 1941," *HGS* 15:1 (Spring 2001), pp. 75–76, 78.

17. Peter Hayes, *Industry and Ideology: IG Farben in the Nazi Era*, 2nd ed. (Cambridge and New York: Cambridge University Press, 2001), pp. xii–xvi; Joseph Robert White, "IG Auschwitz: The Primacy of Racial Politics (unpublished Ph.D. dissertation, University of Nebraska-Lincoln, 2000), p. 30; hereafter, White, "Primacy."

18. Faust quotation in T-301/118/NI-14556(S)/708, IG Auschwitz Weekly Report No. 30, 15–21 Dec. 1941.

19. On management's frustration with the Four-Year Plan authorities, White, "Primacy," pp. 50–51. On "Crimes against Peace" allegations against IG Farben, Josiah DuBois, *The Devil's Chemists: 24 Conspirators of the International Farben Cartel Who Manufacture Wars* (Boston: Beacon Press, 1952); and Mark E. Spicka, "The Devil's Chemists on Trial: The American Prosecution of IG Farben at Nuremberg," *The Historian* 61:4 (Summer 1999): 894.

20. As summarized in White, "Primacy," chap. III.

21. NARA, RG-242 (Captured German Documents), Nuremberg Organizations (NO-) 1501, Gerhard Maurer, SS-WVHA Office DII Rundschreiben, Abschrift, DII/1 23 Ma/Hag., 5 Oct. 1942.

22. On the infirmary's genocidal role, White, "Primacy," chap. IV and pp. 328–342.

23. United States Strategic Bombing Survey, Oil Division, *Powder, Explosives, Special Rockets and Jet Propellants, War Gases and Smoke Acid (Ministerial Report No. 1)*, 2nd ed. (NP: Oil Division, Jan. 1947), pp. 3–4, 22, 54, Exhibit H.

24. White, "Target Auschwitz," p. 72 n. 23.

25. On the IG Auschwitz workforce, see NARA, RG 238, microfilm publication M-892, *USA v. Carl Krauch, et al.* (IG Farben Case), roll 65, frame 813, Walther Dürrfeld Exhibit 136, Document 1505, Five Personnel Charts for IG Auschwitz, 1941–1944.

26. Christopher Duffy, *Red Storm on the Reich: The Soviet March on Germany, 1945* (New York: Atheneum, 1991); on IG Auschwitz's last days, White, "Primacy," pp. 310–314.

GLOSSARY

APPELPLATZ   (German) The place for roll call (Appel) in the camps.

AUSCHWITZ The original Auschwitz camp (Auschwitz I) was built in 1940 in the suburbs of the Polish city of Oswiecim. On June 14, 1940, the first convoy of Polish political prisoners—728 men— arrived at the camp. By 1943, Auschwitz was the largest Nazi camp complex, with three main camps—Auschwitz I, Auschwitz II-Birkenau, and Auschwitz III-Monowitz—and some forty subcamps. Over 50 percent of the registered *Häftlinge* in the Auschwitz complex died; 70 to 75 percent of each transport was sent straight to the gas chambers. Untold numbers of victims of the gas chambers were never registered. The total number of Jews murdered in Auschwitz will never be known, but estimates range from 1 million and 2.5 million. The next highest groups were Poles and Russian POWs, most of them dying in the construction of the I.G. Farben plant and as gas chamber "guinea pigs," and *Gypsies*. Auschwitz was liberated by the Soviet army on January 27, 1945.

BIBELFORSCHER (German) A Jehovah's Witness, a purple triangle. German Jehovah's Witnesses, because of their beliefs, refused to use the Hitler salute, salute the Nazi flag, bear arms as soldiers, or participate in affairs of the government. Viewed as enemies of the state, many Jehovah's Witnesses lost their jobs, homes, businesses, and pensions. If they renounced their faith, they could avoid persecution. Over 900 Jehovah's Witness children who refused to join the Hitler Youth were thrown into penal institutions and juvenile homes. Jehovah's Witness publications wrote many scathing articles on Hitler's regime and on the concentration camps. In 1937, the magazine *Consolation* ran an article on poison-gas experiments in Dachau, and in June 1940, the magazine stated, "There were 3,500,000 Jews in Poland when Germany began its *Blitzkrieg* . . . and if reports are correct their destruction seems well under way." Auschwitz camp commander Rudolf Franz Höss saw the *Bibelforscher* in his camp as "poor idiots who were quite happy in their own way." Over 10,000 German and European Jehovah's Witnesses were shipped to concentration camps. It's estimated that between 4,000 and 5,000 Jehovah's Witnesses were murdered during the Nazis' reign, more than 1,500 of them in the camps.

BIRKENAU (German)   Literally "birch grove," this was Auschwitz II, an extermination camp built in October 1941 and located near the Polish village of Brzezinka. In the spring of 1942, the "showers" and crematoriums were operational. On October 10, 1944, there was the uprising of the *Sonderkommando*, during which the prisoner crew of crematoria IV revolted and destroyed the crematories. In November 1944, Heinrich Himmler shut down the gas chambers and made efforts to conceal the mass murder that had taken place there.

BLOCK/BLOCKS (German)   Barracks.

BLOCKAELTESTE/R   (German) Barracks supervisor/s.

BLOKOWA (Polish)   Female barracks supervisor.

BLOKOWY (Polish)   Barracks supervisor.

BOCHE/BOCHES (French/slang)   A derogatory term for a German citizen/s.

BUNA   Acronym for butadiene natrium, or synthetic rubber. The I.G. Farben plant was called "Buna" by the inmates. The plant was built to produce synthetic rubber and fuel. When the Nazis abandoned Auschwitz, not an ounce of synthetic rubber had yet been produced.

CROIX DE FEU   Literally, Cross of Fire. A right-wing organization founded in 1915 by a group of French officers. Original members were all holders of the Military Cross. Many conservative Catholics joined the nationalist, monarchist, and revanchist ("revenge") organization in the 1920s. Membership peaked at 750,000 in 1937. Widely regarded as the counterpart of Germany's and Italy's fascist organizations.

DER STÜRMER Literally "The Attacker." An anti-Semitic Nazi weekly newspaper first published on April 20, 1923. Based in Nuremberg, its publisher and editor, Julius Streicher, used the paper to spread Hitler's doctrine of hatred with crude, simply written articles and "Jew-baiting" cartoons. The final edition of *Der Stürmer* was published on February 1, 1945. After the war, Streicher was tried at the Nuremburg trials for inciting hate and was hanged on October 16, 1946.

DORA, MITTLEBAU-DORA (Also known as Dora-Nordhausen) Established in August 1943 near the southern Harz Mountains and north of the town of Nordhausan, Dora was originally a subcamp of Buchenwald. The first *Häftlinge* were forced to build the underground factory for the production of the V-1 and V-2 rockets. In November 1944, the camp was renamed Mittelbau. About 60,000 men were used as forced or slave laborers, and more than 20,000 died there. Mittelbau-Dora was liberated on April 11, 1945, by the U.S. 33rd Armored Regiment.

DRANCY A transit camp located in the suburbs of Paris. Almost all Jews rounded up in France passed through Drancy before being shipped to Auschwitz and other concentration camps. It wasn't until 1995 that the French government acknowledged the culpability of the Vichy regime in the Nazis' "Final Solution."

FLIC (French/slang) Policeman.

FRONT POPULAIRE A broad coalition of leftist French political parties and major trade unions formed in July 1935. The three main parties were the French Socialist Party (SFIO), the French Communist Party (PCF), and the le Parti Radical. The head of the Front Populaire was Leon Blum, leader of the SFIO. The coalition headed the French government from June 1935 to March 1940.

FUSSLAPAN (German) Foot rags.

GARDES-MOBLES French Federal Police.

GENDARMES French Military Police.

GESTAPO Short for Geheime Staatspolizei, or Secret State Police. Allowed to work above the law, the Gestapo was the tool of terror in Germany and all Nazi-occupied countries. Its primary task was to round up Jews and other "undesirables." At the Nuremberg trials, the entire organization was charged with crimes against humanity.

GRAND GUIGNOL (French)   Used to describe any dramatic entertainment designed to shock, horrify, and sicken and usually featuring the violently gruesome and gory. The phrase comes from the Theatre du Grand Guignol in Montmarte, Paris, which specialized in "shock theatre."

HÄFTLING/E (German)   Inmate/s.

HIMMLER, HEINRICH   The man responsible for the implementation of the "Final Solution." Hitler appointed him Reichsführer-SS (Reich SS leader) in 1929. In Aprir 1934, Hermann Göring, the president of the Reichstag, gave Himmler power over the Gestapo. All the concentration camps were under his command. In the summer of 1942, he ordered the Warsaw Ghetto to be emptied because the Jews were dying too slowly in the confined area. In 1943, he was named Minister of the Interior, then in 1944, was appointed the chief of the Replacement Army. On May 23, 1945, Himmler was captured by British forces and committed suicide.

HKB/HÄFTLINGSKRANKENBAU (German)   Inmates' infirmary.

I. G. FARBEN   A German conglomerate formed in 1925. Major companies included Bayer, Agfa, and BASF. Seeing great postwar potential, I.G. Farben funded I.G. Auschwitz without any government money. It was their largest plant and cost more than 900 million Reichsmark (over $250 million). Zyklon B was produced by the I.G. Farben company Degesch. After the war, the Allies disbanded the conglomerate, but allowed the original companies to continue doing business.

JUDE (German)   Jew, a "yellow triangle." The only group of human beings the Nazis wanted to annihilate completely. When Hitler took power on January 30, 1933, German Jews were systematically stripped of all political, economic, and social rights. On September 15, 1935, the Nuremberg Racial Laws were decreed, which banned Jews from being German citizens. On February 21, 1939, German Jews were forced to hand over all their gold and silver items. With the invasion of Poland and the start of World War II, the Nazis rounded up the Jews in all the countries they occupied, putting them into ghettos or concentration camps. As Nazi forces tore into the Soviet Union, the Einsatzgruppen (Special Forces under the control of Heinrich Himmler) began the mass killing of Jews (along with Gypsies and Communist leaders). On January 20, 1942, the Wannsee Conference was held and the "Final Solution"(Endlösung der Judenfrage) was set in motion. In the Shoah (Hebrew term for "calamity"), over 6 million Jewish men, women, and children were murdered by the Nazis.

KANADA KOMMANDO (German) The work detail that gathered and sorted the belongings of the new arrivals to Auschwitz. Anything of value was earmarked for shipment to Germany, but some items found their way to Auschwitz's black market. The inmates nicknamed the Kommando "Kanada" because Canada was seen as a country of wealth and prosperity.

KIPP LORE (German) A coal car with a container that can be tilted to easily empty the load.

KOMMANDO (German) Work detail.

KAPO (German) Inmate supervisor of a *Kommando*. Assigned by the SS and usually a German convict.

KRÄTZEBLOCK (German) Barracks for inmates with scabies, skin mange, or contagious itch.

K.L. Abbreviation of *Konzentrationslager*, the German word for "concentration camp."

LAGER (German) Camp.

LAGERÄLTESTER (German) Camp elder, most of the time a German convict in charge of discipline in the camp.

LAGERFÜRHER (German) A warden, usually an SS officer who oversaw discipline in the camp

LANDSTURM (German) German reserve forces that are called on last, composed of men not in the armed forces (mainly elderly veterans and teenagers).

LEBENSRAUM (German) Literally, "living space." One of Hitler's excuses for invading Poland and the Soviet Union was to acquire land to be colonized by Germans.

LEICHENWAGEN (German) Hearse.

MAKHORKA (Russian)   A harsh Russian tobacco composed of to-bacco leaf stems.

MALHEURE (French)   Horrible or bad luck.

MAQUIS (French)   Literally "sage brush," the name for the French Resistance. The resistance was given that name because most of the men and women lived or hid in the French mountainsides.

MAQUISARDS (French)   French Resistance fighters.

MAUTHAUSEN   A concentration camp 20 kilometers from Linz, Austria, which was opened in August 1938. The total number of *Häft-linge* who passed through the camp is estimated at 199,404, and of that number, 119,000 died. The camp was liberated by the U.S. 11th Armored Division on May 5, 1945.

MESSERSCHMITT   The Messerschmitt BF-109 was the standard German fighter plane. It had a water-cooled Daimler-Benz 12-cylinder engine with over 1,000 horsepower.

MON AMI (French)   My friend/buddy.

MONOWITZ   Auschwitz III , operational in May 1942. A slave labor camp built in the town of Monowice, Poland, whose name was Germanized into Monowitz. The camp supplied workers for the I.G. Farben plant. At the roll call before the death march out of Auschwitz, there were 10,244 inmates.

MUZHIK   (Russian) A term for a Russian peasant, especially be-fore the 1917 Revolution.

MUSELMANN/MUSELMÄNNER (German)   Literally, Muslim/s, but camp slang for an inmate near death, who has given up on life.

ORGANIZE   Camp slang for stealing anything from the Nazis that could help in one's survival or for illicit trade in stolen items. If a prisoner was caught with an "organized" item, it could mean a beating, the *Stehbunker*, or execution.

PAJAMAS   Camp slang for the thin gray-and-blue striped uniforms given to *Häftlinge*.

PÈRE LACHAISE   The oldest and largest cemetery in Paris. Named after Père François de la Chaise, the confessor of Louis XIV, the ceme-tery was built on an old quarry. Père Lachaise holds the remains of many famous people, including Molière, Balzac, Sarah Bernhardt, Chopin, Proust, Oscar Wilde, Isadora Duncan, and Jim Morrison.

PIEPEL (German)   Errand boy, although in the K.L., it also implied a juvenile prostitute.

PITCHI POI   A legendary village in Yiddish song, used by Jews and other inmates of Drancy as the name of the secret destination the Nazis were shipping them to.

PUFF (German/slang)   Bordello, whorehouse.

RAVENSBRÜCK   The Nazi's only major women's camp, located 56 miles north of Berlin. The camp was built in 1938, and was liberated by the Soviets on April 30, 1945. About 92,000 women died at Ravensbrück.

REICHSFLUCHTSTEUER   A German "flight" tax that was established on December 8, 1931. For anti-Semitic reasons, the Nazis perverted the laws passed before the Seizure of Power, which were originally designed to prevent large amounts of capital from leaving the country during the Great Depression. By 1933, there were a number of laws with the sole purpose of eliminating the Jews from the German economy.

ROMANI   An ethnic group, commonly known as Gypsies, whose roots can be traced to India. About 23,000 Romani from eleven countries were shipped to Birkenau, where a special Romani family camp had been built. About 21,000 were either gassed or died from malnutrition, disease (especially typhus), or mistreatment. It is estimated that between 20 and 50 percent of European Romani were murdered by the Nazis. *Gypsy* is a pejorative term.

SCHREIBSTUBE (German)   Administration office.

SELECTION   Euphemism (*Selektion* in German) for being chosen for work or, more commonly, death.

SONDERKOMMANDO (German)   Special work team. In Auschwitz, the *Sonderkommando* was responsible for leading people into the gas chambers, extracting their bodies, and burning them in the crematoriums. Members of the *Sonderkommando* usually worked in the crematoriums for a few months before being sent to their deaths, as part of the Nazis' attempts to leave no witnesses to their crimes.

Speckjäger (German/slang)   Bacon hunter, or someone who chases lard, a scavenger.

SS (Schutzstaffel) (German)   Security Detail. Originally formed to protect Hitler and other Nazi officials. Under Heinrich Himmler, the SS became military units, the Waffen-SS. By 1944, nearly 40,000 SS were assigned to concentration camps.

Stehbunker (German)   Standing bunker, or very small cell. One of the Nazis' forms of punishment for *Häftlinge* who broke their arbitrary rules and regulations. A narrow cell, 90 cm by 90 cm, in which a man couldn't turn around or move his hands. *Häftlinge* were kept in these cells from 10 to over 24 hours at a time.

Stubendienst/e (German)   Barracks foreman/men.

Sudetendeutsch, Sudeten German (German)   A German national living in the Sudetenland, which became part of Czechoslovakia after World War I. There were 3,2 million Germans living in this area, which bordered Germany (11,000 square miles). In September 1938, the Munich Agreement, which was signed by Hitler, Britain's Neville Chamberlin, France's Edouard Daladier, and Italy's Mussolini, permitted Germany's annexation of the Sudetenland. Czechoslovakia was given no say in the matter. In March 1939, Germany annexed the rest of the country.

Untermensch/Untermenschen   (German)   Subhuman/s, used generally to refer to prisoners and Jews.

Verboten (German)   Forbidden.

Vorarbeiter (German)   Foreman.

Wehrmacht   German Armed Forces.

Zyklon-B   Crystalline hydrogen cyanide, used in the Nazi gas chambers. Originally developed as a pesticide, and first used in September 1941 on Soviet POWs.